OUTSOURCING LIBRARY TECHNICAL SERVICES OPERATIONS

Practices in Academic, Public, and Special Libraries

Edited by

KAREN A. WILSON

MARYLOU COLVER

Sponsored by the
Commercial Technical Services Committee
Association for Library Collections
and Technical Services

American Library Association
Chicago and London 1997

While extensive effort has gone into ensuring the reliability of information appearing in this book, the publisher makes no warranty, express or implied, on the accuracy or reliability of the information, and does not assume and hereby disclaims any liability to any person for any loss or damage caused by errors or omissions in this publication.

Cover by Image House

Text design by Dianne M. Rooney

Composition by the dotted i in Optima and Fenice using QuarkXpress v 3.32.

Printed on 50-pound Victor Offset, a pH-neutral stock, and bound in 10-point coated cover stock by Victor Graphics

The paper used in this publication meets the minimum requirements of American National Standard for Information Sciences—Permanence of Paper for Printed Library Materials, ANSI Z39.48-1992.∞

Library of Congress Cataloging-in-Publication Data

Outsourcing library technical services operations : practices in academic, public, and special libraries / edited by Karen A. Wilson and Marylou Colver.
    p. cm.
   "Sponsored by the Commercial Technical Services Committee, Association for Library Collections and Technical Services."
   Includes bibliographical references (p.) and index.
   ISBN 0-8389-0703-2
   1. Processing (Libraries)—Contracting out—United States.
2. Processing (Libraries)—Contracting out—Canada.   3. Academic libraries—United States.   4. Academic libraries—Canada.
5. Public libraries—United States.   6. Special libraries—United States.   I. Wilson, Karen A.   II. Colver, Marylou.   III. Association for Library Collections & Technical Services. Commercial Technical Services Committee.
Z731.094   1997
025'.02'0687—dc21   97-22901

Printed in the United States of America.

01 00 99 98 97   5 4 3 2 1

CONTENTS

Part One ■ Academic Libraries ....

FOREWORD

In their Preface, editors Karen A. Wilson and Marylou Colver refer to a rapidly growing interest in library technical services outsourcing in both Canada and the United States. This increasing interest is evident in the volume of programs and articles on outsourcing appearing in the mid-1990s. During this decade, the universe of presentations and publications within the library profession has offered us both useful and sometimes not-so-useful commentary on this topic. In addition, although the burgeoning body of information has been enlightening, it has often lacked structured, objective examination of real-time outsourcing programs.

Outsourcing Library Technical Services Operations: Practices in Academic, Public, and Special Libraries is a valuable addition to library literature. This presentation of case studies will be useful as librarians begin to explore a wider range of technical services options. However, the value of this collection extends beyond simple identification and presentation of case studies. Wilson and Colver apply structure and editorial rigor to all the cases included. Moreover, the editors provide a convenient vehicle to aggregate actual experience. Here is a storehouse of practice in one volume, which provides readers with the ability both to understand a variety of options and opportunities, and to compare a particular type of outsourcing application in different institutions. In that regard, this work is as much to be appreciated as a compendium of comparative experience, as it is to be sampled case study by case study.

Before reading these cases, it is important to understand the editors' guidelines for these chapters. First and foremost, the case studies were to be of successful library technical services outsourcing initiatives that had been operational for at least one year. Ultimately, readers will define success on their own, as they examine each case in the context of its individual library setting. In its entirety, however, this work represents a digest of mid-decade best practices in outsourcing, useful as a guide to present practitioners and invaluable as a benchmark in the chronicle of ongoing development.

The editors also supplied their contributors with one final instruction, which may well frame the long-term usefulness of this work. It is worth quoting in full: "We need to keep in mind that outsourcing is an activity that has an impact on both a vendor and a library. Staff at both organizations are involved in making the process work. In writing your chapters, you may want to share your content with your vendor(s) for a number of reasons: It keeps the vendors in the loop as to where their names will be appearing in the library literature; it gives the vendors an opportunity to suggest any additional comments about your project; and it gives the vendors a chance to review your data for accuracy, clarity, and completeness. Since this is a book about successful outsourcing programs, which can serve as models for others, we need to be sure that the content of the book accurately reflects the entire scope of your outsourcing ventures." The degree to which these guidelines were followed further enhances the usefulness of the case studies.

In reading this collection of cases, what can be learned from the experience of our contributors? A first lesson removes the prejudice that considerable scope and scale of operations determine benefit. A perception exists within the library community that the benefits of outsourcing are confined to medium and large institutions, whose initiatives, almost by definition, are of a significant size. This perception is colored by well-publicized initiatives, including those at Stanford University, Wright State University, and the University of Alberta, and the statewide public library initiative in Hawaii. Some of those programs are described in this work; others are not.

In evaluating successful outsourcing programs on the basis of scope and scale, we can conclude from the experience presented in this book that larger is not necessarily better. Carol Henderson, instructional dean in the library of the Central Oregon Community College, advises us of the benefit in outsourcing original cataloging for as few as 50 titles per year. Aimee Ruzicka, manager of the Chubb Law & Business Library, identifies the significant value of outsourced cataloging for 1,200 titles. In addition, Ellen Crosby, head of cataloging at the Indiana Historical Society Library, demonstrates advantages in outsourcing the cataloging of 1,000 trade ephemera. These three initiatives are in juxtaposition to the thousands of titles involved in the combined Claremont Colleges program and the experience of the Florida Atlantic University Libraries.

Other authors describe outsourcing of tens of thousands of volumes at the Albuquerque/Bernalillo County Public Library System, the University of Alberta, and the University of Manitoba. If the number of volumes processed in an outsourcing environment is a determinant of success, however, these large-scale examples are all dwarfed by the experience of the

Houston Public Library, which receives as many as 40,000 books per month. Clearly, as the variety of cases in this book reveals, benefit is relative and accrues independently of the size of the outsourcing venture.

What about other benefits of outsourcing? Anecdote would suggest that reduction in cost is a driving consideration. As might be expected, it is certainly true that a number of the contributed case studies suggest that a budgetary savings was a desired end. Staff at the Central Oregon Community College Library looked explicitly for cost savings from their vendor, Small Library Systems, and found that "outsourcing has provided the library's managers with original cataloging services at 40 percent of the former cost for creating original records in-house." Both Canadian initiatives were conceived assuming a cost reduction as well. Based on their cost analysis of pre- and postoutsourcing experience at the University of Manitoba, Lynne Partington, head of the cataloguing section, and George Talbot, cataloguer, report that outsourcing of cataloguing with Information Systems Management "has substantially reduced cataloguing costs." Similarly, Kathy Carter, head of cataloguing at the University of Alberta, cites a 25 percent to 35 percent reduction in cost, based on a blended throughput of copy and original cataloging from the same vendor. There is also the prospect of greater savings in year two of Alberta's initiative, when it is expected that a larger volume of material will drive unit prices lower.

In the public library arena, Gene Rollins, former chief of technical services at the Houston Public Library during their multifaceted outsourcing initiative, reports that, for the ongoing authority control component of the project, "estimated in-house costs would range between $70,000 and $90,000 per year, depending on levels of staff experience. The cost benefit of outsourcing this category of authority control to Blackwell for approximately $7,000 per year has been a major advantage for HPL's managers."

In other case studies, however, the authors found cost savings or cost avoidance a pleasant by-product of their initiatives. Although cost saving was not a stated objective at Florida Atlantic University, Janice Donahue and William Miller, assistant director for technical services and director of libraries, respectively, reached a satisfactory conclusion that OCLC's TECH-PRO service costs "were lower than the amount of salary and training costs that would have been required for in-house cataloging and physical processing." The cost benefits of The Claremont Colleges are indicative of many other outsourcing experiences. Isao Uesugi, former head, OPAC management/INNOPAC system coordinator of the colleges, writes that "the per-title cost of outsourced cataloging does not differ substantially from in-house copy cataloging costs for approval books. . . . Because the primary motivation for outsourcing was not based on reducing cataloging costs, the fact that outsourcing has not resulted in measurable budgetary savings for cataloging of approval books has not been a critical concern."

From the experience represented in these case studies, we know that reducing or eliminating costs was not the sole or, in many cases, even a compelling reason for outsourcing. What, then, was the motivation? There appear to be almost as many different motivations and objectives in these case studies as there are projects. In no particular order, here is a summary of objectives that were either stated or achieved as a by-product of outsourcing:

- reduce original cataloging turnaround time
- improve the quality of cataloging
- provide professional catalogers with more time for public service duties
- reassign cataloging staff to other service areas
- restructure library services
- secure bibliographic control of rare materials
- deal with accumulated backlogs
- access expertise not available in-house
- compensate for lack of available work space
- enhance access to journals published electronically
- leverage value from collections and established services
- improve receipt-to-shelf speed for new books
- create name and subject authority files
- create opening-day collections
- reduce the number of on-the-job injuries
- expand library services without a corresponding increase in resources

Given the diversity of reasons for sourcing technical services capability outside the library, are there any factors common to most or all of these case studies? There are at least two, and they are related: (1) the complexity of the endeavor and (2) the nature of the library-vendor relationship.

A simple reading of each case study demonstrates the complexity of these projects as a whole. The library processes that are being outsourced in these organizations are inherently complex. They are built upon common bibliographic practices, but have often been tailored to local circumstances and requirements. Staff in these libraries are now able to move forward with new and creative approaches to traditional processes. This is accomplished by combining the wisdom of generations of librarians who developed technical services standards and common protocols (cataloging rules, classification systems, authority control, and so on) with the capability of today's powerful information (that is, library systems) and telecommunications technologies.

If complexity of process is the norm, however, do these new approaches to technical services demand different and more involving relationships with vendors? Recall that an acknowledgment of vendors' contributions was mentioned in the editors' instructions to authors. In her Introduction, Karen Wilson also reflects upon the underpinning nature of vendors' roles and the ways in which traditional commercial services constitute the "foundation for library technical services outsourcing programs in the 1990s." She notes that "now, as in the past, these commercial products and services continue to be offered in a variety of modes."

In spite of this link to the past, the case studies published here suggest something beyond "foundation" products and services. A description of the commercial services used in libraries today demands a more dynamic characterization of vendor product and service development in the outsourcing arena than a simple linear representation from the "past" to the "now." Every case study in this volume suggests that something more complex is transpiring in the library-vendor relationship. Ann Fiegen, catalog management librarian, and Stephen Bosch, information access librarian, in the University of Arizona Library, summarize the nature of that relationship when they state that both parties "must align the technical capabilities, the development priorities, and the available resources of each partner." Fiegen and Bosch note that frequently the required service is of such a nature that no established products or services exist. A tolerance for ambiguity and a willingness "to agree on temporary solutions" sometimes characterize this dynamic environment.

Susan Bailey, assistant head of the catalog department, and Selden Deemer, library systems manager, when discussing Emory University Libraries' outsourcing of authority control processing, make a similar observation when they write that "tradeoffs have become a necessary part of the business atmosphere required in today's libraries, especially in an outsourcing environment." Gene Rollins, currently library systems manager for the San Antonio Public Library, also stresses the intimate nature of the new library-vendor relationship when he comments that "vendor personnel should be viewed as extensions of library staff and should be kept apprised of changes in policies, procedures, and practices. . . . The more knowledge each partner has, the more successful outsourcing will be."

This recognition of vendor as partner is an emerging phenomenon and evidence of the fact that something different is happening. This is perhaps best expressed by the library staff responsible for the outsourced document delivery service developed at Stanford University's J. Hugh Jackson Library. Those authors note "how staff in a traditional library teamed with a commercial vendor to produce a dynamic synergy, which benefited the staff and clients of both organizations."

What might be the determining nature of these evolving relationships? In this early period of outsourcing, two key attributes appear: strongly perceived mutual self-interest and shared risk, underpinned by a significant resource commitment. We are also enlightened by the Stanford contributors as to why this is happening: "In times of financial stress, even libraries may be expendable. Document delivery and the outsourcing effort, as well as TQM (total quality management) and other customer-motivated strategies, have become pieces in the overall strategy to secure for the library a lasting place."

Readers have reason to applaud all contributors to this collection of case studies for sharing important experiences. This knowledge will guide the initiatives of staffs in other libraries in the United States and Canada. Individuals in the libraries represented in this book, as well as a handful of others not represented here, have indeed taken a risk in their outsourcing ventures. They have established precedent and are jointly creating new capabilities with vendor partners.

Will the ongoing outsourcing projects described here continue? Will staffs in those libraries that have completed successful projects engage in more ambitious initiatives? Will the overall outsourcing trend continue? Will outsourced technical services ever be a dominant model for North American libraries? These are only a few questions that individuals in the library profession have been asking. Because this is only a foreword, these questions must remain rhetorical. We can rest assured, however, that this collection of current practices certainly will not be the last word on library technical services outsourcing.

Ernie Ingles
Executive Director, Learning Systems
University of Alberta

PREFACE

Outsourcing of library technical services functions to commercial vendors has been widely examined and discussed in the library profession during the 1990s. This is not a new concept for those librarians who have outsourced parts of their technical services activities for decades. However, the magnitude of current interest in this topic is evidenced by the fact that over 90 articles on various aspects of technical services outsourcing appeared in library literature from 1993 to mid-1996, preceded by almost no information on this activity during the previous two decades.

The concept for this book emerged in 1995, amid discussions about outsourcing among members of the American Library Association's ALCTS (Association for Library Collections and Technical Services) Commercial Technical Services Committee. Committee members were aware of the lack of published case studies on technical services outsourcing in the 1990s, at the same time as they were witnessing the increasing interest in evaluating outsourcing as an option for managing technical services functions. This book was conceived to provide readers with greater insight on managerial aspects of outsourcing, based on a variety of successful experiences in different kinds of library settings. The authors aim to provide library directors, technical services managers, and other library staff with a greater understanding of the outcome of contemporary outsourcing programs in the United States and Canada.

This book represents only one effort on the part of the Commercial Technical Services Committee's members to provide more information on outsourcing practices. The Committee also sponsored an outsourcing program at the March 1996 Public Library Association Conference in Portland, Oregon. That activity was followed by another program at the July 1996 American Library Association Conference in New York City. Authors of four case studies in this book participated as speakers at those two events. In addition, the Committee's previous book, *Outsourcing Cataloging, Authority Work, and Physical Processing: A Checklist of Considerations,* published in 1995 by the American Library Association, provides other guidelines for outsourcing library technical services operations.

ACKNOWLEDGMENTS

We are grateful to the following former and current members of the Association for Library Collections and Technical Services (ALCTS) Commercial Technical Services Committee for their contributions to this book: J. Randolph Call, Chair 1993–95, Detroit Public Library; Nancy Davey, Indianapolis-Marion County Public Library; Dawn Hale, Chair 1992–93, Johns Hopkins University; Sandra Herzinger, Chair 1995–96, University of Nebraska–Lincoln; Roxanne J. Sellberg, Chair 1996–97, Northwestern University; and Karen Wilhoit, Wright State University. Special thanks are extended to Randy Call for his role in establishing initial contact with authors of the outsourcing case studies and for his efforts toward planning the Committee's two conference programs on outsourcing during 1996. Nancy Davey is also recognized for preparing the preliminary indexes for the manuscript version of this work before it was submitted to the publisher. Her efforts in drafting both the author-title index and subject index are greatly appreciated.

Other individuals who were also members of the Commercial Technical Services Committee at some point during the evolution of this book include: Marie A. Kascus, Central Connecticut State University; Stuart Rosenthal, Queens Borough Public Library; Lynn D. Shrewsbury, Southwestern Library Network; Robert L. Watkins, Amigos Bibliographic Council, Inc.; and Gretchen Whitney, University of Arizona.

This book is a collaborative effort representing contributions from 28 individuals in 18 organizations. We wish to thank the contributors of the 16 case studies for their willingness to share insights about their outsourcing programs and for their cooperation and patience during the writing and editing stages of this project. All vendor representatives who provided input to authors are also acknowledged for their support in gathering management data for this book.

Members of the ALCTS Publications Committee, staff in the ALCTS Executive Office, and ALA Editions' staff are acknowledged for their efforts toward the successful publication of this case studies book. The entire membership of the ALCTS Commercial Technical Services Committee is indebted to all individuals in these organizations who supported the committee members' interests in creating this book and in developing other avenues of library education on the topic of outsourcing.

We wish to acknowledge our employers, and the employers of all contributors, for their support for this project. Special appreciation is extended to Timothy Wei at the Stanford University Graduate School of Business, and to Fred Philipp and David Papkoff at Blackwell North America, Inc. Technical services staff members in the J. Hugh Jackson Library at Stanford University who also offered assistance and moral support during the completion of this book include Kent Abbott, Helen Athey, Tom Holt, Minson Liu, Richard Musante, Victor Nielepko, Pat Sandoval, Zina Shapiro, and Jill Standbridge. Staff members at Blackwell North America, Inc. who were instrumental in supporting this publication include Allan Graham, Jennifer Kosta, Jennifer Madsen, Holly Schmidt, and Dale Simon. A special word of thanks is also extended to Greg Cutting and Mary-Elise Diedrich at the Lake Oswego Public Library.

We know that numerous lives were impacted in one way or another during the year in which this book was compiled. The following individuals are acknowledged for their words of advice or encouragement during this process: Elizabeth Bringman, Sib Farrell, Barry Hinman, Carolyn Sheehy, Kim Simmons, Aline Soules, Jack Walsdorf, and David Wilson. A final word of thanks is extended to unnamed individuals who made accommodations to their schedules or offered other supportive contributions during the course of this publication. Your willingness to share in this experience enabled us to sustain our momentum in this endeavor.

Karen A. Wilson
Marylou Colver

INTRODUCTION

The case studies in the following chapters include a variety of library out-sourcing programs in the 1990s. These case studies offer insight on critical aspects of managing outsourcing activities, by providing a special focus on the results and effects of outsourcing in each library.

In order to demonstrate the effectiveness of technical services out-sourcing in various library environments, the case studies in this book were selected from university, college, community college, public, and cor-porate libraries in the United States and Canada. The 16 case studies are assembled into three major categories: academic libraries, public libraries, and special libraries. Some cases cover outsourcing of a single function to a single vendor. Other cases offer information on outsourcing of multiple activities to as many as five different vendors. An abstract, which summa-rizes the scope and accomplishments of outsourcing within each organi-zation, is provided at the beginning of each case.

A wide range of outsourcing programs is explored in these chapters, including authority control (retrospective and ongoing), book selection, collection enhancement and expansion, database maintenance for added copies and all cataloging, document delivery and tables of contents deliv-ery, federal depository document cataloging and authority control, foreign language and pamphlet cataloging, Hypertext Markup Language (HTML) editing of tables of contents and book reviews for electronic journals, item record creation, original and copy cataloging of books, original and copy cataloging of audiovisual material and music scores, physical processing, and record enrichment with tables of contents.

The case studies include examples of outsourcing for opening-day collections, processing of unique gift collections in different formats, and outsourcing of all cataloging department functions. The use of commercial vendors for reducing cataloging backlogs and managing other retrospec-tive processing needs is also explored. Two chapters contain information about the use of existing or former staff on a contract basis for "insourcing" activities. Some outsourcing reports consist of completed projects that had to be accomplished within a specified time frame. Those cases relate to a limited set of material for processing. For the most part, however, ongoing outsourcing programs constitute the majority of activities reported in this book.

These case studies illustrate opportunities for outsourcing in both automated and manual technical services environments, using a variety of vendors and automated library systems. Outsourcing contracts with over 15 commercial technical services vendors are represented in the book, including bibliographic utilities, booksellers, cataloging agencies, information vendors, and audiovisual media providers.

One common factor among these cases is that they pertain to either a completed project or an ongoing program that represents at least one year of outsourcing. The chapter authors also possess firsthand knowledge of the outsourcing programs described, and they address aspects of their outsourcing experiences that extend beyond basic operational issues. There is an emphasis on describing the results and effects of outsourcing activities in each library, as well as on providing a basic description of the nature of the outsourcing activities. Authors describe the objectives that library administrators and staff expected to achieve from outsourcing, provide an evaluation of how well those objectives were accomplished, and discuss the impact of outsourcing on staff and other aspects of library operations.

Standard bibliographic tools, which are cited frequently throughout the cases, are consolidated in a listing that follows the entire case studies section. An annotated bibliography serves as a resource guide for learning more about other case studies and for outsourcing information in library literature. Over a dozen other case studies from academic, public, and special libraries are included in the bibliography, as well as general articles on outsourcing by librarians and vendors. Outsourcing checklists, manuals, and surveys provide further guidelines for obtaining information on library technical services outsourcing.

Background on Commercial Library Technical Services

Throughout most of this century, commercial library technical services have been a valued commodity. Several library technical services outsourcing programs in the 1990s utilize commercial services that have been available for some time. In the area of acquisitions and collection development activities, booksellers have been offering approval plans since the 1960s. Similarly, shelf-ready books, with full processing and catalog records, have been available from booksellers since the late 1950s. The range of services and programs available to librarians when developing outsourcing activities is captured in the following description of services obtainable from commercial vendors.

COMMERCIAL ACQUISITIONS AND COLLECTION DEVELOPMENT SERVICES

Commercial acquisitions and collection development services available in the marketplace include: book approval and slip notification plans, blanket and standing order plans, collection analysis, out-of-print services, antiquarian and rare-book services, serials subscription plans, serials check-in and claiming programs, deposit account plans, online ordering and electronic invoicing, fund accounting, document delivery services, and automated acquisitions and serials control systems.

COMMERCIAL CATALOGING, PHYSICAL PROCESSING, AND PRESERVATION SERVICES

Cataloging, physical processing, and preservation services offered by numerous vendors in recent decades have included the following: copy and original cataloging, catalog cards, catalog records in MARC (machine-readable cataloging) format, book and computer output microfilm (COM) catalogs, record enrichment, authority control, reclassification, retrospective conversion, binding, physical processing, barcoding, item record creation, conservation services, preservation microfilming and photocopying, and automated cataloging and circulation control systems.

SCOPE OF COMMERCIAL LIBRARY TECHNICAL SERVICES PROGRAMS

The scope of past and present outsourcing programs is as varied as the kinds of commercial services offered by vendors. Librarians have used commercial services to create opening-day collections, manage technical services backlogs, and expend unanticipated funds quickly. Other applications have included collection replacement following disasters, and processing of special format collections, foreign language material, and gift collections. The scope of vendor services has varied from outsourcing on a temporary to an ongoing basis, from partial to full outsourcing of specific functions, and from the provision of in-house to remote services.

This vast array of acquisitions, cataloging, collection development, physical processing, and preservation services, many of which have long been available from commercial vendors, constitutes the foundation for library technical services outsourcing programs in the 1990s. These commercial products and services continue to be offered in a variety of modes. In addition, centralized and cooperative library programs provide other avenues for acquiring technical services from an outside source.

Outsourcing in the 1990s

In the early 1990s, the word *outsourcing* emerged in the library profession to describe the use of commercial library technical services. From 1992 to 1993, this term was used with increased frequency in professional association meetings and appeared regularly in online library discussion forums about technical services operations. By the mid-1990s, the technical services outsourcing concept ranked as one of the hottest topics in the library profession. Outsourcing seminars were being held across the country with increasing frequency. In July 1996, a one-day American Library Association preconference, devoted to the topic of evaluating strategies for improving in-house services and examining outsourcing options for managing technical services operations, was sponsored by members of the Association for Library Collections and Technical Services (ALCTS).

Amidst the debate within the library profession about the rapid emergence of this trend, a few points about outsourcing were well known by the mid-1990s. Outsourcing might have been a new term for librarians, but the concept of contracting with outside sources for the purchase of library technical services and products had existed for decades. The 1990s, however, saw electronic technology advance services to new levels. Outsourced services in 1996 far exceed the scope of traditional commercial products and services offered as recently as 1992. New directions in technical services outsourcing were evidenced by almost monthly announcements in 1995 and 1996 about recent developments in the scope of services available from vendors.

The new focus that emerged from a few academic and public library outsourcing activities, ranging from contracting for a single product or service to outsourcing of an entire operation or department, garnered considerable national attention as well. The annotated bibliography at the end of this book includes references for these and other outsourcing case studies discussed in library literature during this decade. Among the most notable case studies in libraries during the early to mid-1990s are the following:

1992   J. Hugh Jackson Library staff at Stanford University's Graduate School of Business contracted with Blackwell North America, Inc. and B. H. Blackwell, Ltd. to acquire copy cataloging and physical processing for monographs. Jackson Library was the first academic library to partner with these vendors for this full complement of outsourcing services on an ongoing basis.

1993   Wright State University staff contracted with the Online Computer Library Center (OCLC) for cataloging services and became the first academic library in the United States to outsource its entire cataloging operation. In the same year, individuals at Michigan

State University Libraries, Yankee Book Peddler (YBP), and OCLC jointly tested OCLC's PromptCat service for acquiring OCLC cataloging for approval books purchased from YBP.

1994   In Canada, staff at the University of Alberta Library and University of Manitoba Libraries outsourced cataloging and physical processing with Information Systems Management/Library Technical Services, a venture that represented new frontiers in outsourcing for all parties.

1995   Stanford University Libraries' staff implemented an outsourcing program with YBP, launching the first ongoing, large-scale outsourcing program at a major research library system in the United States.

1996   Within public libraries, full-scale outsourcing of collection development and acquisitions activities to a bookseller occurred when the Hawaii State Public Library System contracted with Baker & Taylor for book selection, cataloging, and physical processing.

By 1996, most library directors, technical services managers, and technical services staff were well aware of emerging outsourcing trends. At the very least, individuals monitored new developments to determine how these changes might affect their operations. At the other end of the spectrum, scores of library managers initiated outsourcing to some degree within their organizations and became leaders in the further development of commercial technical services. All these events have confirmed that outsourcing of library technical services operations, in one form or another, will continue into the twenty-first century.

Conclusion

This book is the first comprehensive resource for studying the widespread impact of contemporary library technical services outsourcing activities. The case studies and the annotated bibliography provide library managers and staff with a tool for learning more about their colleagues' experiences and achievements in outsourcing. The successful programs described here can also serve as models, as librarians consider various ways of using commercial technical services within their organizations.

Karen A. Wilson

Part One

Academic Libraries

Outsourced Cataloguing and Physical Processing at the University of Alberta Library

Kathy Carter

In early 1995, the University of Alberta Library's staff began an ongoing outsourcing program for cataloguing and physical processing of most newly acquired monographs with ISM/LTS (Information Systems Management/Library Technical Services), located in Winnipeg, Manitoba. During the first year of full-scale operation, over 30,000 titles were catalogued by the ISM/LTS staff. The vendor's quality of copy and original cataloguing, adherence to standards, and turnaround time have been acceptable to library staff, based on contractual expectations and reports on quality that were provided by an independent consultant. As a result of outsourcing, the library's Cataloguing Division was reduced from 59 FTE to 29 FTE, and staff were retrained and reallocated to other library areas. There were no layoffs, and the library's managers have benefited from the availability of additional staff in public services areas. Cataloguing costs were reduced by an estimated 25 percent to 35 percent. The library also receives tables of contents and record enrichment data from Blackwell North America, Inc. as part of the ISM/LTS agreement. During the first year of outsourc-

The author wishes to thank fellow University of Alberta librarians Sieglinde Rooney and Merrill Distad, and Deb Wallace of ISM/LTS, for their help and advice with the preparation of this chapter.

ing. approximately 25 percent of catalogue records were enhanced with tables of contents and summary information.

In 1994–95, following several years of incremental budget reductions, administrators at the University of Alberta faced a three-year, 21 percent provin-
cial funding reduction. In order to maintain the library's strategic directions,
which included concentration of resources in direct user-centered services, protection of job security to avoid layoffs, and development of partnerships with service providers, the library's managers decided to make a
drastic and innovative response to the budgetary challenge. Outsourcing
of cataloguing held the promise of meeting their objectives, without a no-
ticeable reduction in the quality of services.

Background

The University of Alberta Library is the second-largest library in Canada
and is a founding member of the 20-library NEOS consortium. The name
"NEOS" comes from the Greek word for "new." In the 1990s, between
35,000 and 40,000 titles were acquired and catalogued annually at the
university's library, in a centralized operation that includes the law and
medical libraries. Before outsourcing, there were 59 FTE in the library's
Cataloguing Division.

   In October 1993, a small outsourcing project was initiated with one
of the library's major book vendors, John Coutts Library Services, located
in Niagara Falls, Ontario. Coutts's staff provided shelf-ready books and
MARC (machine-readable cataloging) bibliographic records for most
books ordered from them for the university's Humanities and Social Sciences Library. Coutts did not provide original cataloguing. Although this
project was largely successful, it was limited in scope. When the magnitude of the university's budget cuts became known, and the library's managers decided on a more radical form of outsourcing, the Coutts project
was terminated in November 1994. At that time, senior library staff envisioned outsourcing the entire cataloguing function and maintaining only
two or three in-house staff to manage vendor contracts.

Outsourcing Project Description

The decision to outsource the cataloguing operation was announced to library staff in February 1994. An advisory team was immediately formed to
reengineer cataloguing functions. The team consisted of senior catalogu-

ing staff and representatives from Acquisitions, Financial Systems and Analysis, and public services units. They were assisted by staff from an external firm, Campbell Consulting Ltd., in Ottawa, Ontario. Conferring with other library staff as needed, the team identified outsourcing strategy options, drafted cataloguing and physical processing specifications, provided cost analyses, prepared an implementation plan, developed procedures, and designed a new, smaller Cataloguing Division.

Cost analyses were based on previous output statistics and no attempt was made to gather additional data. Because individual staff members performed a variety of functions, it was impossible to establish reliable costs for most discrete processes. However, the team estimated that outsourcing could reduce the aggregate cost of cataloguing and physical processing by about one third.

The advisory team also compiled the following documents:

- Cataloguing Standards and Practices: Survey of Unit Libraries, May 1994
- Issues Related to Outsourcing the Cataloguing Function, May 1994
- Cost Analysis of Cataloguing Processes, May 1994
- Review of Available Purchased Processing Options, July 1994

Vendor Selection and Contract Negotiations

A decision was made in July 1994 to select ISM/LTS (Information Systems Management/Library Technical Services), located in Winnipeg, Manitoba, as the primary outsourcing vendor. At that time, ISM/LTS's staff had not yet developed a cataloguing service, but ISM was a well-established bibliographic utility providing various other services, primarily to Canadian customers. ISM had a large bibliographic database with a cataloguing and authority processing system (CATSS), which library staff used for cataloguing support before installation of the DRA (Data Research Associates) system in 1993. By committing to a large-scale, long-term partnership with ISM/LTS, the library's managers not only wanted to outsource for their immediate needs, but also wanted to contribute to the development of a firm that could serve other Canadian libraries as well. Negotiations between the vendor's managers and senior library staff extended through the summer and fall, and culminated with a five-year contract signed in November 1994. During this time, a manager was hired by ISM/LTS to build its cataloguing unit and the resulting MARC*ADVANTAGE* service.

During negotiations, it became apparent that ISM/LTS's staff were not initially prepared to assume responsibility for the library's entire cataloguing operation. This was due in part to the skills ISM/LTS's managers thought their staff would possess. For example, they were not anticipated to have serials cataloguing skills or the capacity to package and label audiovisual material according to the library's requirements. It was also due to the intention of ISM/LTS's staff to complete the cataloguing in their own database. Unless they worked directly in the library's database, it would have been impractical for them to edit existing records or create holdings records, partly due to DRA's system limitations.

Although there are some exclusions in the outsourcing contract, the vendor's staff are expected to provide original and copy cataloguing, as well as physical processing, for most new material acquired by the library. Physical processing includes barcodes, property stamps, bookplates, security targets, and date-due slips. The agreement addresses the following contractual categories:

- specifications for bibliographic records, physical processing, and reports
- excluded categories of material
- procedures for delivery of material and records
- volume, type, and throughput of material
- priorities
- turnaround times
- charges
- measures for quality control and remedial actions
- implementation schedules

Although the potential exists for outsourcing remaining in-house activities to ISM/LTS or other vendors, library staff continue to perform the following functions:

- creation of item records for new titles and added copies/volumes
- database maintenance
- authority control maintenance
- cataloguing for all serials, CJK (Chinese-Japanese-Korean) material, and rare books
- cataloguing of material produced or acquired locally, including theses and Alberta school curriculum material
- physical packaging and labeling of audiovisual material
- binding of some material and preparation of others for commercial binders

Shipping and receiving, and transfer/overlay of ISM/LTS's records from a temporary database into the library's catalogue, are new in-house functions performed in outsourcing.

Managerial functions performed in the Cataloguing Division include the following:

- contract administration and development
- quality control
- planning and organization of special projects
- development and communication of cataloguing policies and priorities
- management of the restructured Cataloguing Division
- coordination of cataloguing operations with Acquisitions and other library units
- analysis and training for cataloguing system software changes

The University of Alberta Library staff also provide selected cataloguing functions for NEOS consortium partners. Library staff offer training on the DRA cataloguing software, perform some item and authority maintenance functions, and participate in the development of consortium standards and practices.

Reallocation of Library Staff

In fall 1994, library staff completed plans for the complex process of reallocating Cataloguing Division positions and staff members affected by outsourcing. Library staff had already prepared restructuring plans with projected staffing requirements for all library units. Using these plans, senior library managers reassigned all cataloguing positions to other units or to the redesigned Cataloguing Division. Staff members were placed in new positions that matched their preferences as closely as possible, but which also maintained their job classification levels. All staff began their new jobs on January 16, 1995.

Library managers worked closely with the university's central personnel office to ensure compliance with collective bargaining agreements and job classification systems. The university's two staff associations were consulted and informed about new developments throughout the reallocation process. The associations' executives, as well as central personnel office staff, were also invited to all library staff meetings related to outsourcing in order to further facilitate communication.

Implementation of Outsourcing

Implementation began in January 1995 with a three-month startup period. During this time, some contract provisions were not yet in effect, and ISM/LTS's staff catalogued only English- and French-language books. By April, all contract provisions were in force and the first year of full operation began. At planned intervals during the next two months, ISM/LTS's staff began cataloguing the remaining categories of material: audiovisual material, books in other languages, computer files, gifts, government publications, items catalogued in French, microforms, law material, and music material.

Because the contract includes physical processing and labeling, all material catalogued by the vendor is shipped to their site in Winnipeg, Manitoba. From the outset, the library's five major book vendors were advised to ship books to ISM/LTS and to forward invoices to the library. ISM/LTS's staff are required to review all incoming shipments from vendors, thus performing part of the library's receiving function. Later in the year, the library's smaller vendors also began shipping material directly to the vendor. Other material is received by library staff in Edmonton and forwarded to ISM/LTS, including firm orders from individual publishers, gifts, standing orders, and government publications received on deposit. Commercial courier services are used, and shipping time is two days each way. Material is packed and shipped daily from both sites.

ISM/LTS's staff place completed MARC records in a file on their computer. The file is retrieved and transferred daily by the library's systems staff, using the Internet File Transfer Protocol (FTP). Records are loaded into a temporary DRA database. As items arrive from ISM/LTS, library staff transfer corresponding records individually into the catalogue and create item records. They also check for any existing order records, which they overlay with ISM/LTS's records.

Impact of Outsourcing

Only minor problems occurred with the majority of material catalogued during the five-month implementation period, but delays were experienced with some specialized material (for example, music and Slavic books). Most delays occurred because ISM/LTS was recruiting and training its staff at that time. The library staff reallocations all took place at the start of the implementation period, rather than proceeding in stages corresponding to the outsourcing implementation. However, work performed by the remaining cataloguing staff, including those planning to retire, prevented the growth of backlogs in most categories.

Bibliographic Standards

For the most part, bibliographic standards were not changed by outsourcing. These include use of the Canadian versions of the Library of Congress (LC) classification for Canadian history (FC), Canadian literature (PS 8000 and PS 9000), and common law (KF modified). Some enhancements to bibliographic description, access points, classification, and subject headings, which were previously provided mainly to special material (for example, curriculum and music), are no longer provided.

The most significant changes occurred in classification and call number assignment. The decision to forgo a shelflist check for call number assignment resulted in the loss of uniqueness in numbers and in separation of related works. An important exception is that established numbers for literary authors and composers continue to be used. An initial decision not to require ISM/LTS's staff to check different editions and classify them together has been reversed. These exceptions, although deemed important, add cost to the outsourcing process, because they require the vendor's staff to consult the library's catalogue online via telnet access. Some local exceptions and modifications to LC classification have been abandoned also, resulting in split collections. The largest collection affected was government documents. Most are now classified by LC, rather than by a local scheme based on the CODOC system for Canadian government documents.

ISM/LTS's staff use their CATSS authorities functions to provide current and consistent headings on bibliographic records, but they do not supply new or updated authority records. They also check series in the library's catalogue to ensure conformance with the library's established forms. Maintenance of headings and authority records is performed by the library's staff using DRA's authorities functions. Authority records are imported from LC and from the National Library of Canada databases, accessible through DRA Net.

Quality Control

Quality control is achieved by three processes: automated and manual review at ISM/LTS's facility, in-house review by library staff, and third-party review.

1. ISM/LTS's Script program on CATSS is used to check for accuracy and validity of data and to perform standardized editing according to library specifications. For example, Script checks for matching dates in the 260 field, the 008 field, and the call number; generates a call number from the 050 field; adds the library's identification code to two fields; and transforms 440 fields into a 490 field and an 830 field to improve authorities updating. These functions reduce errors at little cost. ISM/LTS's cataloguers supplement the automated processes with manual review.

2. Library staff review all ISM/LTS records to ensure that each record and book match, and that the author, title, imprint, and spine label

are correct. Library staff have never conducted a thorough quality review of all records. However, during the implementation period, all items in selected categories were reviewed until library staff were satisfied that their quality was satisfactory. The categories included children's literature, government publications, music, and books catalogued in French. By mid-1996, approximately 10 percent of original and non-LC records also received a more detailed review, focused on subject headings and call numbers. Errors are corrected by library staff and are communicated weekly to ISM/LTS's staff to assist them in improving performance.

3. An independent consultant, selected jointly by ISM/LTS's staff and the library's staff, performs periodic reviews of selected records. Detailed reports, which calculate error rates and identify problem areas, are supplied by the consultant. Reviews are to continue through the life of the contract, but will probably be reduced in frequency from quarterly to annually, if ISM/LTS's quality continues to be satisfactory.

Determination of acceptable error rates has been difficult for several reasons. The library's managers did not have significant data on in-house error rates prior to outsourcing. There is also a lack of concise and widely accepted standards in the profession, as well as a paucity of data on actual cataloguing error rates in libraries. Nevertheless, the library's contract defined errors and acceptable error rates in detail. In addition to providing quality expectations for cataloguing, the contract included quality standards for receiving, processing, and turnaround times. Escalating dispute-resolution provisions were also included.

Library staff have not attempted to calculate, on the basis of their manual reviews, the error rates of ISM/LTS's staff. This is because not all records are reviewed in detail, nor are there any random or systematic selection processes for the records that are reviewed in detail. The two third-party reviews, conducted before July 1996, produced reliable cataloguing error rate calculations, which have exceeded the initial contractual thresholds. Library staff, however, have determined that the overall number of errors is well within tolerable limits. Instead of focusing on raw error rates, a more fruitful approach has been for the library's staff and ISM/LTS's staff to identify patterns of recurring errors and means for reducing the most common problems. In this context, the third-party reviews have become useful over time as an indication of trends, both in overall error rates and in specific problem areas. Throughout this process, the vendor's staff have demonstrated a commitment to quality and continuous improvement.

An unanticipated problem for the library's managers has been the challenge of assuring quality with a reduced cataloguing staff. The difficulty relates more to the skills of staff remaining in the Cataloguing Division, in terms of the reduced pool of language, subject, and format specialists, than to the actual number of staff available for quality control work. This problem has resulted in some reliance on specialists in public service areas for identification and reporting of cataloguing errors. Given the lack of data on previous or current error rates for in-house cataloguing, the library's managers have been unable to determine if error rates have changed as a result of outsourcing.

Turnaround Time

The outsourcing contract stipulates turnaround times for different categories of material, including rush titles. Items with available catalogue copy are to be processed within two weeks. Items requiring original cataloguing are to be completed within six weeks. ISM/LTS's tracking system permits immediate identification and retrieval of rush items. These turnaround-time requirements have not always been met, but the vendor's performance is improving. Because library staff have limited data on past turnaround times, it has been impossible to determine if overall turnaround times were affected by outsourcing.

Production and Hit Rates

During the first year, ISM/LTS's staff catalogued 30,397 titles and library staff catalogued 9,780 titles. The monthly production rates of ISM/LTS's staff for that year are illustrated in Exhibit 1.1.

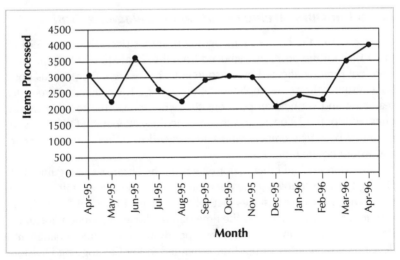

EXHIBIT 1.1 Items Processed by ISM/LTS, April 1995 to April 1996.

In the second year of the contract, library staff anticipate that 45,000 to 50,000 titles will be catalogued by ISM/LTS's staff. The vendor's staff are scheduled to complete the cataloguing of a 10,000-item gift collection in the future as well.

In addition to using their own database as a source for cataloguing copy, ISM/LTS's staff use the Research Libraries Information Network (RLIN) database and the Online Computer Library Center (OCLC) database. A 90 percent hit rate was achieved using these three databases.

Vendor Relations

From the earliest planning stages through full-scale outsourcing, relations between the library's staff and ISM/LTS's staff have been excellent. In addition to frequent communication by telephone and electronic mail, representatives from both organizations meet quarterly to resolve larger issues. During the beginning months of the contract, numerous procedural matters, and other issues that were not addressed in the contract, required prompt attention. The professionalism and responsiveness of ISM/LTS's staff, together with the company's technological capacities, have inspired confidence in library staff. These conditions have resulted in a close and productive working relationship. Because the University of Alberta Library was one of ISM/LTS's first customers for outsourcing of cataloguing and physical processing, as well as their largest customer, the library's contract and relationship with the vendor have also had an impact on the development of ISM/LTS's outsourcing staff and services.

Impact of Outsourcing on Library Cataloguing Staff

The number of the library's cataloguing positions decreased from 59 FTE to 29 FTE. Of the positions removed from the Cataloguing Division, nine were not directly affected by outsourcing. They were either surplus positions resulting from the implementation of the DRA system, or pre-order searching and verification positions that were transferred to other library units. Four of the 29 positions remaining in the Cataloguing Division were occupied by staff members who had decided to retire within two years and would not be replaced.

Outsourcing had other major effects on the library's cataloguing staff. During the year following the decision to outsource, most staff members experienced the classic stages that follow a major loss: denial, anger, depression, and acceptance. By the time staff reallocations were made, most staff were more optimistic about the opportunities for career change and development, whether or not they remained in the Cataloguing Division. The library's managers ensured that funding for an active staff training and development program would be available, which eased the transition process. The program included workshops on change; orientation programs about individual unit libraries presented by public services staff; and basic training in collections, reference, and circulation. Although many cataloguing staff had worked part-time in public service before outsourcing, this program gave all cataloguing staff a broader perspective about other aspects of the library. It also introduced them to potential colleagues in other units.

Staff members had the freedom to apply for whatever positions at their classification levels they desired, after having had the opportunity to participate in the orientation and training sessions. Commitments to job security and retraining remained throughout this process. In spite of these measures, however, there was a period of anxiety, disappointment, stress, and uncertainty. Eighteen months after their reallocation, some individuals who left the Cataloguing Division are pleased with their new positions, while others believe that their skills and aptitudes are not as well matched to their new duties.

The jobs of staff members who remained in cataloguing also changed. The loss of colleagues, and their specialized expertise, made the transition difficult. Standards for in-house operations had to be updated to conform with standards established for the ISM/LTS's staff. Some tasks remained the same, but most staff were required to assume additional and broader assignments. For many, this was a welcome opportunity to learn new skills, apply existing skills in other situations, or expand their scope of responsibilities.

Impact of Outsourcing on Other Library Staff

Outsourcing has also affected staff outside the Cataloguing Division. Partial outsourcing of the receiving function had an unexpectedly large impact on staff in the Acquisitions Division and the Financial Systems and Analysis Division, where procedural changes and retraining were required. Acquisitions staff worked with ISM/LTS's staff and the library's book vendors to facilitate changes in shipping and to ensure prompt payment of invoices. The level of coordination between acquisitions and cataloguing processes became more important than ever. Simultaneous implementation of the DRA acquisitions module and outsourcing with ISM/LTS also posed some challenges. Other unanticipated outcomes of outsourcing related to the increased shipping/receiving of material to ISM/LTS, sorting requirements, and tracking/coordination with other units and processes.

Impact on Consortium Libraries

The NEOS consortium has a shared database with shared bibliographic records. Staff members at other NEOS libraries had some concerns that the University of Alberta Library's outsourcing might have an adverse effect on the database, either through substandard records, duplicate records, or other problems. In response to these concerns, the library's staff reported on new outsourcing activities and agreements at meetings of the NEOS Cataloguing Standards Group. When the outsourcing specifications were written, the advisory team also ensured that the specifications adhered to NEOS cataloguing standards.

Expansion of Outsourcing Services

A major benefit of the ISM/LTS contract has been a pilot project to add MARC fields for tables of contents and summary information to the library's catalogue records. Through an agreement with Blackwell North America, Inc., ISM/LTS's processing includes the addition of these fields from Blackwell's database to the library's records. Approximately 25 percent of the library's records were enriched in this manner during the first year.

Outsourcing Results

The library's managers have accomplished the major objectives anticipated for outsourcing at the outset: to achieve budgetary reduction targets, to reallocate resources to direct user services and focus on services to library patrons, and to protect job security. Expenditures were reduced by containing costs for temporary staff, continuing a hiring freeze, and encouraging natural attrition through voluntary, early-retirement incentives. Cataloguing costs have been reduced by an estimated 25 percent to 35 percent and can be capped on an annual basis. This has been a significant achievement, although no attempt has been made to estimate cost savings that could have been realized by retaining all cataloguing activity in-house and applying the new cataloguing standards used by the vendor.

Conclusion

Outsourcing of the majority of cataloguing for the University of Alberta Library was a major endeavor. Working together, library staff and ISM/LTS staff devoted enormous efforts to planning and implementation. After more than one year of operation, the arrangement is working well and the library administration's objectives have been met. ISM/LTS's staff have developed a flourishing cataloguing and physical processing service, which now serves several other Canadian libraries. An initiative, which many saw as a leap of faith into the unknown, has proved its viability.

2

Vendor Preprocessing of Approval Material and Cataloging Records for the University of Arizona Library

Ann Fiegen and Stephen Bosch

University of Arizona Library's staff have outsourced copy cataloging, item record creation, and physical processing for domestic approval books since 1996, in collaboration with Blackwell North America, Inc. and Innovative Interfaces, Inc. Outsourcing was accomplished by contracting with each vendor to develop software that resulted in a weekly Internet File Transfer Protocol (FTP) transmission from Blackwell of full-level catalog records, enhanced with table of contents information and fields containing item and invoice data, for loading into Innovative's system. From January to March 1996, 93.77 percent of Blackwell's approval books were supplied with full cataloging and physical processing. The project has resulted in significant savings in costs and staffing for processing of approval titles, while greatly improving the receipt-to-shelf speed for new books. Books that required 30 minutes for in-house cataloging and physical processing in 1993 are now routed through the library's technical services area in 75 seconds per title.

Reengineering, downsizing, process improvement, and outsourcing are tools that have been employed in the 1990s as library managers rethink

This chapter is based on a presentation made by Ann Fiegen at the Association for Library Collections and Technical Services' Commercial Technical Services Committee's program, Creative Outsourcing: Assessment and Evaluation, New York City, July 9, 1996.

ways in which services are delivered to patrons. Technical processing is one aspect of library operations that has come under close scrutiny and pressure for change. In this era of shrinking budgets, library managers have had to scrutinize the total costs of providing technical services and reevaluate service delivery mechanisms.

The University of Arizona Library's staff have been subjected to this pressure for change. Budget reductions during the 1980s and 1990s, and the resultant 11 percent cut in total staff, most of which occurred in technical services, forced the reevaluation of several activities and functions. Technical processing was examined closely for ways to achieve cost savings.

In reengineering technical services, it was necessary to assess the cost effectiveness of the value added by each process. Library managers and staff had to determine if work done at each step actually added value in terms of satisfying customer needs. If customers needed good bibliographic access and wanted material on the library's shelves as soon as possible, at the lowest feasible cost, the primary question was whether this work had to be performed in-house by existing staff. The question was posed as to whether other organizations could do the same work less expensively and as well as or better than in-house staff. The library's approval plan program was one area in which the answers to these questions led to outsourcing with a commercial vendor.

Background

Before outsourcing, library staff used a standard approach for acquiring and processing approval titles. Their approval vendor, Blackwell North America, Inc., located in Lake Oswego, Oregon, shipped books weekly. Temporary records were transferred electronically from Blackwell to the library and loaded into the online catalog from Innovative Interfaces, Inc. These records, with brief bibliographic and invoice data, were used to receive books and process payments. Once received, approval books were placed on a shelf for examination by selectors. Books remained on review for about one week, before they were forwarded for further processing. Rejected books were noted on invoices and returned to the vendor. The average annual return rate was 1.8 percent.

Approval titles that were accepted for the collection were searched by Library Assistant Seniors in the Online Library Computer Center (OCLC) database to obtain catalog records from the Library of Congress (LC) or OCLC's member libraries. Matching copy-cataloging records were edited and holdings information was added in the OCLC database. Two local 949 fields were entered during editing: One was designed to build an item record with location, copy, volume, and barcode information; another issued commands to add records to the library's local system. Cataloged material was forwarded to Cataloging Support for label creation and attachment. After labeling was completed, all books were moved to the Bindery and Preservation area, where book pockets, property stamps, and security system strips were applied. The bindery processed items for commercial binding, and all other material was forwarded to the stacks.

The library received 14,208 Blackwell approval titles in FY 1994/95, the year before moving to outsourced approval cataloging. Full-level LC cataloging was available for 7,166, or 50 percent, of total receipts. An additional 6,050, or 42 percent, of total receipts had Cataloging-in-Publication (CIP) records that required additional editing. The remaining 8 percent of material was cataloged using either OCLC member records or original records.

The processing of domestic approval books was an area that appeared to have real potential for positive change, when this operation was scrutinized in the early 1990s. Approval vendors were known to "handle" books as part of their work, in much the same manner as library staff. To support their approval programs over the years, vendors had also created high-level systems for bibliographic access and control. Technology had advanced to the point that, theoretically, it was possible to export a vendor's bibliographic data to a library's local system. It was this type of strategic thinking that eventually led library staff to explore outsourcing for the processing of this material.

In their quest to improve approval processing routines, library staff envisioned receiving shelf-ready books, full-level catalog records, and fully processed payments, with minimal intervention by staff once material arrived in the library. In this scenario, books would be unpacked and directly forwarded to the stacks. Full-level MARC (machine-readable cataloging) bibliographic records would be supplied by an outside vendor and electronically entered into the local system in packages of whole files, rather than on a manual record-by-record basis. Similarly, invoices would be paid electronically as whole files. For those processes where intervention by library staff might be needed, it was envisioned that computer-programmable solutions would be found. Processes requiring human intervention would be critically examined in this overall plan.

In fall 1993, a decision was made to explore the possibility of obtaining preprocessed approval books according to this vision. To make this vision a reality, however, library staff knew it would be necessary to work closely on system development with both a book vendor and the library's online catalog vendor. Staff began investigating the availability of services from book vendors by informally contacting vendors and staff at other libraries. These inquiries indicated that the combination of services desired was not yet available from book vendors. Although most vendors were experienced in providing clients with "shelf-ready" material at that time, none had experience in transmitting electronic bibliographic, order, item, and invoice information, as one integrated package, to a large research library using Innovative's online system.

Nevertheless, managers at Blackwell, the library's existing approval vendor, were willing to invest the time and effort to develop the service program envisioned by library staff. For that reason, Blackwell was selected as the vendor for this outsourcing project. OCLC's PromptCat service was evaluated as a possible alternative when it became available in 1995. At that time, however, PromptCat did not include the full spectrum of physical processing and electronic connectivity desired for this particular project.

Outsourcing Objectives

In fall 1994, a project team, consisting of five staff members from systems, acquisitions, and cataloging, was assigned the task of planning the transition to a preprocessed domestic approval plan. The Blackwell North America Project Team established three primary outsourcing objectives:

1. Reduce the operational costs for cataloging and physical processing of approval plan material.

2. Reallocate staff from technical services processing activities to the library's public service areas. Two library assistant seniors spent most of their time processing Blackwell approval material.

3. Increase the delivery speed of approval plan titles to library patrons.

To achieve these objectives, the project team completed the following steps:

■ A contract was negotiated with Blackwell to receive their MARC-PLUS records (that is, LC MARC bibliographic records plus invoice information), for all Blackwell approval titles. Library staff chose to accept MARC-PLUS records derived from LC MARC only. CAN MARC and UK MARC, from Canada and the United Kingdom, respectively, were not in the cataloging profile.

■ In addition to receiving full catalog records from Blackwell, library staff requested that books be as fully processed as possible. The library's specifications called for each piece to have a spine label, barcode, book pocket, property stamp, and security system strip. Paperbacks were to be included in this program as well. Initially, only books with matching catalog records would receive physical processing. Changing the in-house workflow for books without catalog records was beyond the scope of the project.

- Although the initial contract excluded CIP records, the team agreed to purchase Blackwell's CIP upgrade product once that service was released in fall 1995. That process includes changes to the MARC leader and modification of all relevant variable fields, to upgrade the record to encoding level "p" in Leader byte 05 (record status). As many as 19 different fields would be reviewed and changed as part of the CIP upgrade service.

- Whenever possible, catalog records would also be enhanced with Blackwell's tables of contents information by the vendor's MARC Record Enrichment service.

- A separate file, consisting of LC data for fully cataloged records received from Blackwell, would be transmitted via the Internet File Transfer Protocol (FTP) to OCLC to update the library's holdings in the OCLC database.

- Invoices and payment information for individual titles acquired in this new arrangement would continue to be transmitted via FTP.

In addition to this outsourcing strategy, Blackwell's staff developed specific software that would create proper shelving locations, item records, and order records, as files from Blackwell were loaded into the library's local system. These steps were accomplished by making the following modifications to MARC records during the vendor's MARC customization process:

- An 049 field, with an appropriate OCLC holding-library symbol (based on a call number conversion table supplied by library staff), was added to each record.

- A 949 field was added to build item record information. The 949 field had a second indicator of "1" and subfields to hold location, barcode, and copy data. The 049 field information was used to create location data in the 949 subfield.

- A 980 field, with subfield information on list price, selling price, invoice number, invoice line item number, and so forth, was used to build an order record.

The project team worked with Innovative's staff to design special loading software for entering Blackwell's data into the library's local system. The specifications for this work with Innovative included the following requirements:

- Two separate files for full and brief MARC records from Blackwell needed to be fully integrated into the local database. The file containing brief MARC records would be loaded as a standard, temporary-approval file. The file containing full MARC records would be loaded in the same manner as OCLC catalog records had traditionally been loaded into the library's system.
- Bibliographic, order, and item records would be created for each book with a full MARC catalog record.
- Items from Blackwell, for which full LC MARC copy was unavailable, would be entered into the local system with brief records only. Those records would contain bibliographic and order information components.

It was assumed that invoicing and payment processing for both files would be accomplished in the same way they had been done in the past.

Outsourcing Scope and Constraints

Once the software development requirements had been established, library staff identified internal measures needed to support outsourcing.

Approval Plan Scope

To enhance the cost effectiveness of the project, the approval plan's scope had to be broadened to include as many titles as possible. In cases where books were published in both the United States and Great Britain, it was decided that the domestic edition would be obtained preprocessed from Blackwell. Staff knew that this approach could result in a delay in receiving these items, due to the publishing lag time for domestic editions. The decreased time for technical processing of this material was viewed as adequate compensation for this delay. In addition, standing orders for monographic series were reviewed to determine which items were treated in the approval plan. If titles were available on an approval basis, the corresponding standing orders were canceled and items were added to the library's regular approval program. This change ensured that more books in the standing-order category would arrive preprocessed.

Local Practices and Processing Limitations

The original goal of outsourcing was to acquire as many shelf-ready books as possible and to minimize the amount of time that in-house staff handled books. However, library managers realized that only a certain percentage of approval titles would qualify for preprocessing. It was estimated at the beginning of the project that Blackwell would be able to supply LC catalog records and physical processing for 90 percent of approval books, and that the other 10 percent of titles would be shipped to the library without cataloging or physical processing. Other categories of material were also expected to be preprocessed by Blackwell, which would require further in-house work to provide correct bibliographic access. Procedures needed to be devised to identify the following types of material among preprocessed shipments:

- Parts of multivolume sets, which would need individual volume information for item records or spine labels
- Records with nonbibliography call numbers in LC's Z classification schedule, which would need reclassification to appropriate subject classifications
- Records treated as analyzed serials by LC, which might need reclassification to other call numbers in order to conform with the library's local practices
- Records for reference material, which would need to be assessed for inclusion in various reference areas and modified accordingly
- Duplicate copies of material already in the collection or on order
- Oversize material

Outsourcing Outcomes

Much of what the project team envisioned as they developed their specifications has been realized, although the team needed 16 months to implement cataloging and physical processing of Blackwell's approval plan material. Planning began in September 1994. Testing began in April 1995 with 86 records, and gradually increased to full weekly shipments of 250 records through December 1995. Full production began in January 1996.

Cataloging

From January 1996 through May 1996, fully processed material and records with LC cataloging copy were delivered for 93.77 percent of books acquired from Blackwell. Enhanced tables of contents information was included for 80 percent of those records. Among 2,519 titles received between January 1996 and March 1996, only 157 titles, or 6.23 percent, arrived without cataloging copy. In addition, only 106 books and records for the 2,362 cataloged items required further in-house processing. Modifications to those items included seven call number changes to nonbibliography Z classification numbers, one call number change pertaining to numeration in the call number, 10 changes in records for multivolume set records, one change for oversize material, and 22 changes to records for duplicate copies. A total of 65 books were reviewed for addition to the library's reference collection. An additional 114 CIP records required local upgrading, because Blackwell's CIP upgrade service was not in full production during the initial part of the January to May 1996 time frame.

The Blackwell approval plan represents 33 percent of yearly monographic receipts. Given the volume of material cataloged by Blackwell in the new outsourcing arrangement, the library's business relationship with OCLC changed. This shift from using OCLC's bibliographic database for cataloging books to acquiring vendor-supplied bibliographic records implies a basic shift in the way in which library staff use the OCLC database. This change resulted in the library becoming a tape-loading member of OCLC. Blackwell's records are currently used to update OCLC holdings in an automated process, via FTP.

Although there were minor problems with record loading in general, library staff have continued to address issues associated with loading Blackwell's records into the local system. Data from the MARC record (location, material type, bibliographic level, language codes, and country codes) did not initially map into the local database under INNOPAC Release 9.1. An interim solution was adopted, which required library staff to manipulate the files globally as they were loaded into the system. This solution will no longer be needed following Release 10 implementation of INNOPAC.

Physical Processing and Binding

Library patrons report that Blackwell's spine labels are easier to read and more attractive than the library's in-house labels. The vendor's other physical processing services, including barcodes, security strips, and pockets, have been consistent and excellent.

There was a modest reduction in bindery costs as a result of outsourcing, because paperbacks received on approval are no longer rebound before release to the stacks. Paperbacks are now preprocessed in the same way as other material, and are shelved "as is" when shipped from Blackwell. Although staff in the library's Bindery and Preservation area had major misgivings about processing paperbacks in this manner, items supplied by Blackwell in the first few months of outsourcing included a minimal number of exceptionally thin paperbacks. It is anticipated that there will only be a small increase in book repairs and bindery costs, if for any reason these specific titles are damaged over time.

Costs

Blackwell's pricing is based on the library's unique cataloging and physical processing specifications. Because outsourcing charges vary among libraries, depending on the specific options chosen, the library's following per-book costs are not universally applicable:

$ .25   MARC-PLUS Record

$ .75   MARC Enrichment (as applicable)

$ .50   MARC Customization

$1.35   Book Processing

$2.85   Total (Add $1.50 for records with CIP upgrade)

Outsourcing costs are paid from the library's materials budget. Accounting staff created a single line, separate from the regular approval lines, for outsourcing costs. Historically, the materials budget was used to purchase many types of bibliographic records, including payments for OCLC services. Based on this precedent, library staff determined that outsourcing costs were part of the materials budget. There was no negative impact on funds for other areas, since base increases were received during fiscal years 1994/95 and 1995/96. A portion of the new funds were added to cover the costs associated with this project.

Comparative in-house costs are unavailable. However, library staff have engaged in a structured Process Improvement Plan for technical services operations. A key component of that plan is data collection and analysis of in-house cataloging and physical processing costs for books with LC copy cataloging records.

Approval Plan to Blanket Plan Strategy

One change that was difficult for library selectors to accept was the fundamental shift from an approval plan to a "blanket" plan for collection development. The standard practice of returning a certain percentage of approval books was curtailed when outsourcing was implemented, in order to maintain a low discount rate for the library. The discount rate would have been greatly reduced if books were returned to Blackwell. Because Blackwell's preprocessed books are customized with property stamp markings and other processing products, those items cannot be resold by the vendor or returned to a publisher.

Library staff had several discussions with selectors to educate them about the background for this fundamental change to a blanket order plan. One positive aspect of this issue was that the library's rate of returns was only

1.8 percent before implementation of outsourcing. Consequently, the over-all financial impact of possibly acquiring that additional percentage of material was minimal, when compared with the overall benefits of outsourcing.

After outsourcing began, all preprocessed material was accepted for the collection, unless damaged during shipment. Preliminary data suggest that there was no automatic 1.8 percent increase in receipts. Reports indicate that from January to June 1996, 75, or less than 1 percent, fewer books were received from the approval plan than during January to June 1995. Discussions with selectors indicate that they were not returning "marginal" notification slips, because corresponding items could not be returned. Since outsourcing began, all approval plan books have been accepted by library staff to be absorbed into the collection. Overall, the initial impact of shifting to a blanket plan has not adversely affected the overall cost for the approval plan nor has it had a negative impact on shelving.

During discussions with selectors, library staff stressed that the approval profile must be actively managed, because the option of returning unwanted items would no longer exist. Staff suggested ways to manage approval plans other than weekly hands-on evaluation of new material. For example, management reports from the vendor and catalog-generated lists that describe material supplied by the program can be used by selectors to assess approval plan performance. Exceptionally broad or narrow categories can be examined for modification. In addition, these reports can be used to clarify the plan's long-term performance, instead of relying on data from weekly evaluation decisions.

Staff Teamwork

One consequence of outsourcing was an increase in the interaction between Acquisitions Department staff and the library's selectors. Before the preprocessing project, selectors were not fully aware of the details for the library's approval plan profile. Because they had previously evaluated all titles for acceptance or rejection, they always had the option of returning unwanted items to the vendor. The only incentive for selectors to work with Acquisitions Department staff on modifying the approval plan profile occurred when individual selectors became tired of repeatedly rejecting similar items.

With the implementation of outsourcing, however, selectors had to manage the approval profile instead of managing the results of the profile. Consequently, selectors needed to understand the profile structure and learn how to assess the profile for modification. In addition, need increased for budget reports, activity reports, and book lists produced from the online catalog by Acquisitions Department staff. These reports aided selectors with monitoring approval plan activity in their assigned subject areas.

Library staff demonstrated more teamwork in the process of developing an integrated approach for managing their approval plan. Instead of returning unwanted material, staff systematically assessed the overall activity of the plan. The profile was changed when material that was out of scope with the selectors' collection interests consistently appeared in book shipments. In addition to obtaining a better approval plan in this process, staff saved considerable time. The library's selectors, a group of 50 librarians, no longer need to spend an hour each week reviewing approval books. Instead, selectors now spend a few hours each quarter assessing management reports about material received from the approval plan, and modifying the plan as needed. Although approval plan modification has created an increased workload for acquisitions staff, the cost and time savings among the library's selectors have more than offset the additional work in the Acquisitions Department.

Staffing, Turnaround Time, and Productivity

Concurrent with the implementation of the library's outsourcing project, a fundamental shift has occurred in the way that staff at the University of Arizona work in general. All staff have the opportunity to serve on cross-functional project teams. The work of the cross-functional teams varies from long-range planning and budget allocation for the whole library to such projects as implementation of outsourced cataloging. Through the work of these teams, the library's direction is determined and new services are implemented. It is also crucial to the success of these new services that significant savings in staffing and other costs be found wherever possible.

Three staff on the six-member Order Receiving Team, which processes weekly Blackwell shipments, spend much of their time on work related to one or more other teams. Significant time savings have been realized by the entire Order Receiving Team as a result of outsourcing, because most work previously performed by two team members is now done by the vendor. Data from a time-analysis study conducted in 1993 indicated that each title required about 30 minutes for receipt, cataloging, and physical processing, using an LC copy catalog record from the OCLC database. In 1996, the average processing and cataloging time for titles in three weekly shipments from Blackwell was 75 seconds per title. This work involves transmitting and loading files from Blackwell into INNOPAC, verifying receipt of books, printing and identifying lists of titles to receive local work, and making those changes.

Interviews with staff affected by outsourcing indicate an immediate effect on productivity when preprocessed books began arriving. Approval material was released from the technical services area much faster. The average weekly shipments of Blackwell's approval books, ranging from 200 to 250 items, are now processed within 48 hours of receipt, compared to a previous average turnaround time of five days. Instead of processing approval titles, cataloging staff now have more flexibility to assist each other, to process backlog material, and to catalog multimedia material. All staff in technical services spend from two to seven hours weekly at circulation desks, general information desks, or reference desks. Time saved by outsourcing allows affected staff to add a few more hours weekly to other tasks.

Preliminary data indicate that the library has saved 60 hours per week of staff time in the cataloging and physical processing areas as a result of outsourcing. Furthermore, there is a fundamental change from working as a copy cataloger, responsible for performing simple repetitive processing of LC records, to managing electronic file transfers. When asked about their plans for the future, several copy catalogers and other staff have indicated new interest in learning about emerging technologies. Staff are also being trained to manage more complex multiple-file electronic transmissions and to manipulate files for global updating in the online catalog. The net result is that staff have a more integrated view of their work and no longer view themselves only as copy catalogers.

Library staff look forward to learning more about outsourcing, as contracts for additional outside services from vendors are established. Library staff also plan to reduce the in-house turnaround time for Blackwell material that arrives each Friday. Essentially, the goal is to provide a 24-hour turnaround time for Blackwell material and to release new books from technical services by the following Monday. Other short-range staffing plans include the opportunity for reassignment to other areas of the library. This will occur once the Process Improvement Plan activity is fulfilled, the corresponding data analysis is completed, and decisions regarding redesign of technical services are made.

Conclusion

As librarians in general seek avenues for reducing costs and collaborate in development partnerships with material vendors and system suppliers, an intricate arrangement is created that must align the technical capabilities, the development priorities, and the available resources of each partner. When embarking on a major service change with no established products, system vendors and their clients often need to agree on temporary solutions. The solutions may not be ideal, but might be sufficient for project implementation. Products can be finalized as work continues during additional phases of development. As products are developed, flexibility on the part of all partners is essential for success.

For this project, the automatic creation of bibliographic, order, invoice, and item records has not yet been completed. Eventually, this process will evolve through a phased approach, as software enhancements from Blackwell North America, Inc. and Innovative Interfaces, Inc. make this possible.

This was a seminal outsourcing project. Now that an awareness exists that this type of processing can be successfully accomplished outside the library, other outsourcing applications will be explored at the University of Arizona Library. Newly acquired knowledge and expertise will be used to extend the outsourcing process to other approval plans and other types of orders, including notification slip plans, firm orders, standing orders, and the acquisition of audiovisual material. In these future expansions of the library's outsourcing program, vendors will be assessed on the basis of their ability to meet standards established in this groundbreaking project.

3 Authority Control and Record Enrichment Outsourcing at the University of California, Santa Barbara

Cecily Johns

Library staff at the University of California, Santa Barbara (UCSB) have outsourced authority control and MARC (machine-readable cataloging) record enrichment to Blackwell North America, Inc. Retrospective authority control processing of nearly 1 million bibliographic records was performed during 1989–90, in preparation for UCSB's migration from a card catalog to the NOTIS online catalog. Outsourcing expanded in 1990 to include ongoing processing of approximately 6,800 newly created bibliographic records per month and the delivery of matching authority records. In 1993, UCSB Library's staff opted to acquire Blackwell's monographic MARC Record Enrichment service with tables of contents (TOC). The TOC record enrichment rate for eligible titles ranged from 45 percent to 55 percent of the library's current cataloging during 1996.

Library staff at the University of California, Santa Barbara (UCSB) have had a long and fruitful relationship with Blackwell North America, Inc., located in Lake Oswego, Oregon. Blackwell's services have included an approval plan, retrospective and ongoing authority control, tables of contents record enrichment, receipt of Library of Congress (LC) MARC (machine-readable cataloging) records for matching books, and physical processing of books. The outsourcing services covered in this chapter include authority control processing, launched in 1989–90, and bibliographic record enrichment, which began in 1993.

Background

The UCSB Library is a member of the Association of Research Libraries and has over 2.3 million volumes, representing 1.9 million unique titles, in its collection. The campus and the library have operated in an environment of staff downsizing throughout the 1990s. Since implementation of the NOTIS online catalog in 1989–90, there has been a 30 percent reduction in the size of the Cataloging Department's staff. In FY 1996, the department had 28.25 FTE career employees (5.5. FTE librarians and 22.75 library assistants), with an additional seven FTE student assistants. Since 1989–90, the library's staff have cataloged an average of 37,817 titles annually.

Before contracting with a vendor for authority control processing, UCSB Library's staff performed all authority work manually in a card environment. This work involved the ongoing creation of a series file and a separate name authority file. Staff also relied on the LC authority file, once it became available through the Research Libraries Information Network (RLIN) database. In addition to those procedures, a subject catalog editor (a high-level library assistant) routinely made extensive changes and updates to the subject card catalog. As new cards were filed in the author-title catalog, errors in headings were also identified by that quality control check. This manual authority control management system was in place until the end of the 1980s.

Authority Control Strategy for the NOTIS Online Database

In 1989, UCSB's campus administrators funded the acquisition of an integrated library system and the NOTIS system was selected for implementation. Technical services librarians, together with the library's systems staff, began intensive planning for establishing the online catalog. A NOTIS Implementation Team and a separate Authority Control Task Force were formed to plan and execute the complex set of tasks required to install an online system. Task force members included the head of cataloging, the principal cataloger, and the library automation librarian. The associate university librarian (AUL) for technical services and the AUL for administrative services worked closely with the task force to coordinate and facilitate financial and administrative details.

The task force investigated two authority control services vendors. Based on information gathered in early 1989, both directly from vendors and through references at academic libraries, the task force recommended Blackwell as the outsourcing vendor. Because UCSB Library's staff were pleased with Blackwell's performance as their approval vendor and were familiar with the company's reputation for reliability and quality in database processing work, the NOTIS Implementation Team selected Blackwell as the vendor of choice as well.

The task force's proposal to the library's administrators emphasized that authority control management was a critical requirement for the NOTIS online catalog, in order to facilitate and optimize bibliographic access to name, series, uniform title, and subject entries. In addition to the benefits of standardized and updated headings, catalog users would benefit from a cross-reference structure based on LC name and subject authority files. In justifying their strategy for outsourcing authority control processing, the task force described this approach in a written report by stating that the vendor could "create an automated bibliographical file of quality [which] ensures optimum access to the collections by patrons" (Memorandum of October 6, 1989).

Another factor for establishing authority control for the online catalog was that library staff had previously completed a database retrospective conversion project using Carrollton Press/Utlas's REMARC product, a machine-matching service for pre-LC MARC (machine-readable catalog) records, for a large portion of its catalog-record conversion. Staff knew that many of the converted records contained older forms of headings, which needed updating for compatibility with more recent catalog records. The updating of those access points was viewed as another benefit of authority control processing.

Cost savings were not considered as a goal when the decision was made to contract with a vendor for authority control processing. The expense of creating an authority file and cross-reference structure was considered an essential part of the online system. When the proposal was made by the head of cataloging to outsource authority processing with Blackwell, however, the library's administrators determined that this expense should be a "no cost" item in the budget. Therefore, a position was left vacant to pay for the service.

Outsourcing Objectives

Based on input from the task force, the NOTIS Implementation Team established the following objectives for the retrospective authority control outsourcing program before NOTIS implementation:

- Create a name and subject authority file developed from UCSB Library's bibliographic records, which would provide a cross-reference structure for the online catalog through links between the authority file and the bibliographic file.
- Update the name, series, and subject heading entries in UCSB's catalog to the latest forms of heading used by LC.

Retrospective Authority Control Processing

The task force members recommended that a snapshot tape of UCSB's bibliographic records be acquired from the Research Libraries Group (RLG) RLIN database for processing by Blackwell. In preparation for the project, a snapshot tape of 825,000 bibliographic records was acquired from RLG for the period through the end of May 1989. Three supplemental tapes, totaling 72,489 records and covering from June 1989 through February 1990, were also ordered from RLG and forwarded to Blackwell. During the following months, several supplementary tapes, containing about 120,000 additional records, were generated by RLG as well.

It was estimated that the library's database of approximately 1 million bibliographic records would produce 3 million name, series, and subject entries. On the basis of those estimates, an authority file of 1.38 million records was anticipated to be generated by Blackwell's staff. The library staff's expectations of the work to be completed in the authority control processing were as follows:

1. Upgrade name, series, and subject entries to the latest LC form and standardize variant forms of headings.
2. Reconcile cataloging variations resulting from use of both the *Anglo-American Cataloging Rules* and *Anglo-American Cataloguing Rules,* second edition, 1988 revision, guidelines.
3. Generate collection-specific LC name and subject authority files.
4. Create minimal authority records for headings that did not have matching LC records. These records were intended to serve as the basis for adding local cross-references to the NOTIS catalog.

In addition to having Blackwell's staff perform machine-matched authority control processing, the library's staff opted to outsource the manual review of nonmatched and partially matched headings to Blackwell.

Retrospective Authority Control Processing and NOTIS Implementation

It is important to identify unanticipated issues that emerged in outsourcing. The library's staff had originally planned to implement the NOTIS online catalog in the fall of 1989, before the beginning of the university's academic year. However, manual review of authority records is labor-intensive. The vendor estimated that review of the nearly 1 million records in UCSB's database would require seven months, from the receipt of RLG's tapes to the delivery of Blackwell's output files. It became obvious that the time required for manual review of the library's bibliographic records would extend beyond the catalog's scheduled implementation date. Because the library's staff wanted to activate the online catalog with bibliographic records that had already received authority control processing, the catalog implementation schedule was adjusted to accommodate the vendor's manual editing schedule.

Because the library's circulation system from CLSI, Inc. needed to be replaced before the beginning of the academic year, however, the library's administrators decided to implement the NOTIS circulation module before implementing the NOTIS online catalog. Although most libraries activate online catalogs before activating their circulation and acquisitions modules, UCSB's staff chose an alternate plan for NOTIS system implementation in order to accommodate the authority control outsourcing schedule.

Budgeting for Retrospective Authority Control Processing

Another outsourcing challenge was the difficulty in budgeting for authority control processing, since the final number of bibliographic records that would be processed by Blackwell was not easy to predict. Several factors contributed to this problem. One factor was that successful efforts to accelerate retrospective conversion projects before NOTIS implementation generated more MARC bibliographic records than anticipated during the budget preparation phase. The library's staff had to estimate outsourcing costs based on a projected number of MARC bibliographic records at the time the RLIN snapshot tape would be produced. The record count was higher than predicted.

Another determinant, not realized until after the budget had been completed, was that location changes made by staff in the library's database triggered the inclusion of a record on the output file supplied to Blackwell. A large, ongoing project to move material to a storage facility inadvertently increased the number of records and the cost of authority control processing.

Furthermore, the date for implementation of the online catalog was delayed. It was difficult to estimate the final count of records for authority processing, since this delay affected the number of records for shipment to Blackwell. Although task force members were able to estimate the number of records cataloged annually with reasonable accuracy, the output from retrospective conversion and catalog maintenance projects was harder to predict.

In addition to the inability to predict with accuracy the final number of records, the unit cost per record varied for the snapshot tape and the supplementary tapes. The initial batch of records on the snapshot tape cost $.127 per record for machine-match and manual review processes. The unit costs for the supplemental batches of records ranged between $.162 and $.176. The difference in the unit cost was due to the application of minimum charges, depending on the size of the batch. The only cost data available at the time the outsourcing budget was prepared was the $.127 figure.

All these factors had a major impact on the budget planning process for the subsequent fiscal year. Ultimately, the total cost for the outsourcing of authority control work was substantially more than originally budgeted. Nevertheless, a major investment in the online system had been made. The library's administrators agreed that a corresponding investment should be made to improve the bibliographic database, in order to create an online catalog with a cross-reference structure. The expense was justified with the belief that it would substantially reduce future bibliographic maintenance costs as well.

Results of Retrospective Authority Control Processing

The task force made spot checks once the database and authority files were loaded. During the retrospective project, collection-specific LC and minimal name and subject authority files of 1.28 million records were generated. Based on the task force's evaluation of the updated bibliographic records and authority files, the library's administrators and the NOTIS Implementation Team members agreed that all objectives of the outsourcing project were met. However, the objective to create minimal-level records was eliminated, because they were not as essential as had been anticipated originally.

Ongoing Authority Control Processing

Because the decision to contract with Blackwell for ongoing processing of new catalog records had to be reached before the retrospective authority control work was done, there was no opportunity to complete a cost-benefit analysis before taking that action. Nevertheless, the task force and the library's administrators agreed to a commitment for ongoing processing, if a funding source could be determined at the time the decision was made. Consequently, the salary savings from a vacant position in the Cataloging Department were reallocated to fund the costs of the ongoing service. The objectives of the ongoing processing are the same as those of the initial retrospective project. Each month a tape of approximately 6,800 bibliographic records for current cataloging is exported to Blackwell for processing. One month after receiving the tape, Blackwell's staff provide machine-updated and manually reviewed bibliographic records, as well as new collection-specific authority records.

Ongoing Authority Control Maintenance Requirements

One factor affecting ongoing authority processing is that UCSB Library's catalog database is composed of both bibliographic records created by in-house staff and a large number of records purchased from outside vendors. Records from MARCIVE Inc. and from the Online Computer Library Center (OCLC) database are among the files from external sources. During the first five years since the online catalog was created, 500,000 records from outside sources have been acquired and loaded in the database.

For each subset of records loaded, an oversight committee for the NOTIS system also must decide whether that particular group of records should be outsourced to Blackwell for authority control. Generally, the committee has decided not to send records that will be upgraded later and then sent to Blackwell. Catalog records acquired and loaded as a source of copy cataloging only, which are suppressed from display in the public catalog, are not sent for processing either. The NOTIS output program, which generates monthly tapes for ongoing authority control processing by Blackwell, needs to be modified occasionally to include or exclude groups of records from external sources. This modification process was an unanticipated aspect of outsourcing, the impact of which has been absorbed by the library's systems staff.

In addition, the catalog database is comprised of a large number of brief serial records, which emanated from an automated serial union list that was loaded at the time the online catalog database was created. As these records are upgraded, the recataloging effort creates another source of new records for ongoing authority control processing.

Another in-house operation affected by ongoing authority processing is the procedure for catalog maintenance on records that are currently being processed by Blackwell's staff. When catalog records are supplied to the vendor on a monthly basis, any updated bibliographic records returned by Blackwell are matched by control number and overlay the library's original record. Because an entire bibliographic record is replaced in the overlay process, whole-record replacement necessitates the modification of workflow and procedures in the Cataloging Department. However, item record maintenance, and bibliographic record maintenance for records created after shipment of the last monthly tape, are unaffected by the overlay process and can continue uninterrupted.

New procedures have been established to address this aspect of ongoing authority processing. Cataloging staff do not modify bibliographic records that were created during the monthly time frame corresponding to the tape of records currently being processed by Blackwell, because modifications might be lost in the overlay process when Blackwell's output tape is loaded into the NOTIS system. For similar reasons, recent records are not deleted either, since they could reappear when the Blackwell records are loaded.

In-House Staffing for Authority Control Maintenance

As has been the case at other large research libraries with online catalogs, UCSB Library's managers have reassigned staff from other areas of technical services to the authority control unit following online catalog implementation. In mid-1996, the authority control unit contained 1.25 FTE and was composed of staff from the serials cataloging and retrospective conversion areas. Further allocation of staff from other areas of technical processing is planned, as special catalog maintenance, or retrospective conversion and cataloging projects, are completed. Authority work, such as global changes to headings, which is now performed in the unit, had not been done since the library's staff maintained a card catalog.

As stated by Allen Cohen, the library's head of cataloging in 1990, "In short, we and other libraries are faced with the paradox of automation potentially increasing access and service, but only if there is sufficient staffing to make it work" (Memorandum of May 7, 1990). No matter how much an authority control vendor improves a library's database, the local system's authority control module will dictate in-house staff time requirements for authority control maintenance. Ideally, records supplied by Blackwell would overlay existing authority records and automatically generate all corresponding bibliographic changes. In reality, most online library systems vendors have not yet automated all aspects of authority maintenance.

Outsourcing Tables of Contents Record Enrichment

In 1992, Blackwell's staff introduced a service to enrich monographic records with tables of contents (TOC). It was apparent that this new enhancement could be added to UCSB's ongoing authority control processing from Blackwell, without disrupting the routine workflow or affecting the established delivery schedule. In spring 1993, a test of the new MARC Record Enrichment service was conducted. Blackwell's staff matched one of UCSB's monthly authority control processing tapes against the TOC database. In that test, 25 percent of UCSB's MARC records were enhanced with TOC data.

A decision was made to contract for TOC records on an ongoing basis beginning in May 1993. The UCSB Library thus became one of the first academic libraries in the United States to use this service. By May 1996, 29,690 records had been enriched with TOC. The enrichment rate for eligible titles ranged from 45 percent to 55 percent. The unit cost for this service is $.75 for each record enriched with TOC data. The library's annual expenditure is approximately $7,700, covered by funds obtained from salary savings.

The benefit of acquiring this service is that author names and chapter titles from tables of contents in books are indexed by keyword in the NOTIS online catalog. At the record display level, catalog users can view tables of contents without having to retrieve books from the library's stacks. However, the access and display of TOC data in an online catalog is a function controlled by features in a library's local system. The NOTIS online catalog displays the MARC 505 field containing TOC data as a paragraph of text. Although this format can be difficult for patrons to read, the library's staff and patrons agree that the addition of keyword access to contents information more than offsets the display issue.

Before outsourcing TOC data, the idea of adding this operation as part of the in-house cataloging process had never been considered. Nevertheless, when the service was introduced, the benefits of enriching bibliographic records in this manner appealed to both the library's administrators and public services staff. Administrators concluded that Blackwell's unit cost was reasonable and well worth the benefits. Because expediting in-house processing is an established goal at UCSB, obtaining services such as TOC, which are more efficiently done in an outsourcing mode, will always be an attractive option.

Conclusion

To ensure success in outsourcing, it is critical that a planning group engage in thorough preparation before initiating an outsourcing project. This planning process includes studying vendor literature on the service being evaluated, asking questions when information is not clear, surveying staff at other libraries using the service, and testing the service whenever possible. Questions should be submitted not only to the outsourcing vendor, but to the vendor for the library's local online system as well.

If the outsourcing vendor requires a profile, it is important to study that document carefully and to provide the vendor with complete and accurate information. In most cases, the profile becomes part of the final outsourcing contract. It is also important to anticipate all outsourcing costs. The planning group should make a detailed analysis of vendor cost projections before making a final commitment. In addition, in-house costs should be assessed for performing the same process, even if the ultimate decision is to outsource.

One last key to a successful outsourcing program is to develop a good working relationship with the vendor and communicate regularly throughout that relationship. To facilitate this communication process, it is best if library managers designate a single individual to serve as the library's liaison with the outsourcing vendor, relaying problems and questions to a single vendor contact. At the UCSB Library, the chair of the Authority Control Task Force served as the liaison. Both the library's liaison and the vendor's representative must be responsive to each other to sustain this relationship. Occasionally, both parties will need to acknowledge their strengths and weaknesses. Building this trust between the vendor's staff and the library's staff is crucial to the overall success of any outsourcing effort, as it has been between Blackwell's staff and UCSB Library's staff.

Freelance Cataloging: Outsourcing Original Cataloging at Central Oregon Community College Library

Carol G. Henderson

Small Library Systems, in Silver Springs, Idaho, has provided off-site original cataloging for Central Oregon Community College Library's books and audiovisual material since 1994. The goals of this outsourcing project were to reduce original cataloging turnaround time, to improve cataloging quality, to decrease cataloging costs, and to provide the library's professional cataloger with more time for public service duties. After two years, turnaround time and cataloging error rates decreased substantially, and a staff member no longer needs to maintain expertise or time for original cataloging. Outsourcing also resulted in a 60 percent reduction of original cataloging costs.

Since spring 1994, staff at the Central Oregon Community College (COCC) Library and Media Department in Bend, Oregon, have used a freelance cataloging professional for original cataloging of books and audiovisual material. This outsourcing program was launched in an effort to reduce turnaround time for original cataloging, to improve the quality of original records, to decrease the cost of original cataloging, and to provide the cataloging librarian with more time for other duties in bibliographic instruction and library supervision.

Background

The COCC Library has a collection of approximately 42,000 volumes, with a staff of four (3.5 FTE) professionals and seven (7 FTE) library technical assistants. In FY 1996/97, the library's total budget was $617,000. The acquisitions budget was $81,000. Based on routine acquisitions patterns, library staff typically receive fewer than 50 titles per year requiring original cataloging. Most original cataloging is for older, gift items, as opposed to new material acquired through the library's purchase process. Original cataloging of recently published acquisitions is limited to about five items per year. Library staff use the Library of Congress classification system and obtain most of their catalog records from the Library Corporation's Bibliofile database. In addition, records are selected from the Online Computer Library Center (OCLC) database.

As is often the case in a small academic library, each staff member is responsible for a variety of duties. The in-house librarian who used to perform original cataloging also supervised the cataloging operation, supervised and trained paraprofessional reference staff, worked 10 hours each week at the reference desk, searched online reference databases, taught four sections of a library skills class, and served as the instructor of an Internet course. In addition, the original cataloger was a member of faculty committees and provided Internet training for individuals across campus and in the local community. The time available to maintain cataloging skills and create original records, while meeting all the public services demands of this position, was limited.

Turnaround time for original cataloging was problematic as well. Because of the relatively small number of items cataloged each year, the catalog librarian often waited until 10 or more items requiring original cataloging had accumulated before allocating time for cataloging. The cataloger preferred this strategy because it reduced the need to alternate frequently between public services work and cataloging tasks.

However, processing time for original cataloging was considerably slower than desired. Often, cataloging was done near the end of a 10-week term, when there were fewer demands for online searching, teaching, and reference work. As a result, turnaround time for original cataloging was usually six to eight weeks longer than for copy cataloging or adaptive cataloging. From June to September, when there were no contractual provisions for employing the cataloger, turnaround time for original cataloging ranged from three to four months. Consequently, outsourcing of original cataloging was viewed as one solution for reducing turnaround time throughout the calendar year.

Outsourcing Project Description

Small Library Systems (SLS), located in Silver Springs, Idaho, was selected as the library's vendor. This choice was made after one of SLS's catalogers was introduced to library staff at an annual telecommunications conference in Oregon. The outsourcing program began as a pilot project. Ten items, representative of the type of material typically earmarked for original cataloging, were sent to SLS's freelance cataloger for cataloging and evaluation. The test material included older titles that had been received as gifts, locally published material unlikely to be cataloged elsewhere, and foreign-language literature. The freelance cataloger also received a copy of the library's cataloging manual.

After the 10 items were cataloged, the records were reviewed for accuracy by the library's technical assistant responsible for adaptive cataloging, by the catalog librarian, and by an experienced professional cataloger from another institution. The review of sample records established that the freelance cataloger provided high-quality work. Library staff also concluded at the end of the pilot project that outsourcing was cost effective and could be performed on a more timely basis than in-house cataloging.

After the pilot project, routine procedures were established for outsourcing original cataloging on a regular basis. The first step in that ongoing process is to identify all library material that requires original cataloging. When a new item arrives in the Catalog Department, the copy cataloger searches the Bibliofile database for a catalog record, using the record identifier assigned in pre-order searching. If an acceptable catalog record is found, it is captured for cataloging. If no record is found, the item is then sought in the OCLC database.

If no matching catalog record is found in either the Bibliofile or OCLC databases, the item is evaluated by the adaptive cataloger as a candidate for original cataloging. If the adaptive cataloger is unable to locate a matching record during a second search of the databases, or a near-match record from which a new record can be created with minimal changes, the item is forwarded to SLS. Catalog records for similar items in the Bibliofile and OCLC databases are often printed during the search processes and shipped with original cataloging material. These database records serve as an additional resource for the freelance cataloger.

New material requiring original cataloging, which has been ordered by library staff or requested by COCC faculty, is shipped to SLS as soon as the pre-cataloging search process has been completed. Gift material is held until at least 10 items are accumulated. As a result, gifts can be shipped to SLS as late as six months after arrival at the library. Gifts usually consist of older titles, which are not deemed in need of urgent cataloging. Gifts that include information on a subject currently in demand, however, are handled as exceptions and are immediately forwarded to SLS. If more than two weeks elapse after the first round of pre-cataloging searches on the Bibliofile and OCLC databases, database searches are repeated to verify that all items still require original cataloging before items are shipped to SLS. This final search is conducted for both new purchases and gift titles.

Library staff ship material to SLS using United Parcel Service (UPS). The freelance cataloger performs all original cataloging with the item in hand, rather than working from photocopied title pages or other sources of cataloging information. SLS's staff return cataloged items via UPS, together with catalog records. COCC pays for shipping of material to SLS, and SLS pays for return shipping charges.

The vendor's catalog records are stored on floppy disks, which are preformatted for loading into the Bibliofile system used at COCC. The freelance cataloger prepares the records in a form that is also appropriate for uploading to OCLC. COCC's staff upload SLS's catalog records to the Bibliofile hard drive and process them in the same manner as other records from the Bibliofile CD-ROM database.

Impact of Outsourcing

The outsourcing goals were to reduce the amount of time required for processing material needing original cataloging, to improve the quality of original records added to COCC's catalog, to reduce the cost of original cataloging, and to allow the original cataloger more time for public services work. All goals were achieved during the first two years of outsourcing.

Turnaround Time

The average turnaround time for outsourced original cataloging is 20 days from date of mailing to date of receipt. Although low-priority gift items might still be held in the library as long as six months before being shipped to SLS, high-interest and newly purchased items are routinely cataloged within 20 days. This turnaround time is far superior to the 10 weeks previously required for material cataloged during the academic year and the three to four months previously required during the summer. With outsourcing, turnaround time for original cataloging is more comparable to the processing time for adaptive cataloging performed by library staff.

Record Quality

The quality of original cataloging records has improved significantly since library staff contracted with SLS. Before implementation of outsourcing, the in-house cataloger was unable to maintain a high level of skill while cataloging only 35 to 40 items annually. In comparison, the SLS cataloger assigned to work on the library's titles creates dozens of original catalog records every week, and effectively monitors and adheres to the latest changes in cataloging practices.

Cataloging errors by the library's in-house original cataloger, which occurred most frequently in records for nonstandard formats and foreign-language material, often required between two and four corrections each year in the three years before outsourcing. The library's formatting error reports in the Bibliofile database have decreased to zero since outsourcing for original cataloging began. Two typographical errors in outsourced records were identified and corrected by COCC's technical assistants during the past two years. However, because library staff have no records of typographical errors before outsourcing, no data are available for comparing the level of typographical errors between the in-house cataloger and the freelance cataloger.

Comparative Costs per Item

In addition to all other improvements in original cataloging, library managers have determined that outsourcing has been more cost effective. COCC's librarians have nine-month, faculty-contract appointments. The annual budget for a librarian averages $46,800 for salary and benefits. Based on a 45-hour week, the approximate hourly cost for a librarian is $27.

A brief time study of in-house original cataloging, in the year prior to outsourcing, revealed that the library's original cataloger required an estimated average time of 1.2 hours per item. The estimate included the time required to review and research cataloging rules each time cataloging was done. During the 45-hour time study, original catalog records were created for 37 items. Multiplying the 45 hours by the average $27 hourly cost for a professional cataloger, and dividing the sum by the number of items cataloged during the study, yields an approximate original cataloging cost of $32.84 per item.

Comparative outsourcing costs per item are considerably less. SLS charges $12 per item for catalog records in a format compatible with COCC's local cataloging system. COCC's shipping costs average $1.37 per item, with return shipping costs paid by the outsourcing provider. This amounts to an average outsourcing cost of $13.37 per item.

Based on these figures, it was estimated that the vendor would charge $535 for original cataloging of 40 items during a given year, compared with a total annual cost of $1,314 for in-house original cataloging of the same number of titles. The difference amounts to a $779 annual cost savings for COCC. Given the small size of COCC's operation and the limited number of titles that require original cataloging, the dollar savings is minimal. Cost savings in terms of overall percentages, however, are more significant. Outsourcing has provided the library's managers with original cataloging services at 40 percent of the former cost for creating original records in-house.

As with any cost comparison, it is important to recognize that the 60 percent cost savings in this case study cannot be viewed as universally applicable for other libraries. Staff in other libraries would need to conduct their own in-house cost studies and compare their costs with the contract rates from their specific outsourcing service providers. Local processing requirements and costs, as well as shipping fees and other overhead costs, would also need to be factored into any cost analysis.

Professional Staff Time

Because the library receives fewer than 50 titles per year for original cataloging, the savings in terms of staff time as a result of outsourcing is not significant. The library's cataloger used to spend an average of 10 to 12 hours per quarter on original cataloging. In the past, approximately 45 hours per year were devoted to this technical services function. At best, public services staff have received about one extra week of professional staff time as a consequence of outsourcing.

Beyond the immediate advantage of acquiring this additional time, however, outsourcing has provided a benefit to library managers that can hardly be quantified. It is no longer necessary to ensure that at least one professional reference librarian also possesses original cataloging skills. Instead, managers are able to focus on hiring faculty librarians with exceptional abilities in bibliographic instruction and reference service, in order to meet the increasingly complex demands for direct services to the library's patrons. The current primary objectives of the institution are to enhance public services operations and to dedicate as much professional staff time as possible to public services efforts. Outsourcing of original cataloging ensures that a professional library staff member no longer has to devote time to maintaining cataloging and database skills for technical services work.

Outsourcing Results

Much has changed at COCC since outsourcing of original cataloging began in 1994. The college is building a new library, scheduled to open in the fall of 1997. Plans are also being developed to begin offering baccalaureate degrees by the year 2002. These two events have produced considerable concern over the size of the library's collection. The collection has been inadequate for years, but the problem of large-scale collection upgrading is now at the forefront of these issues.

Faced with the challenge of adding 20,000 volumes to the library between 1998 and 2002, in order to meet the Association for College and Research Libraries' standards for libraries in baccalaureate-degree-granting

institutions, an outsourcing project considerably larger than the one outlined in this chapter has been suggested. A proposal has been made to purchase a large block of additional volumes from a major bookseller and
simultaneously acquire vendor-supplied cataloging for all material at the
time of purchase. Some library technical services staff are concerned that
this action might dilute the quality of catalog records in COCC's database,
if significant numbers of vendor-supplied records are added without adequate review for accuracy. The staff time and costs required for in-house selection and cataloging of 3,000 more volumes per year, however, make
outsourcing an attractive option for achieving this goal.

Although the library's original cataloging outsourcing activity is limited in size and scope, it is a program for which quality objectives carry as
much weight as cost considerations. More recent outsourcing proposals
have focused considerably on cost comparisons alone. Library staff understand that quality control issues in outsourcing can be difficult to monitor
and capture, whereas initial cost savings figures are easier to determine.
Cost savings data are also quite persuasive when evaluating outsourcing as
an option for obtaining copy cataloging records.

Given the cost savings approach that is being emphasized on campus,
library staff are in the process of thoroughly investigating available vendor
services for outsourcing of copy cataloging on a large-scale basis. It is important to staff engaged in that process for managers to ensure that quality considerations are not compromised in favor of overall cost savings. Given the
fact that COCC's staff likely will not be in a position to screen all vendor-
supplied cataloging in a large-scale program, quality control for future outsourcing is the greatest challenge facing COCC's technical services staff at
this time.

In the meantime, outsourcing of original cataloging has succeeded
with little negative impact on library operations. SLS's managers have assigned only one cataloger for COCC's material, and that cataloger's work
is performed with high quality. Procedures for uploading records received
from SLS are scheduled for eventual notification, as COCC's library staff
migrate to using Innovative Interfaces, Inc. for their public access catalog
and cataloging module. However, this change is not expected to present
major problems. The outsourcing program and procedures for original cataloging are expected to remain unchanged.

Conclusion

This case study suggests several caveats for librarians considering outsourcing as a management approach for certain technical services operations. First, it is important to gather accurate data on current in-house

procedures and costs before replacing in-house processes with outsourced services. Local cataloging costs vary widely, and using average cost data from other libraries, including COCC's, is not representative of true costs within every institution.

Second, librarians are encouraged to conduct a pilot test of a vendor's outsourcing services before committing to long-term contracts. It might even be necessary to seek advice from a third party about the quality of the proposed vendor's services, if in-house staff lack the appropriate level of expertise to make these determinations.

Third, library managers should continue to gather data on their vendor's turnaround time and error rate on a regular basis, for continuous evaluation of outsourcing services over time. It is important to ensure that the quality control standards of outsourcing service providers are maintained after a pilot project is completed and full-scale outsourcing has begun. If the primary objective of outsourcing is to save money, for example, quality standards could easily be compromised over time, without overt intention of doing so. Periodic monitoring of quality and costs helps to address these management issues.

Finally, continuous reflection on a library's overall mission and goals is essential, in terms of the role that outsourcing plays in the organization's strategic plan. It is important to ensure that outsourcing programs serve those goals better than in-house alternatives.

COCC's library staff achieved their overall goals of providing better bibliographic instruction and a more-focused quality of instruction to library patrons, without increasing the number of librarians. Outsourcing also resulted in a better quality of cataloging, without compromising local standards designed to provide the best possible access to material in a limited collection. At COCC, outsourcing met the particular original cataloging needs of a library with a relatively small staff. It also enabled COCC's library staff to focus on more critical and increasing public services demands in the 1990s.

Strategic Planning for Technical Services: Outsourcing Copy Cataloging at The Libraries of The Claremont Colleges

Isao Uesugi

In 1994, The Libraries of The Claremont Colleges began outsourcing copy cataloging of approval titles, in an effort to reassign cataloging staff to other service areas. This outsourcing program was part of a strategic plan and commitment to the Colleges to incorporate both external and internal resources into the libraries' operations. Printouts of order-level records for approval books acquired from Yankee Book Peddler were shipped to the Online Computer Library Center's TECHPRO staff for matching with catalog records. TECHPRO's full-level records were subsequently loaded into the libraries' INNOPAC database to overlay the order-level records. All physical processing for books with outsourced cataloging was completed in-house by the libraries' staff. TECHPRO's staff have supplied the libraries with catalog records for over 16,000 books, contributing to an increase in cataloging productivity. As a consequence of outsourcing, five FTE copy catalogers were also successfully reassigned to public services positions.

The Libraries of The Claremont Colleges have outsourced copy cataloging of monograph approval titles since March 1994, at which time the Online Computer Library Center (OCLC) in Dublin, Ohio, was selected as the outsourcing provider. OCLC was chosen for two reasons: (1) the libraries' staff had used OCLC as their bibliographic utility since 1975, and decided to remain with the same source of catalog records; and (2) the OCLC record number, which is a key control element in the libraries' bibliographic database, could not be supplied in bibliographic records from other vendors. OCLC's TECHPRO service staff cataloged books acquired from the libraries' approval vendor, Yankee Book Peddler (YBP), located in Contoocook, New Hampshire. Outsourced records were loaded into the libraries' INNOPAC automated library system from Innovative Interfaces, Inc.

Background

The 1994 decision to outsource copy cataloging of approval titles at The Libraries of The Claremont Colleges was part of a strategic plan to restructure library services. Restructuring began with the Council of Presidents' mandate to reduce the libraries' operations budget, without substantially diminishing the level of library services. Because the personnel budget was a major component of the operations budget, creative approaches to managing staff workloads were essential for successfully fulfilling this mandate.

With extensive input from staff, the director of the libraries identified the following strategic principles of operation to meet this challenge:

1. Expand applications of technology in all aspects of library work.
2. Redeploy staff from traditional technical processing functions to direct delivery of information services.
3. Maximize the use of outsourcing for appropriate library processes.

Outsourcing Strategy and Objectives

The ultimate goal of outsourcing within the technical services area was to relieve copy cataloging staff from cataloging responsibilities for approval plan material and to reassign those staff to specific public service areas. It was anticipated from the outset that the remaining cataloging staff would continue to process other material on-site, including firm orders and standing orders. In that regard, outsourcing was not viewed as a substitute for all cataloging processes, nor was it intended as a means of staff reduction or budgetary savings for copy cataloging operations. The primary reason for exploring the effectiveness of outsourcing was to determine the impact that this strategy would have on the libraries' overall services.

With concurrence from the Council of Presidents, the director of the libraries decided that the additional costs for outsourcing of cataloging would be charged to the materials budget, as part of the overall costs for new acquisitions. Additional funding for approval books was provided to cover outsourcing costs. In proposing this new budgeting strategy for copy cataloging costs, the director of the libraries emphasized the fact that new books do not magically appear on library shelves. It was well acknowledged that the delivery of information in books is mediated by costly cataloging processes, whether the cataloging occurs on- or off-site. This education process resulted in realigned budgetary practices, which ensured that library services would not be diminished in terms of the ability of the libraries' staff to provide patrons with fully cataloged acquisitions in a timely manner.

Based on these policy decisions and objectives, the following guidelines were established for outsourced monograph cataloging of approval titles:

1. Obtain outsourced cataloging at a cost that approximated, or was lower than, existing costs for in-house cataloging.

2. Provide library staff with the ability to bypass the outsourced-cataloging work flow and process any item urgently needed by staff and patrons.

3. Redesign the cataloging process for approval titles and rely on outsourcing services, augmented by enhanced in-house automated processes.

Outsourcing Project Description

TECHPRO and YBP's staff worked with the libraries' catalogers in developing procedures for loading OCLC records into INNOPAC. The first step in the outsourcing process is loading YBP's order-level records into the local system by means of the Internet File Transfer Protocol (FTP). A file is staged by YBP's staff on their server each Tuesday for the weekly shipment of approval titles. Each file is numbered consecutively, so that the libraries' staff can develop easy FTP access logic. The libraries' acquisitions staff transfer the approval records file every Wednesday. This step results in the creation of brief bibliographic and order records, each of which is displayed in the INNOPAC online public access catalog (OPAC) as "1 copy UNDER CONSIDERATION for HON." HON is the designation for the Honnold/Mudd Library. The status code is an INNOPAC feature that the libraries' staff opted to use for this procedure.

After bibliographers have completed the selection of approval titles for specific collections or branches, and have assigned specific funds for payment of titles, acquisitions staff pay for accepted titles in the INNOPAC system and enter location codes for appropriate collections. A system-generated payment process automatically changes the OPAC display for accepted approval titles to "1 copy being PROCESSED for HON." All accepted titles are shelved in the technical services area, according to payment dates, item locations, and titles.

The libraries' staff select about 600 approval titles each month from YBP. In agreement with OCLC, the libraries' cataloging staff submit 600 titles to TECHPRO each month, in two shipments, near the beginning and middle of the month. OCLC's staff are responsible for providing MARC (machine-readable cataloging) records for as many books as possible in each shipment of titles.

An important feature of this outsourcing program is that books are *not* shipped to TECHPRO's operation in Ohio. Instead, printouts of YBP's order-level records in INNOPAC are sent to TECHPRO. The following critical bibliographic information exists in each order-level record: author, title, publisher, publication date, series title (if applicable), and International Standard Book Number (ISBN). During contract negotiations with OCLC, TECHPRO's staff verified that order-level records contain sufficient data to ascertain matching MARC bibliographic records in OCLC's online union catalog (OLUC).

Before shipping printouts to OCLC, the libraries' staff apply barcodes to books and their corresponding printout entries. Staff use "double barcodes," which originally were intended solely for use on books for which dust covers are retained. For that application, a range of 11-digit barcode numbers was reserved for double barcodes. Each unique number in the range was printed on a pair of barcode labels for application on both a book and the book's jacket.

In order to implement outsourced cataloging, without shipping books to OCLC, a decision was made to utilize the double barcodes to link each book and its corresponding order-level printout entry. One label is applied to each approval book and another label is applied to the matching printout. TECHPRO's staff enter the barcode number on the printout in the catalog record's 945 "‡d" subfield. The same number is added to the book's item record in INNOPAC after full-MARC records are loaded. For tracking purposes, the libraries' staff retain an INNOPAC file of titles in each shipment to TECHPRO.

Cataloging Requirements and Procedures

Cataloging requirements, including the MARC fields and subfields for item-level data, are specified in detail in the OCLC contract. The libraries' staff agreed to accept LC MARC, Cataloging-in-Publication (CIP), and full-level OCLC member-contributed records. If a bibliographic record found in OCLC's OLUC lacks a subject entry, except in literature, TECHPRO's staff are to assign appropriate LC subject headings. CIP records are accepted with a blank 300 field, as well as with incomplete 504 fields. OCLC's staff are instructed to enter item-level information in the 945 field in the following manner: location code in the "‡a" subfield, optional volume information in the "‡c" subfield, a full 11-digit barcode in the "‡d" subfield, and an optional non-circulating code of "k" in the "‡e" subfield. Item-level data are included in the order-record printout supplied to the vendor. The "k" code, used for reference titles designated for in-house library use only, generates a "NON-CIRC" message on the libraries' OPAC screen at the time catalog records are loaded.

Because books are not shipped off-site, any title that is needed urgently for reserve or other purposes can be retrieved from the outsourced processing workflow and cataloged in-house. This enables the libraries' staff to bypass outsourcing and immediately respond to patron needs for specific titles, with minimal impact on overall cataloging operations. The order-level printout for any title submitted to OCLC for cataloging, which is subsequently cataloged in-house, is given to the libraries' manager of outsourced cataloging. TECHPRO's bibliographic records for titles cataloged in-house in this manner are easily detected when OCLC's records are loaded into INNOPAC. The duplicate TECHPRO record automatically overlays existing bibliographic records, but creates an additional item record from the 945 field. The manager of outsourced cataloging uses the order-level printout to verify superfluous item records that need to be deleted manually. Due to the option to catalog selected titles in-house, the libraries' staff have not lost control of the entire cataloging process in the outsourcing scheme.

The libraries' staff receive MARC records from TECHPRO on diskettes. TECHPRO's staff also return printouts of titles for which full-catalog records are not found in OCLC's OLUC. OCLC's staff systematically discard printouts for titles that are captured in their database and processed. TECHPRO's full-MARC bibliographic records replace YBP's order-level records in the libraries' local system in an overlay process, using ISBNs as the match key. During the loading process, item information in a 945 field is automatically converted to an item record in the libraries' catalog.

The loader to perform this ISBN matching and replacement process was purchased from Innovative as a TECHPRO load profile. During initial testing of the loader, it was discovered that the MARC records contain additional data following the ISBN in the 020 field, for example, acid-free paper. Order-level records contain only ISBN numbers in this field. Because the loader was designed to match the entire 020 field, and not specifically the ISBN, the libraries' programmer modified the edit stage of the loader so that it strips data after the ISBN.

As full records are loaded, order-level records are automatically upgraded to full bibliographic records. However, uncataloged titles remain as order-level brief records, which are sorted and printed for matching with uncataloged books. Books without catalog records from OCLC are sent to the libraries' Cataloging Services Department for a second search of OCLC's OLUC by in-house staff. Eventually, all material not cataloged by OCLC is processed by the libraries' staff. Approval books with TECHPRO catalog records are forwarded to the libraries' Physical Processing Unit for labeling.

Physical Processing

The decision to handle physical processing in-house, instead of using TECH-PRO for both cataloging and physical processing services, was prompted by four factors. First, the expense and time requirements involved in shipping 600 books per month from California to Ohio and back to California were unacceptable. Second, by storing approval books in-house during the cataloging process, the libraries' staff retained the option of retrieving selected titles for rush cataloging, if urgently needed by the libraries' staff or patrons. Third, TECHPRO's staff were unable to customize their operation to provide the same kind of spine label data used by the libraries. One customized requirement includes a "NON-CIRC" message for reference titles and music biographies. This message appears on the spine label immediately below the call number, separated by a dotted line. Fourth, an in-house program already existed for batch processing of spine labels and creation of customized labels for various item locations.

Impact of Outsourcing

The three outsourcing objectives established by the director of the libraries in 1994 were successfully accomplished. First, the per-title cost of outsourced cataloging does not differ substantially from in-house copy cataloging costs for approval books. An in-house cataloging cost was calculated on the basis of staff productivity over a 12-month period, including time spent referring to manuals and other tools, checking with the supervisor on rule interpretations, and taking formal, as well as informal, breaks. This analysis provided the libraries' administrators with a realistic comparison between the cost of in-house cataloging and OCLC's outsourcing costs. Because the primary motivation for outsourcing was not based on reducing cataloging costs, the fact that outsourcing has not resulted in measurable budgetary savings for cataloging of approval books has not been a critical concern.

Second, TECHPRO's agreement to provide catalog records from printouts of order-level records, rather than using a book-in-hand approach, enables the libraries' staff to store books locally and retain some control of the cataloging process. Nevertheless, there are tradeoffs in this approach.

One disadvantage is that OCLC's staff supply incomplete CIP MARC records for selected titles, because the vendor's staff cannot upgrade CIP records without items in hand. However, during the first three months of outsourcing, fewer than five CIP records were found for each monthly batch of 600 approval books. This amounts to less than 1 percent of all titles cataloged by OCLC's staff, and has been viewed by the libraries' administrators and staff as an acceptable tradeoff in outsourcing.

Third, the use of double barcodes, one for books and the other for corresponding entries on printouts, enables INNOPAC's TECHPRO load profile to create bibliographic and item records from each batch of MARC records. The libraries' programmer developed a program to transfer MARC records from a diskette to a Macintosh file, which is subsequently loaded into the libraries' OPAC by means of INNOPAC's TECHPRO load profile. The in-house loading of TECHPRO's records is fully automated in a packaged program. The only manual portion of the cataloging process at the libraries is the physical application of barcodes to books and printouts to enable OCLC's staff to link books to bibliographic records. This barcoding work is performed primarily by student assistants. The in-house development of a packaged process was consistent with the first of the three strategic principles of operation mentioned earlier, namely, expanded application of technology in library operations.

Staffing

Outsourcing of copy cataloging for approval titles also enabled the libraries' administrators to successfully achieve another strategic principle of operation: redeployment of staff. Within the Cataloging Services Department, the staffing level was reduced from nine full-time positions in 1993–94 to four full-time positions in 1994–95. Five full-time staff members at the Library Assistant II level were reassigned, in varying FTE allotments, to other functional areas of the libraries, including interlibrary lending and borrowing, the information desk, and the bibliographic search center. Public services units increased their staffing as a result of these reassignments. However, the overall operations budget was reduced, because positions have not been filled as staff retire or resign.

In addition, outsourced cataloging is managed now by a staff member outside Cataloging Services. The head of the Cataloging Services Department, who has served as the manager of outsourcing from the beginning, subsequently became the head of OPAC Management and the INNOPAC system coordinator. Approximately 20 percent of that individual's time is devoted to tasks related to loading of TECHPRO's records and overall management of the outsourcing program.

Productivity

Another of the strategic principles of operation, maximum use of outsourcing, was evident in the overall cataloging productivity for the libraries. The total number of new titles cataloged in the first year of outsourcing increased from 15,853 in 1993–94 to 17,681 in 1994–95. This increase was largely due to outsourcing, since the number of approval titles cataloged by TECHPRO's staff within those two years increased from 1,170 to 7,341 books.

The overall increase in the number of new titles cataloged was also due to other factors, including work restructuring in Cataloging Services. Retrospective conversion activities were temporarily halted during that period, and the bulk of staff time was redirected to cataloging new books. Due to the reduction in copy cataloging staff, however, outsourcing was the single most important factor that contributed to the increased number of new titles cataloged in that time frame.

Quality

Relatively few cataloging errors by TECHPRO's staff have been detected by the libraries' staff. One type of error, which did occur several times in the early stages of outsourcing, was the addition of incorrect barcode numbers in the 945 field. This problem was identified by the libraries' Physical Processing Unit staff as they generated spine labels. If barcodes had more or less than the required 11 digits, labels would not be generated. If barcode numbers were incorrect, spine labels would not match books. When these problems were reported, the libraries' staff discovered that TECHPRO's staff keyed barcode numbers manually, instead of scanning them, into OCLC records. As this concern with barcode conflicts surfaced, however, the problem was resolved by OCLC's staff.

Turnaround Time

Once printouts are mailed to the vendor, TECHPRO's staff average a three-week turnaround time from the date the libraries' staff mail printouts to the date full-MARC records arrive at the libraries. However, an additional delay occurs at the front end of this process, due to the bimonthly shipping schedule stipulated in the terms of the outsourcing contract. For each 300-title shipment at the beginning and middle of every month, several of those titles are also held at the library for up to two weeks before the corresponding printouts are submitted to TECHPRO for cataloging. The net result is an overall turnaround time that varies from three to five weeks.

TECHPRO's records are loaded into INNOPAC within one day after receipt. Another two to five days are required for book labeling. After technical services processing has been completed, approval titles with outsourced cataloging are shelved in the libraries' new-books collection within one day.

The increased cataloging turnaround time was anticipated from the outset and has not been a major problem for the libraries' staff. To ensure that faculty and students are aware of this specific problem, however, the increased turnaround time has been communicated by the director of the libraries to members of the campus community. It is generally understood by the campus constituency that the outsourcing program implemented by the libraries' staff is the best practicable solution to the particular budgetary constraints and requirements faced by the libraries' administrators. To remedy problems caused by the turnaround time, in-house staff have cataloged 88 urgently needed approval items from 1994 to mid-1996, instead of waiting for OCLC's records.

Order-Record Discrepancies

One unanticipated problem that surfaced during outsourcing is YBP's use of distributor names in order-level records, rather than actual publisher names. This problem is particularly acute in the area of museum publications. As TECHPRO staff originally encountered these distributor names in printouts, they corresponded with the libraries' staff by electronic mail to verify publishers of certain titles. After analyzing the initial results of this process, the libraries' managers notified TECHPRO's staff to accept records with this publisher and distributor conflict as found in OCLC's OLUC, as long as other bibliographic data in printouts matched the online catalog record. The terms of the libraries' original contract were revised later to accommodate this exception.

Diacritics

A second unanticipated problem with outsourced cataloging involved the corruption of certain diacritics during the in-house processing of MARC records. MARC records are shipped from TECHPRO on a diskette and are loaded into a Macintosh file at the libraries, before they are loaded into the local INNOPAC system. In the beginning, the libraries' programmer discovered that diacritical marks on records were corrupted in the ASCII transfer from the TECHPRO diskette to the Macintosh file. A table was created to convert corrupted diacritical marks to the correct ones. Once the file transfer process was altered to a binary mode, the problem was solved.

Outsourcing of Other Cataloging

Given the overwhelming success of the outsourcing program for monograph copy cataloging of approval plan titles, the libraries' managers began two additional TECHPRO projects in August 1996. Each month surrogates are sent to TECHPRO staff for original cataloging of 20 dissertation and theses titles plus 15 to 18 Russian-language titles. As of July 1997, both projects are still in progress and double barcodes are being used for these materials.

Conclusion

From March 1994 to June 1996, 16,105 YBP approval titles were submitted to OCLC, for which 16,026 MARC records were received by the libraries. TECHPRO's staff cataloged 99.5 percent of the titles supplied to them for cataloging. They assigned call numbers in 90 records, or 0.56 percent of titles cataloged, and assigned LC subject headings in 26 records, or 0.16 percent of titles cataloged. From July 1994 to June 1995, 41.5 percent of the libraries' overall copy cataloging was outsourced to TECHPRO. In September 1996, following one month of beta-testing the INNOPAC Prompt-Cat record load program, outsourcing of copy cataloging for approval titles was switched from TECHPRO to PromptCat. With PromptCat, the libraries retrieve FTP files matching approval titles shipped by YBP and load them locally into INNOPAC.

In spite of this successful contracting experience with OCLC, The Libraries of The Claremont Colleges' outsourcing program neither justifies nor invalidates outsourcing of cataloging in general. It does, however, illustrate one application of outsourcing within the context of conditions unique to Claremont.

A key element in the Claremont experience was that outsourcing of cataloging was an extension of the libraries' policy to utilize a full range of resources, both external and internal, to provide the best possible services to their community. The libraries' staff have traditionally relied on in-house, as well as borrowed, print resources to address the information needs of the libraries' patrons. They have also incorporated full-text and other commercial databases into their reference operation to enhance the libraries' information services.

Outsourcing of cataloging is considered as another opportunity for utilizing available external resources. From the time at which the concept of technical services outsourcing was originally proposed, to the present day, the question was not *whether* to use outsourcing, but rather *how* to incorporate outsourcing into the critical processes of providing effective library services.

6 Authority Control: Outsourcing Retrospective and Ongoing Processing at the Emory University Libraries

Susan B. Bailey and Selden Deemer

Both retrospective and ongoing authority control for the Emory University Libraries has been outsourced to Library Technologies, Inc. (LTI). In 1994, during Emory's migration from DOBIS to the SIRSI integrated library system, 1,063,118 bibliographic records were processed through automated Library of Congress (LC) name and subject authority control. The new system was implemented with an authority file composed of both LC and provisional authority records. Provisional records were needed to take advantage of a SIRSI system feature that automatically checks headings as records are loaded. As a result of outsourcing, much authority work previously done at the time of cataloging has been eliminated. Relatively few headings are verified locally, and updates to records already in the system are based on the vendor's reports. LTI's Authority Express service, which allows for authority processing of current cataloging via the Internet File Transfer Protocol, has significantly improved the timeliness of authority record updates.

The decision to outsource authority control processing at the Emory University Libraries was announced in 1994, shortly after a 1993 decision to implement SIRSI's Unicorn integrated library system. SIRSI implementation offered Emory's staff the first opportunity to provide full authority control for the library's catalog of more than 1 million bibliographic records. Library Technologies, Inc. (LTI), located in Willow Grove, Pennsylvania, was chosen to supply both retrospective and ongoing authority control in a state-of-the-art electronic environment.

Background

Emory's first integrated library system, DOBIS, was not compatible with the United States MARC (machine-readable cataloging) Authorities format. When the SIRSI implementation decision was made, only bibliographic records from an Online Computer Library Center (OCLC) retrospective conversion project had been brought under authority control by a vendor. The conversion project, which had been completed well before the SIRSI decision was reached, included authority control processing by Blackwell North America, Inc. For that reason, those were the only vendor-supplied authority records in 1993.

For years, however, in-house authority processing, consisting of name, subject, and series authority control, had been performed by the library's staff during the cataloging process. The OCLC Name Authority File was routinely checked by catalogers. A subject heading editor also verified subject headings in the microfiche edition of *Library of Congress Subject Headings* and on OCLC. Nevertheless, because in-house authority processing was limited to current cataloging only, no effort was made to correct older forms already present in the catalog as new forms emerged. The net result was a database that had considerable inconsistency among forms of access.

During the planning stage for migration to the SIRSI system, there was basically no debate among library employees at Emory on the need for authority control. Although some librarians may feel that "online retrieval has challenged the need for authority control as traditionally practiced in library cataloging departments" (Park 1992, 75), that was not the case at Emory. Library staff well understood that "authority control helps a patron find information by providing consistent headings, or access points, which lead to all works in a database by a given author, about a given subject, or under a collective title. In addition, reference headings contained within authority records provide links to other access points and between varying forms of access points" (Younger 1995, 135).

Emory's library staff not only wanted to place their catalog under full authority control, which had not been practical under DOBIS, but also wanted to do so by contracting with an authority control vendor. In debating whether the Library's managers could justify the expense of using an outside vendor, much of the thinking at Emory was consistent with the approach used at Harvard University. Robin K. Wendler, in describing Harvard's decision to purchase commercial authority control, stated that "we did not justify the expense of authority control at all. It was a given, something so basic to a successful library catalog as to make justification un-necessary" (Wendler 1995, 5).

Without using a vendor for authority control processing, it would have been impractical for staff to have created a collection-specific authority file for a catalog with over 1 million bibliographic records. The potential lack of full authority control, in turn, would have meant that a key benefit of SIRSI's system, support for a syndetic reference structure, would not have been realized.

The only remaining question was whether a vendor could process the entire database in the required time frame. Two to three months is not suf-ficient time for a vendor's staff to manually review unmatched headings on a file of over 1 million records; strictly automated processing was the only option. Staff debated other options: (1) loading their database without au-thority control processing, and sending it to an authority control vendor at a later date; and (2) creating a partial authority file by loading the existing authority records, and manually exporting authority records from OCLC to build the remainder of the file. Automated authority processing was cho-sen, because these other options were viewed as unacceptable.

Retrospective Authority Control

There was no time for a formal bid process. Potential vendors were con-tacted by telephone and estimates were requested. LTI was selected, based on the company's ability to meet Emory's turnaround time requirement. In mid-February 1994, managers at Emory and LTI negotiated a contract to complete the authority control processing of the library's database and de-liver a tape of authority records for loading into SIRSI by May 1, 1994.

Authority Control Options and Provisional Records

Specifications for creating collection-specific authority files differ among systems and within a given system, depending on supported functions and selected options. Basically, two options exist in SIRSI's Unicorn authority control module. One option is to use online authority records in a manner analogous to manual files. Catalogers can check the local file to determine if the form of entry being reviewed has already been used. In that approach, there is no automatic, system-generated review of new headings. There is also no need to have records in the authority file for each access point in the database. The other Unicorn option is to have all headings automatically checked by the system as they are loaded into the database. The latter option requires an authority record for every controlled access point in the database.

Emory decided to take advantage of the second option, using Uni-corn's automated, authority-checking feature. That option required the availability of Library of Congress (LC) name and subject authority records, as well as provisional records for headings with either a partial match or no match with LC authority records. LTI's staff were required to provide provisional records for headings that did not match LC or only matched the "‡a" subfield of LC authority records. Provisional records did not have to contain cross-references, however, because such records exist primarily to support the automated-checking process.

Provisional authority records could have been machine-generated by Unicorn, but SIRSI's staff cautioned against using that option in Emory's case. That recommendation was made because of the online processing workload associated with creating the more than one million provisional records needed for Emory's database. From the standpoint of the SIRSI system operators, the best approach was to create the records off line. Consequently, Emory outsourced the creation of provisional records to LTI.

Another aspect of the SIRSI system also had a major impact on the outsourcing of authority control processing. At the time Emory's staff implemented SIRSI, subject processing was limited to LC headings only. This was done because Unicorn did not support the use of multiple subject authority files, including the combination of LC and MeSH (that is, medical subject headings that represent the National Library of Medicine's controlled vocabulary). Conflict often occurs between MeSH and LC forms. Because of this, Emory's managers decided to process medical subject headings and create a MeSH authority file after SIRSI supports separate subject heading thesauri.

Results

By May 1994, LTI provided automated LC authority control for 1,063,118 bibliographic records. They delivered 624,641 LC name and subject authority records that matched headings in Emory's catalog. There was a ratio of .587 matching authority records for each bibliographic record in the database. LTI created 685,424 provisional records as well. All vendor records were loaded into EUCLID, Emory's local name for the Unicorn system. The retrospective authority control match rates were: 84.7 percent of headings linked to LC, 10.3 percent of headings linked to LTI records, and 5 percent of headings that were not linked at all. The total cost of processing the 1,063,118 records was $59,167.

Authority Control Maintenance

Retrospective authority control necessitates a commitment to ongoing maintenance, in order to retain the benefits of authority control and protect the initial investment. Emory's staff had to address two issues in ongoing maintenance: (1) ensuring that authority control was performed during all subsequent cataloging, and (2) keeping the retrospective authority file updated.

Much of the rationale for Emory's plan for ongoing authority control was predicated on receiving additional services from an authority control vendor. Library staff anticipated that vendor reports would provide the bulk of information relating to heading changes, updates, and revisions. Managers expected that maintenance tasks would be performed by in-house staff, based on requirements stipulated by vendor-supplied reports. Although cataloging occurs at individual libraries on Emory's campus, and each library effectively operates independently, Emory's authority file exists as one shared file. Consequently, an Authority Control Working Group, composed of members from all the Emory libraries, agreed to establish a database maintenance unit to handle ongoing authority control after the retrospective project was completed.

Authority Control for Current Cataloging

Emory's staff add approximately 55,000 bibliographic records to their database each year. In early 1994, when discussions about authority control processing of new cataloging first occurred, library staff planned to send new cataloging records to LTI once a year for processing. The major drawback with that approach was that a considerable number of unauthorized headings were expected to appear in the database annually, some of which were anticipated to be in the catalog for almost the entire 12-month period.

Authority Express Service

By late 1994, however, LTI introduced its Authority Express service. That program offers librarians the option of using Internet File Transfer Protocol (FTP) to transmit records for processing at any chosen frequency. Authority Express provides updated bibliographic records and matching authority records within a 24-hour turnaround time on files of 5,000 records or less.

In spring 1995, Emory's library systems manager decided to pursue the Authority Express option. As a first step, SIRSI staff developed two custom processing reports. One report extracted catalog records from the system for transfer to LTI, and the other reloaded authorized records after processing. These procedures involved staff participation in the extraction and reloading phases. By summer 1995, however, Emory's system support staff had developed enough expertise with Unicorn to modify and extend SIRSI's custom reports to enable both processes to occur without staff intervention.

Weekly authority processing began in mid-1995 and has continued to date. Shortly after midnight each Friday morning, current-cataloging records are extracted from SIRSI in a batch process. This includes all records created during the previous seven days, with the exception of temporary or provisional records. That file is staged to LTI's server on the same day. Later that day, LTI's online notification service prompts Emory's computer to retrieve the following seven files from LTI's server:

1. New LC Name Authority Records (EMORYnnn.LCN)
2. New LC Subject Authority Records (EMORYnnn.LCS)
3. New Provisional Name Authority Records (EMORYnnn.PRN)
4. New Provisional Subject Authority Records (EMORYnnn.PRS)
5. Updated MARC Bibliographic Records (EMORYnnn.OUT)
6. Authority Control Statistical Report (EMORYnnn.ACF)
7. Unlinked Headings List (EMORYnnn.ULH)

The first five files are loaded sequentially into the catalog between Friday afternoon and Saturday afternoon. LC authority records are loaded first, followed by provisional records, to ensure that all authority records are present before the authorized bibliographic records are reloaded. This load sequence reflects the operational requirements of SIRSI's authority control module. The last two files, consisting of processing reports, are forwarded, via electronic mail, to Emory's authority control unit. The authority control statistical report lists headings by MARC tags, detailing the link results obtained during authority processing. The unlinked headings list includes all headings in which subfield "‡a" did not link to an LC or LTI authority record.

The Authority Express service has been used for processing other bibliographic records as well. In addition to records for new cataloging, Emory staff periodically obtain batch-load records from outside sources, including government-document records from MARCIVE, Inc. and special-project microform records, all of which are sent to LTI for authority control processing before they are loaded into Unicorn. The bibliographic record and authority control process flow for the daily, weekly, and monthly flow of records for the entire Authority Express service is outlined in Exhibit 6.1.

Results

The match rates for Authority Express, based on a random survey of eight batches, average 87.1 percent of headings that link to LC, 6.0 percent of headings that link to LTI records, and 6.9 percent of headings that do not link at all. In terms of costs for authority control processing of new cataloging, LTI's charges for this service have been $10.00 per file, plus $.10 per record. Cost studies were not conducted to compare in-house costs with outsourcing costs.

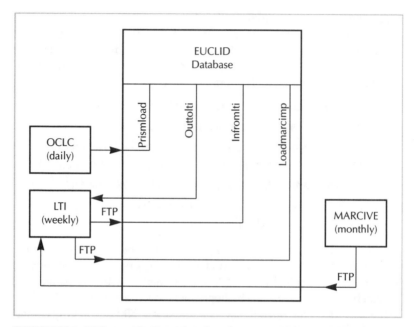

EXHIBIT 6.1 Bibliographic Record and Authority Control Processing Flows for Emory University Libraries, Using Library Technologies, Inc.'s Authority Express Service. The flow of authority control records and bibliographic records in and out of EUCLID, Emory's Unicorn system database, is illustrated in this figure.

At the time of Emory's original contract with LTI, which called for authority processing of new cataloging once a year, Emory's staff never imagined that new catalog records could be authorized weekly. In that regard, the timeliness of updates provided by Authority Express is a most welcome benefit of outsourcing. Emory's staff also find that the only manual processes to be performed in-house consist of reviewing the unlinked headings list, generated by LTI each week, and reviewing an authority record load report automatically produced by Unicorn each time authority records are loaded.

Ongoing Maintenance of Bibliographic Headings and Authority Records

In addition to using LTI's Authority Express for new cataloging, Emory's managers elected to use LTI's Update Notification Service for ongoing maintenance of bibliographic headings and retrospective authority control records. The Update Notification Service provides two paper reports, each separated into sections by names, series, and subjects. One report lists bibliographic heading changes during the previous six months. The second report lists new, revised, or deleted LC authority records.

During the first year of using the Update Notification Service, Emory's staff received only print reports from LTI and manually exported corresponding authority records from OCLC into SIRSI. Beginning in the second year, library staff requested LC authority records on diskette from LTI, to experiment with loading LTI's records directly into SIRSI. The purpose of this study was to determine in-house staff requirements for manual review of conflicts in records and manual corrections to effect overlay results. It was anticipated that this experiment would also answer questions about the need to change entries with subject subdivisions, in those cases when primary subject headings change.

Results

Emory's staff learned that loading of authority records provided by LTI into a system with an automatic authority-checking feature resulted in fewer problems than had been anticipated. The Unicorn authority-checking process monitors each change made to an authority record, and automatically makes corresponding changes to all bibliographic records in which the exact heading occurs. The cascading of authority updates to bibliographic headings minimizes the amount of in-house, manual correction, and global updating by Emory's staff.

Advantages also accrue from using LTI for both retrospective authority control processing and ongoing maintenance processing. To achieve maximum benefit of a notification service for authority control maintenance, either all authority processing for a library must be done by the same vendor, or the maintenance vendor must receive a copy of the bibliographic database and collection-specific authority files. The current version of a library's files is needed in order for a vendor to limit reports of changed headings only to those used by the library. Using the same vendor for authority processing of both the retrospective database and current cataloging simplified outsourcing procedures.

Emory's annual subscription for LTI's Update Notification Service has been $1,875, based on a reporting frequency of semi-annual updates. At present, cost studies have not been conducted to compare in-house costs and Notification Service costs, or to make comparisons to the costs of other options.

Impact of Outsourcing on Staffing

The assistant head of Emory's main Catalog Department, who chaired the Authority Control Working Group and serves as the vendor liaison for outsourcing, has continued to be responsible for overseeing local aspects of the authority control function. Authority control and related database maintenance activities are dispersed among staff in the Catalog Department. Work is distributed among individuals who check LTI's Update Notification Service reports and weekly lists of unlinked headings. Approximately 40 hours of staff time and about 20 hours of the assistant department head's time are devoted to managing and performing authority control work each week. Staff assigned to this effort vary from clerical to higher level, depending on availability. Student time, usually ranging between 7 and 15 hours per week, is also used for basic checking.

A goal has been to distribute the volume of in-house authority control work among various staff, so that no one person works more than half time on this task. There are both advantages and disadvantages to this approach. Staff are more effective if they have some variety in their daily workload. However, staff turnover, and the occasional need to devote more time to special projects, often result in staff being reassigned temporarily to other tasks. These staffing fluctuations have made it difficult for individuals to develop expertise in authority control maintenance.

In terms of authority maintenance processing, the most beneficial place to begin is with subject heading changes. However, a greater understanding of cataloging records and MARC tagging is required for subject authority control processing than is needed for changing personal and corporate name headings. Because Emory's additional staffing for authority control maintenance is mainly allocated in student and clerical staff hours, library managers have found that those individuals are better able to address name-heading issues than subject headings. As a result, subject headings do not receive attention in as timely a manner as name headings. Series receive the least attention, because of their complexity. In terms of the overall workflow, it has also been a challenge to keep four or five people working on independent projects, while balancing the distribution of work and ensuring that each person is able to proceed without affecting the work of another.

Unfortunately, the 67 to 75 hours per week of in-house staff allocated for authority control maintenance has not been sufficient for the amount of cleanup and ongoing manual review needed to achieve the desired level of database quality. A backlog of maintenance work has developed, due to the time required for manual review of headings listed on the LTI unlinked headings report and for training on the EUCLID authority control module. Even with outsourcing a significant portion of authority control processing, the library's staff have found that maintaining full authority control in a large, online catalog requires a significant amount of in-house staff time. This personnel situation continues to evolve, as managers become more aware of staffing needs. Extra hours have been added gradually, but the level of staff varies by availability. Staffing pattern and workflow changes resulting from outsourcing of authority control are expected to continue for some time, until the proper staffing balance is achieved.

Other Impacts of Outsourcing

One key challenge of Emory's authority control program is working closely with both LTI's staff and SIRSI's staff to achieve the best results during outsourcing. The initial outsourcing of authority control processing was slower and more problematic than expected, in large part because of problems associated with the implementation of the SIRSI system. In working with Unicorn, Emory's staff also discovered the following unexpected problems:

- Incoming authority records were not updating and replacing existing records as effectively as was desired.
- Series checking did not operate as expected, because of the way Unicorn handled punctuation marks.
- Checking of uniform titles was not achieved as expected.
- Non-unique heading problems, represented by multiple uses for a given term (for example, "Dance" can be both a subject heading and series title), were not handled correctly and an authority record would display for only one heading.

Because of these problems, library staff temporarily stopped loading records and making corrections, since results were uncertain and unnecessary cleanup work was being generated. Several of these problems were resolved by working with SIRSI's Customer Support representatives during initial implementation. Other problems are expected to disappear following a future software release.

Emory staff are fully aware of the importance of examining the quality of commercial authority control processing services for retrospective files, as well as the quality of authority control maintenance services, while planning any authority control outsourcing program. Equally important, however, is a full understanding of the library's authority control module in the local automated system. Each automated system has its strengths and weaknesses in the area of authority control, which impact immensely on authority control outsourcing.

Librarians contemplating outsourcing of authority control processing are advised to research areas of concern in advance with their local system vendor and their authority control vendor. It is also important to consult with staff in other libraries who are familiar with both vendors, although the experiences of others are beneficial only to a certain point. Even in the best of circumstances, the "right" question might not be asked or answered in each investigation. Furthermore, depending on which local system is used and what choices were made during implementation of that system, outsourcing can result in significantly different outcomes.

Conclusion

Although there have been challenges during outsourcing, there is no doubt that the catalog at Emory University Libraries has improved considerably from authority control processing by a commercial vendor. LTI's Authority Express service and Update Notification Service have contributed to continuous improvement of the catalog as well. However, the quality of Emory's in-house authority control maintenance program still needs much improvement. It will take some time to eliminate the backlog of authority control cleanup work.

Although improvements are still to be made at Emory, the overall authority control operation has been successful. This success is due to significant commitments from a variety of staff and the willingness of key personnel to investigate and embrace the opportunities afforded by new options. Individuals involved with authority control processing at Emory continue to evaluate possibilities, and much has been learned during the outsourcing process. Vendors of authority control services have also enhanced their services in the mid-1990s. Because of these factors, outsourcing substantial portions of authority control has become an even more attractive option since Emory first began this program.

In reflecting on the overall benefits of outsourcing authority processing, the words of Robin K. Wendler are most appropriate:

> Automating a portion of the authority control process, like automating any aspect of our work, involves tradeoffs. Corrections will make the database cleaner overall and provision of authority records will free staff to work on other tasks, but you will relinquish a certain amount of control. Many headings are improved, a few are made worse—and we know that other people's mistakes are always more heinous than our own (Wendler 1995, 10).

Tradeoffs have become a necessary part of the business atmosphere required in today's libraries, especially in an outsourcing environment. Staff at Emory University Libraries have accepted these tradeoffs. They have also learned that a cooperative relationship between library staff and an authority control vendor can provide a successful working arrangement that involves a combination of outsourcing and some degree of local control.

Works Cited

Park, Amey L. 1992. Automated authority control: Making the transition. *Special Libraries* 83, no. 2: 75–85.

Wendler, Robin K. 1995. Automating heading correction in a large file: Harvard's experience. In *The Future Is Now: Reconciling Change and Continuity in Authority Control: Proceedings of the OCLC Symposium, ALA Annual Conference, June 23, 1995.* Dublin, Ohio: OCLC Online Computer Library Center.

Younger, Jennifer A. 1995. After Cutter: Authority control in the twenty-first century. *Library Resources & Technical Services* 39, no. 2: 133–41.

7 Cataloging Music Scores and Foreign Language Material: Outsourcing at Florida Atlantic University Libraries

Janice E. Donahue and William Miller

In 1993, Florida Atlantic University Libraries' staff contracted with TECHPRO's staff at the Online Computer Library Center (OCLC) for copy cataloging and original cataloging of 900 music scores and over 6,000 monographs and other publications, some of which were rare material. OCLC's staff supplied cataloging and physical processing for the following languages: English, French, German, Russian, and Spanish. The outsourcing program progressed through Phases I and II from 1993 to 1996. Phase III, focused on cataloging of Yiddish, Hebrew, and English-language Judaica, began in 1996. An extension of Phase II was also launched in 1996. Outsourcing has provided bibliographic access to material that would otherwise have languished unknown and unused by the scholarly community. Cataloging backlogs of gift material and other acquisitions were also eliminated as a consequence of outsourcing, without a permanent investment in staffing that would have been unwarranted for ongoing acquisitions.

Since 1993, staff in the Technical Services Division of Florida Atlantic University (FAU) Libraries in Boca Raton have been engaged in a multiphase outsourcing program with the Online Computer Library Center (OCLC) TECHPRO unit, located in Dublin, Ohio. Two outsourcing phases were completed by 1996. In Phase I, TECHPRO's staff cataloged 700 music scores in a 12-month period from 1993 to 1994. Phase II, from 1994 to

1996, consisted of cataloging 6,000 monographs in English, French, German, and Spanish, as well as 200 music scores in French, German, and Russian. Phase II monographs were primarily pre-1981 imprints received as gifts, but other books, technical reports, and conference proceedings were also included.

Because of the successful results of Phase II, an extension was negotiated with TECHPRO's staff for cataloging 5,000 additional monographs. This extension began in July 1996 and should be completed by December 1997. Phase III, which also began in 1996, focuses on cataloging Yiddish, Hebrew, and English-language Judaica. The outsourcing work and evaluative processes for Phase III are expected to be completed by 1997 as well.

Outsourcing Project Goals

The goals of the first two phases of outsourcing were as follows:

1. Secure formal bibliographic records for rare, donated scores printed in the eighteenth and nineteenth centuries; secure full bibliographic records for hundreds of previously purchased scores and thousands of monographs, in a variety of languages, in the cataloging backlog; and convert records for previously cataloged scores to full-MARC (machine-readable cataloging) records for inclusion in NOTIS, FAU's online public access catalog (OPAC).

2. Accomplish the aforementioned in a manner that would not affect the cataloging productivity of the libraries' routine workflow.

3. Evaluate the effectiveness of outsourcing for further cataloging projects, including the backlog of gifts, foreign-language material, conference proceedings, and technical reports, in order to develop a strategy for maintaining a small cataloging arrearage in the future.

Phase I: Background and Project Description

In the early 1990s, FAU Libraries had few technical services employees with scores cataloging expertise or a music background. Furthermore, the libraries had never employed a fully qualified music cataloger. As a result of this staffing situation, the libraries had a cataloging backlog of purchased and gift scores. The donation of 100 rare scores in 1990, some with title pages in Cyrillic, presented a challenge that compounded the overall scores cataloging problem.

A strong desire by the libraries' administrators to acquire a formal record of the donors' generous gift of 100 scores, and the donors' wishes that the scholarly community be made aware of this material in a timely manner, were major factors in the decision to pursue outsourcing of cataloging for music scores. Additional factors included a monographs cataloging backlog that was increasing from a combination of donations, an aggressive gift program, and supplemental funding. An ongoing in-house retrospective conversion project was also in process, but previously cataloged scores had been omitted. Outsourcing presented the best opportunity for addressing the overall dilemma with scores, especially given the lack of funding for a music cataloger and the downsizing atmosphere prevalent at FAU in the early 1990s.

Outsourcing Strategy and Vendor Selection for Phase I

Three people worked together to select material for outsourcing, design the outsourcing workflow, and evaluate the vendor's quality. The outsourcing team, all permanent staff members, included an entry-level cataloger, who was also a musician; the head of cataloging, who prescribed the cataloging workflow; and the supervisor of the libraries' Processing Unit. The team met weekly for six weeks to discuss categories of material for outsourcing, workflow implications, and physical processing issues. Team members identified items with the highest cataloging priority and designated the approximate number of materials in the following three categories for inclusion in Phase I: 100 uncataloged rare gift scores, 200–300 other uncataloged scores, and 250–350 cataloged scores in need of retrospective conversion to machine-readable format.

The libraries' staff limited vendor selection options to two choices: (1) hiring a local music cataloger for part-time, in-house work during evening and weekend hours; or (2) contracting with OCLC's TECHPRO service for off-site cataloging and physical processing. No other commercial vendor was considered, because of the successful long-term partnership that FAU had enjoyed with OCLC and the assurance of compatibility with existing cataloging and invoicing operations.

OCLC was selected as the vendor for the following reasons: the satisfactory long-term relationship between the libraries' staff and OCLC, the assurance of compatibility with existing cataloging and invoicing operations, a desire to avoid the inevitable learning curve in training a new cataloger on local practices, the difficulty of integrating a new cataloger into the over-committed workflow of technical services staff, the difficulty in training and communicating with a new cataloger during hours that did not overlap with the schedules of regular staff, and an inability to devote additional in-house supervisory time to overseeing a part-time professional cataloger.

Preparation and Shipment of Material for Phase I

Because of the extreme vulnerability of some rare scores in Phase I, the outsourcing team decided that only photocopies of pages significant for cataloging the scores would be sent to the vendor. Discussions with TECHPRO's project manager produced an agreement for the libraries' staff to submit photocopies of the score cover, title page, verso, first and last pages, and other relevant pages to be determined by an FAU cataloger on a case-by-case basis. The need to reduce several oversized scores in the photocopying process, as well as the need to retain all relevant photocopied pages of a score in one surrogate package, added complexity to the photocopying process. In addition, it was of primary importance to copy the rare scores as soon as they were removed from the Special Collections Department, and to return them promptly to Special Collections' staff after each photocopying session. Due to the time involved in photocopying, the outsourcing team decided that non-rare scores would be shipped directly to the vendor.

Communication with the cataloger assigned to the project at TECHPRO was primarily via electronic mail. This proved to be both convenient and efficient. A schedule was developed for delivery of the scores, which included shipment numbers, date of packing, shipping date, and projected return date. One category of information on the schedule was designated for recording the actual date on which scores were returned to FAU Libraries. The shipping/receiving schedule allowed for the transmittal of 20–25 titles to TECHPRO and the return receipt of 20–25 titles from TECHPRO every two weeks. Surrogate cataloging material for rare scores and actual non-rare scores were shipped to TECHPRO via United Parcel Service and returned to FAU Libraries with a diskette containing catalog records.

Quality Control Procedures for Phase I

As OCLC shipments arrived at the libraries, the outsourcing team examined all items and spot-checked for errors to be corrected by the libraries' staff. When the same errors were found in a recurring pattern, those problems were discussed with OCLC's project manager. Quality in Phase I was evaluated by verifying each access point for original and copy cataloging. Fields and headings that were verified included author, title, uniform title, publication data, pagination, bibliographical and series statements, and subject and name headings. For all original cataloging, the field tags, subfields, and indicators were verified as well. Verification of authority work on all headings was performed by an FAU cataloger assigned to this project. Matching authority records were obtained by downloading the Library of Congress (LC) authority records from the resource files maintained by the state university system.

Verification was performed by comparing shelf list cards with material in hand for copy cataloging and by comparing OCLC printouts with material in hand for original cataloging. Standard tools for general cataloging and music cataloging were consulted in the verification process. LC classification numbers were verified against the LC classification schedules and checked for compatibility with the in-house shelf list. During each two-week period, the in-house verification process was supplemented with extensive electronic mail contact between FAU's cataloger and TECHPRO's cataloger to clarify classification and access-point decisions. FAU's head of cataloging and project cataloger reviewed problems or irregularities every week. Each problem was analyzed individually to determine the complexity of correction.

This comprehensive monitoring of the vendor's quality was confined to the 100 rare scores outsourced to TECHPRO in Phase I. Extensive quality control efforts were conducted because of a strong commitment to maintaining the integrity and compatibility of data in the libraries' OPAC. This labor-intensive verification was needed to ensure that TECHPRO's records in FAU's OPAC were of the same quality as those contributed by the libraries' staff.

Outsourcing Results for Phase I

In the early stages of the problem-resolution sessions, it was frequently necessary to consult the contract between FAU and TECHPRO to determine whether problems identified in the quality control checks were truly addressed in the contract. After analyzing the contract and the vendor's quality, in-house staff acknowledged that most problems in the initial stages of verification pertained to conflicts with established local library practices that were not addressed during contract negotiations, either intentionally or unintentionally.

The evaluation process identified two kinds of cataloging problems: (1) real problems and (2) problems that were inconsistencies with FAU's practices, but did not constitute violations of the outsourcing contract. Real problems included typographical errors in indexed and nonindexed fields, and tagging errors. Among the 100 rare scores cataloged by the vendor, there were six typographical errors in copy cataloging records and four typographical errors in original records. Four tagging errors were found in copy cataloging records and one tagging error was found in an original record within the same sample. The second category of problems consisted of conflicts in the editing of note fields, local Cuttering practices, and local practices in tracing name headings. These were not factored into the vendor's error rate.

After six weeks, during which all work was checked for major and minor discrepancies, inconsistencies, and local compatibility, the outsourcing team concluded that the quality of service was more than satisfactory. The libraries' staff were also pleased with their ability to communicate easily and effectively with TECHPRO's cataloger. The outsourcing team had established a good working relationship with TECHPRO's cataloger, who could be relied upon to refer questions and decisions that would affect the libraries' local operation to her FAU counterpart.

Based on those factors, a decision was made to discontinue verifying every access point in OCLC's catalog records after the 100 rare scores were cataloged. The libraries' staff continued to check classification numbers for compatibility with locally assigned classification numbers. However, verifying the suitability of classification numbers assigned by TECHPRO's staff ceased. A decision was made to continue reviewing all original cataloging for errors in tagging, access points, or typographical errors, but only to spot-check other records.

Phase II: Background and Project Description

The Phase II outsourcing project had a different focus and a wider scope than Phase I. The focus was on cataloging general interest material in the libraries' gifts backlog, which included varied subject areas and foreign-language titles. The arrearage also included conference proceedings, technical reports, and other purchased items that required more intensive cataloging treatment than material containing Cataloging-in-Publication (CIP) data. Most gift and purchased titles had pre-1981 publication dates. Also included in Phase II were items from the cataloging "hold" shelf that had no matching records in OCLC and were known to require original cataloging, based on repeated searches for catalog copy.

The OCLC contract for Phase II covered 6,200 titles, including 200 more rare scores received as an additional gift from the previous donors. Among the 6,000 books were 1,200 foreign-language titles in the following categories and percentages: French (25 percent), German (45 percent), and Spanish (35 percent). Because the majority of these books had been in arrearage, the libraries' OPAC already contained provisional records for all titles shipped during Phase II. The plan was to overlay the provisional records with OCLC's records.

Significant differences between the Phase I and Phase II projects included: the larger number of items, and variety of formats and languages, for Phase II material; and the challenge of shipping monographs for processing, as opposed to scores. The large size of the operation demanded an increased emphasis on the production aspect of the project, and required the involvement and cooperation of more staff, at varying levels, than was necessary in Phase I.

As in Phase I, the Phase II contract included specifications for TECHPRO's staff to write call numbers in items and prepare a diskette with all catalog records to be loaded into FAU's OPAC. TECHPRO's staff supplied spine labels for each book, but did not apply the labels. The libraries' staff added labels and barcodes to material, and were responsible for other aspects of physical processing, including property stamps, security targets, and book pockets.

Preparation and Shipping of Material for Phase II

Among all aspects of the outsourcing workflow, the most crucial was the accuracy of the procedure that would result in the overlay of provisional records in FAU's OPAC with fully cataloged MARC records. Cataloging quality and thoroughness were of prime importance, but to ensure the integrity of bibliographic data in the libraries' OPAC, accuracy of the overlay process was essential. If that process did not work, the workflow implications for the libraries' staff would be enormous. To ensure success on both sides of the procedure, it was necessary that the control number of each provisional record in the libraries' OPAC be legibly recorded and included with each volume of outsourced material. TECHPRO's cataloger was required to construct the 035 field in each bibliographic record for the libraries' NOTIS control number. These steps added another layer of complexity, since the Phase I scores did not have OPAC records that were affected by the overlay of OCLC records.

In addition, special effort was made to flag multivolume items for TECHPRO's cataloger, before shipping material to OCLC. Usually, only the first volume of a two-volume set, or the first and last volumes of a multivolume set, were shipped to OCLC. The flag included information indicating the number of volumes in the set and whether the set had been previously cataloged at FAU as part of a series. A base call number was also included for all items to be cataloged as analytics in established series. An extra step before shipping material to OCLC included adding a message to provisional OPAC records indicating that those items were unavailable and had been shipped to TECHPRO for cataloging. These messages contained shipment numbers for items and were useful to staff and patrons in tracking titles requested during this period.

The libraries' original schedule for Phase II called for completion of the project within 12 months. That schedule would have required that approximately 500 volumes per month be received and processed by both FAU's staff and OCLC's TECHPRO staff. The original assumption was based on one shipment per month.

During contract negotiations, both parties realized that the intake and outflow of 500 items per shipment would be prohibitive for FAU's limited amount of staff. A project of that magnitude would entail managing 500 items in a shipment awaiting packing and in the process of being packed, in addition to managing 500 other items arriving from the vendor for receiving, quality control checking, tracking, and processing. Space was inadequate for housing several 500-item shipments in various processing stages, while simultaneously supporting the libraries' in-house cataloging and physical processing operations. An additional negative factor with regard to shipments of that size was the number of items that would be inaccessible to patrons at any given time.

The proposed shipping schedule was a serious problem, since a chief project goal was to outsource cataloging without placing additional burdens on local staff and resources. Therefore, the terms of the contract were amended to include a cataloging time frame of 20 months, as opposed to 12, with total monthly shipments of 300 titles, instead of 500. The original schedule for one shipment per month was also replaced with a plan for two shipments per month.

The libraries' Phase II Request for Price Quote was prepared for TECH-PRO's staff in April 1994. During the ensuing months, workflow procedures for outgoing and incoming shipments were established through several meetings and discussions with the following staff at the libraries: shipping/receiving clerk, catalogers, processing supervisor, processing clerk, and cataloging library technical assistants. Formal procedures were created in July 1994 and the first shipment for Phase II was mailed in September 1994.

Quality Control Procedures for Phase II

Catalog records were closely monitored for errors and irregularities. The libraries' staff also maintained close contact with TECHPRO's cataloger regarding cataloging discrepancies and revisions to both the workflow and contract specifications. In the early stages of Phase II, verification of all descriptive cataloging, subject analysis, authority work, and classification numbers was performed by FAU's staff. A total of 237 titles were scrutinized in this manner from September through November 1994.

Outsourcing Results for Phase II

The most serious and annoying errors in the sampling of 237 items occurred in several batches of books in which call numbers on spine labels did not match call numbers in bibliographic records. Because this problem occurred over several shipments, documentation was established and a series of discussions took place between FAU's staff and OCLC's staff. These discussions resulted in a revision in OCLC's workflow procedures. OCLC's managers also applied a credit to the libraries' account to compensate for the in-house corrections.

Other discrepancies, which required remedial action by FAU's staff, included the assignment and acceptance by TECHPRO's staff of classification numbers that were input by member libraries. In some cases, analytic call numbers with volume designations from member libraries were accepted by TECHPRO's staff. Because FAU's staff would not have provided analytic treatment for specific series, this created in-house filing and shelving conflicts. This type of problem occurred an average of two times per month.

Before outsourcing, the greatest problems were anticipated in potential call number duplication. However, over a 20-month period, only 28 out of 6,298 titles, or .004 percent, contained duplicate call numbers. The libraries' staff were fully satisfied with this low rate, and were pleased that the problem was not as serious as originally anticipated.

The overlay process for replacing the libraries' provisional records with full-MARC OCLC catalog records was one aspect of the workflow in which most errors occurred. These errors were due to a variety of factors, including both illegible and inaccurate numbers supplied to TECHPRO's cataloger, inaccurate keying of the 035 field's control number, and the failure to include the 035 field in the bibliographic records. In each case, the overlay process did not work as records were loaded in the libraries' OPAC. In some cases, the OCLC record replaced the wrong OPAC record. In other situations, an entirely new record was created, leaving a stray provisional record that often contained an attached order record.

The occasional failure to overlay local NOTIS records, and the overlay of incorrect OPAC records by OCLC records, were recurring problems throughout Phase II. This matter was resolved by verifying each record in loading error reports that were generated as OCLC's records were loaded into the OPAC. Loading errors caused by the overlay conflict occurred 88 times during the entire 20-month project, but the libraries' staff do not have data on how many times overlay problems created new records instead of matching provisional records.

The 237 sample records were examined for errors in all bibliographic record fields. The outsourcing team concluded that they were completely satisfied with the overall quality of original and copy cataloging supplied by OCLC after scrutinizing the 237 titles. Intense verification was discontinued at that point, in favor of spot-checking various parts of descriptive cataloging and classification for several items in each shipment. Several issues associated with Phase II, including call number corrections and overlay corrections, occurred throughout the project and were an ongoing part of the workflow.

Outsourcing Costs

TECHPRO's 1993 costs for processing music scores in Phase I were $21.00 for original cataloging, $5.00 for copy cataloging, and $2.50 for transliteration. The 1994 price quote for Phase II was $15.00 for original cataloging of monographs, $21.20 for original cataloging of scores, $5.50 for copy cataloging of monographs, and $7.00 for copy cataloging of scores. The transliteration charge for Phase II was $3.00 per title, and spine labels were $.65 each. Cataloging charges also included writing the call number in the back of items.

All prices quoted by TECHPRO were based on outsourcing requirements established for the unique aspects of the material cataloged for FAU's collections, including language, format, local processing specifications, complexity of material, and project size. The price fluctuations between the two phases reflect the degree of variation in the material cataloged.

Because much of the material in Phase I could not be cataloged in-house, there were no comparative data on in-house costs or error rates for that phase. The libraries' managers did not conduct either an extensive cost analysis or error rate analysis during Phase II, but reached a general conclusion that the vendor's costs for Phase II were lower than the salary and training costs that would have been required for in-house cataloging and physical processing of 6,200 items. The lower outsourcing costs also offset the vendor's error rate, which was determined to have been no greater than would have occurred with local staff.

In terms of indirect outsourcing costs, there was a new learning curve each time a different cataloger at TECHPRO was assigned to the project for material with different formats or languages. The libraries' staff had to develop a working relationship with each OCLC cataloger, as new catalogers became accustomed to contract and workflow requirements. These start-up costs and irregularities, however, were deemed no more disruptive than problems that would have occurred in managing the same kind of operation locally.

The libraries' staff also benefited from the fact that they did not have to devote time and other expenses for hiring, training, and integrating new staff for in-house cataloging on these projects. Furthermore, the lack of work space for additional staff in the libraries' technical services area, and the scheduling problems that would have resulted from working additional staff in different shifts, were factors that were considered in evaluating overall outsourcing costs.

Conclusion

Working with TECHPRO's staff was a good exercise in negotiation. At all times, OCLC's catalogers and managers were accommodating, professional, and concerned with the quality of their work. Each obstacle was addressed on both sides as a friendly negotiation, and the general level of satisfaction with the projects in Phases I and II was high.

Most important, these projects provided FAU's staff with positive outsourcing experiences that increased the staff's confidence in the ability of an outside vendor to handle part of the libraries' routine work and cataloging backlog. Downsizing of the libraries' staff and involvement by staff in arrearage reduction have broadened the staff's understanding of library goals and contributed to their willingness to innovate in order to achieve those goals.

Phases I and II of the outsourcing program with OCLC's TECHPRO staff have demonstrated that outsourcing, despite its inevitable rough spots, is a valuable tool for managing cataloging in an era of downsized staffing, combined with collection expansion. These projects brought external expertise to bear on material that would otherwise have languished unknown and unused by the scholarly community. Outsourcing also helped to eliminate a sizable backlog of gifts and purchases, without a permanent investment in staffing that would have been unwarranted for the level of ongoing acquisitions. In addition, these projects added rare and foreign-language material to the OCLC database for access and use by individuals in other libraries and institutions.

Phase III, cataloging of 1,500 Yiddish, Hebrew, and English-language Judaica, has already begun. Assuming success, the Phase III results will be used to demonstrate, in future grant applications, that outsourcing is a viable way to handle the cataloging of FAU's large collection of uncataloged Judaica.

There is no thought of outsourcing all cataloging at FAU, in large part because the ability to outsource successfully depends on maintaining a certain level of in-house supervision and processing capability. However, outsourcing will be used on a continuing basis to address backlogs and other situations in which outside assistance will maximize resources and provide better access to library collections.

Bibliography

Behara, Ravi S., David E. Gundersen, and Ernest A. Capozzoli. 1995. Trends in information systems outsourcing. *International Journal of Purchasing and Materials Management* 31, no. 2: 46–51.

Chervinko, James S. 1995. Cooperative and contract cataloging of foreign-language materials in academic and research libraries. *Cataloging & Classification Quarterly* 21, no. 1: 29–65.

DaConturbia, Sandra. 1992. Who catalogs foreign-language materials? A survey of ARL libraries. *Technical Services Quarterly* 10, no. 1: 15–30.

Finn, Maureen. 1993. How to plan conversion and contract cataloging projects. *OCLC Newsletter* no. 205: 10–11.

Houk, Gary R. 1991. The vice president for OCLC services discusses conversion and contract cataloging. Interview. *OCLC Newsletter* no. 205: 21–24.

Kemp, Roger L., ed. 1991. *Privatization: The Provision of Public Services by the Private Sector.* Jefferson, N.C.: McFarland.

Minutes of the April 27–28, 1994 [Meeting]. 1994. Minutes of the OCLC Advisory Committee on College and University Libraries. OCLC Online Computer Library Center, Dublin, Ohio. Photocopy.

Murphy, Bob. 1993. Experienced TECHPRO staff catalogs wide variety of materials. *OCLC Newsletter* no. 205: 18–19.

Porter, Anne Millen. 1996. Outsourcing adds complexity, customer focus unifies Unisys. *Purchasing* 120, no. 1: 76–78.

Smiraglia, Richard P. 1989. *Music Cataloging: The Bibliographic Control of Printed and Recorded Music in Libraries.* Englewood, Colo.: Libraries Unlimited.

Chapter 8

Project Muse: Outsourcing Authority Work and Hypertext Markup of Tables of Contents for Electronic Journals Published by Johns Hopkins University Press

Dawn Hale

Librarians at Johns Hopkins University's Milton S. Eisenhower Library have traditionally provided intellectual access to print resources. A new direction was established in 1993, however, when library staff formed a partnership with the Johns Hopkins University (JHU) Press. The goal of the joint venture, named Project Muse, was to publish journals electronically and provide enhanced access to these journals' contents. TeleSec Library Services, Inc., of Wheaton, Maryland, was selected in 1995 to provide authoritative form of names, assign Library of Congress subject headings, and perform Hypertext Markup Language (HTML) editing for online journal tables of contents (TOC). Within one year, TeleSec's staff produced TOCs for 1,101 articles and reviews in 13 titles. The ultimate goal is to publish all 43 of JHU Press's journals electronically and make them available on the World Wide Web, at a lower subscription cost than their print equivalents.

During 1993, staff from both the Milton S. Eisenhower Library and the Homewood Academic Computing Center at Johns Hopkins University (JHU) began a collaborative development project with the JHU Press. The primary

This chapter is based on a presentation made by Dawn Hale at the Association for Library Collections and Technical Services' Commercial Technical Services Committee's program, Creative Outsourcing: Assessment and Evaluation, New York City, July 9, 1996.

goal of this project was to digitize current issues of all journals published by JHU Press and make them available as electronic subscriptions.

This venture, named Project Muse, provided a unique opportunity to bring together a development team from these university units. The key issues the team faced were: (1) the organization and presentation of information in the journals; (2) the technological support required to produce and distribute electronic journals; and (3) the means for providing intellectual access to the contents of the journals. This chapter focuses on the creation of tables of contents (TOC) to facilitate intellectual access.

During the prototype, library staff were instrumental in facilitating intellectual access by performing TOC name authority work, subject heading assignment, and Hypertext Markup Language (HTML) editing for the online prototype journals. When grant funding became available in 1994, TeleSec Library Services, Inc., of Wheaton, Maryland, was selected as an outsourcing vendor to perform tasks originally handled by Eisenhower Library's staff.

Background

Traditionally, librarians have played an important role in the scholarly communication process. They identify, collect, and provide access to information for faculty, students, and researchers (Pintozzi 1996, 89). When staff at JHU Press decided to digitize and disseminate their journals electronically, librarians at the Eisenhower Library were committed to a partnership with them. The shared goal was to create a "strong, competitive, not-for-profit means for publishing scholarly information" (Bennett 1994, 245), while controlling the cost of publishing journals electronically. Central to this partnership was the belief that JHU Press could "deliver scholarly publications in a way that integrates library involvement and feedback, . . . [and] tailor the form of these publications to serve the actual needs of scholars and readers" (Lewis 1995, 174). As a direct outgrowth of this conviction, librarians gathered input from the scholarly community that shaped the development of Project Muse's user interface.

It is clear that navigation and retrieval of Internet resources often produce large, unmanageable results. It is also understood that digital resources have more value when access points are maximized and standardized. Based on these observations, the development team of staff from the JHU Press, the library, and the Homewood Academic Computing Center decided to include a separate, browsable TOC file for each journal issue. In addition to authors and titles, the TOC file contains Library of Congress (LC) subject headings for articles and book reviews in each journal issue. The authoritative forms of TOC name and subject headings are used, with the expectation that libraries subscribing to Project Muse titles could integrate TOCs for the electronic journals with access to conventional material in online library catalogs. As of July 1997, however, this had not yet been accomplished.

Developing the Online TOC Prototype

During 1993, original catalogers in the Cataloging Department of the Eisenhower Library performed name authority work, created LC subject headings, and applied HTML markup to the tables of contents of four issues of three journals that comprised an online prototype: *Configurations, MLN,* and *ELH.* These tables of contents and the full text of the journals were made available, without charge, on the World Wide Web (Web) in February 1994.

Creating the online prototype in-house was invaluable, because it enabled cataloging managers to gain firsthand knowledge of the issues involved in the data creation. Specifically, they learned the mechanics of performing HTML markup, and gained insight into the types of training and tools that expedite staff's abilities to learn and accurately apply HTML codes. In addition, they learned about various management issues, including the level of staff appropriate for markup versus authority work and the amount of time needed to create TOC entries for journal articles and reviews.

Based on a sample of 25 JHU Press journal titles, cataloging managers determined that each journal issue averaged 15.47 articles and book reviews and that each title averaged 3.7 issues per year. Using the figures obtained from that analysis, library staff estimated the data creation requirements for completing 13 journals in a one-year period. Staff calculated that an estimated 744 articles and reviews would need TOC citations created, including name authority work, LC subject headings, and HTML markup during that time frame.

Experience acquired in creating the prototype revealed that a trained cataloger required an average of 20 minutes to create an authoritative TOC entry with subjects for an article. An average of 15 minutes was needed to perform the same work for a book review. An additional 6 minutes of clerical time was necessary for HTML markup of each TOC entry. Revision of the TOC file by cataloging managers served as a quality control checkpoint, and required approximately 15 minutes per journal issue.

After developing the online prototype and analyzing the cost and time data acquired during that process, cataloging managers concluded that TOC creation was an ideal project for outsourcing. Cataloging Department staff, as in many institutions, were balancing a variety of other projects that competed for their time. Furthermore, there would not be a consistent TOC workload during the initial stages of the JHU Press project to warrant hiring a part-time cataloger.

Outsourcing Tables of Contents (TOC) Creation

Funds for Project Muse were awarded by the Andrew W. Mellon Foundation in 1994 and the National Endowment for the Humanities in 1995. The funds were given in support of a three-year project to implement the electronic publishing enterprise. The goals of these grants were threefold: (1) publish all 43 JHU Press journals electronically at a cost lower than their print equivalents; (2) make these journals available on the Web; and (3) develop a subscription base that would sustain the project beyond the grant period.

JHU's staff and the library's staff continued with the production phase of the project. The production schedule for publishing the electronic version of 43 titles within the three-year period funded by the grants was as follows: 13 titles would be published electronically in the first year, 12 more titles in the second year, and 15 additional titles in the third year.

TeleSec Library Services, Inc., located in Wheaton, Maryland, was engaged for the period of March 1995 through February 1996 to provide the authoritative form of names, assign LC subject headings for articles and book reviews, and perform HTML markup of the TOC citations for the first 13 titles to be published online. Cataloging managers were confident that TeleSec's staff would successfully accomplish the outsourcing goals, since they had proven to be a reliable vendor who consistently fulfilled project goals and met production deadlines on previous projects. In addition, TeleSec employs professional librarians who have a solid background in cataloging. The vendor's unit costs for creating the data were based on time-motion averages of Eisenhower Library's catalogers during the prototype.

Training

Because TeleSec's staff had no previous experience with a project of this nature, a close working relationship between TeleSec's staff and the library's staff was critical. In addition, Eisenhower Library's cataloging managers needed to provide TeleSec's staff with HTML training. Because TeleSec's staff would be working off-site, they would not have immediate access to the library's cataloging managers for questions that were expected to arise during the training period. Using in-house knowledge acquired while developing the online prototype, the library's cataloging managers

Shuffles are tuples.

provided TeleSec's staff with detailed written instructions for applying HTML codes and creating linking entries to the full text.

To facilitate the HTML markup for TOC data, the Cataloging Department's managers provided TeleSec's employees with a blank template for each journal title. An example of the blank template for articles in one journal, *Arethusa,* is illustrated in Exhibit 8.1.

In addition to receiving a blank template, TeleSec's staff also were supplied with completed TOC files to use as models. An example of the completed HTML markup for TOC information on an article in *Arethusa* is illustrated in Exhibit 8.2.

When production with the outsourcing vendor began, JHU Press's staff mailed journal galleys to TeleSec. Based on the galleys, TeleSec's staff cre-

---

Template for HTML Markup of TOC: *Arethusa*

<UL>
"Author's Last name, First name."<LI><A
HFREF=/journals/arethusa/v0##.##.#"author's last name".html>
article title</A>

Subjects:
<UL><LI>First subject heading
<LI>Second subject heading
<LI>Third subject heading.</UL></UL>

EXHIBIT 8.1 HTML Markup Template Used in TOC Data Creation for Articles in *Arethusa.*

Completed HTML Markup for Article TOC: *Arethusa*

<UL>
Greene, Ellen.<LI><A
HFREF=/journals/arethusa/v029.29.1greene.html>
Sappho, Foucault, and Women's Erotics</A>

Subjects:
<UL><LI>Sexuality in literature.
<LI>Sappho—Criticism and interpretation.
<LI>Foucault, Michel—Criticism and interpretation.</UL></UL>

EXHIBIT 8.2 Completed HTML Markup for TOC Information on an Article in *Arethusa.*

ated an article TOC entry that included the authoritative form of the author's name, the title proper, and three topical LC subject headings. The TOC entry for book reviews included the authoritative form of the author's and reviewer's names, the title of the review, and one topical subject heading. The authoritative form of translators' and editors' names was also provided, when present on a galley.

Because production deadlines needed to be met consistently, turnaround time for TeleSec's delivery of an issue's completed TOC was established as 10 business days after receiving the galley. TeleSec's staff used WordPerfect word processing software to create TOC files. Cataloging managers at the Eisenhower Library reviewed the files on a diskette before they were uploaded to the Project Muse server. TeleSec's staff obtained Internet access at a later date, to transmit files via electronic mail to staff at the Eisenhower Library and JHU Press.

Impact of Outsourcing

Eisenhower Library's Cataloging Department staff, staff at JHU Press, and TeleSec's staff worked closely together to meet the terms of the grants for the first year of this project. During that time, they gathered meaningful information for managing the operation.

Specification Changes

One aspect of the electronic journals project, which continued to evolve as the outsourcing program progressed, was the stylistic presentation of the TOC and full text. Procedures used during the initial half of the first production year were continually revised, and required extreme flexibility by the vendor. Among other changes, the format of the online files was modified, which affected the structure of the linking entries in the HTML template.

Idiosyncrasies in the way various journals handled reviews also required procedural changes. Consequently, different naming conventions were established for articles, book reviews, performance reviews, essay reviews, and appendixes included in issues. In addition, project managers decided to handle the various types of book reviews differently. In journals that consisted entirely of titled book reviews, for example, *Reviews in American History,* the lengthy reviews were more analogous to articles. These lengthy reviews were presented in the same stylistic manner as article TOC entries. However, journals with separate book review sections, for example, *Configurations,* contained reviews that were considerably shorter. Consequently, decision makers agreed that the shorter reviews would be presented in a style different from article TOC entries.

Refinements of TOC procedures affected the vendor's productivity as new specifications were adopted. There was also an impact on library staff, because they absorbed the work for all changes on journals already completed by the vendor. Having initially reached a good understanding with TeleSec's managers that this project was in an early developmental stage, and having previously established a good working relationship with the vendor, eased the strain caused by changes to coding conventions that occurred midstream during outsourcing.

Communication

Maintenance of good communication among all project participants was another challenge, since staff from the library, JHU Press, and TeleSec were in three geographic locations. An electronic mail table was used to chart the online production process vis-à-vis TeleSec, the Press, and Eisenhower Library. Staff within these organizations were able to facilitate better communication on the status of TOC editing for each journal title by using this method. Using the table, one could easily determine the status of a particular journal galley. The table charted whether the galley had been received by the vendor, if the vendor had completed TOC entries, if library staff had received TOC data for quality review, and if all quality control work was done.

Quality Control

Several different approaches to quality control review were implemented over the course of the outsourcing project. During the initial eight months, procedures were continually modified, and all work by the vendor's staff was reviewed by Eisenhower Library's staff before publication. During the latter four months of the first year, stylistic electronic publishing conventions had become routine. Project managers concluded that postproduction random spot-checking of online TOC entries was adequate for apprising Eisenhower Library's cataloging managers of the vendor's quality.

Before any new title was published online, all work performed by TeleSec's staff on that title's first three issues was reviewed by the library's cataloging managers. This single quality control measure ensured that TeleSec's staff used appropriate procedures and techniques for each title. The review ensured that procedures accounted for the title's idiosyncrasies as well.

Once TeleSec's staff acquired access to the Internet, they were trained to view their HTML markup with a Web browser. Web access enabled them to identify and correct HTML tagging errors affecting the TOC display immediately, before submission of their work. Other preproduction errors noticed by JHU Press's staff and the library's staff were shared with TeleSec's staff via electronic mail. These various approaches to quality control contributed to the vendor's ability to produce high-quality TOC data throughout the project.

Conclusion

After one year, TeleSec's staff produced TOC entries for 1,101 articles and book reviews. This production rate far exceeded the initial projection of 744 TOC files, which had been estimated for the first production year. Careful analysis and planning contributed to the success of this project. As a result of this successful beginning, the vendor's contract was extended into the second production year.

Outsourcing the creation of the electronic TOC for Project Muse was beneficial for all. Several advantages of outsourcing the data creation tasks accrued to the Eisenhower Library's cataloging managers. By not performing this work in-house, they could focus their efforts on monitoring quality control, resolving idiosyncrasies associated with the online release of new journals, and contributing to the ongoing development of Project Muse.

The creativity and overall commitment to the success of the project, which was shared by staff at the library, the JHU Press, and TeleSec, shaped the initial training, assisted staff in overcoming workflow logistics, contributed to the establishment of open lines of communication, and enabled staff to exceed projected production levels. Most important, this project demonstrated that librarians and technical services vendors can play a distinct role in facilitating intellectual access to digitized scholarly information.

Works Cited

Bennett, Scott. 1994. Repositioning university presses in scholarly communication. *Journal of Scholarly Publishing* 25, no. 4: 243–48.

Lewis, Susan. 1995. From Earth to ether: One publisher's reincarnation. *Serials Librarian* 25, no. 3/4: 173–80.

Pintozzi, Chestalene. 1996. Rethinking scholarly communication. *College & Research Libraries News* 57, no. 2: 88–91.

9 Outsourcing Cataloguing and Physical Processing: A Canadian Experience at the University of Manitoba Libraries

Lynne Partington and George Talbot

In 1994, the Bibliographic Database Management Department of the University of Manitoba Libraries began an outsourcing project for copy cataloguing and physical processing of monographs. The MARC*ADVANTAGE* service, offered by Information Systems Management/Library Technical Services (ISM/LTS), was selected for the project. The goals of outsourcing were to redeploy staff elsewhere in the library system, reduce cataloguing costs, and maintain existing cataloguing standards. Initially, ISM/LTS's staff provided copy cataloguing and physical processing for monographs, excluding certain categories, ordered from Blackwell North America, Inc., located in Lake Oswego, Oregon. The project, which evolved through four stages, was later expanded to include original monographic cataloguing, as well as cataloguing of books purchased from John Coutts Library Services, in Niagara Falls, Ontario. The objectives of the project were successfully met. As of February 1996, approximately 10,000 titles had been processed by ISM/LTS in an ongoing outsourcing program.

The University of Manitoba Libraries' Bibliographic Database Management Department (BDM) is responsible for the cataloguing and physical processing of all material for 10 libraries located on the Fort Garry Campus in Winnipeg, Manitoba. The law, medical, and dental libraries, each with its own cataloguing unit, do not rely on BDM for cataloguing and physical processing services. The 1993–94 budget for monographic acquisitions was Can$798,820. This included acquisitions for the law, medical, and dental libraries. Within the same fiscal year, BDM's staff processed approximately 27,000 monographs for the 10 libraries for which they were responsible.

Outsourcing Objectives

In 1993, the libraries' managers began to explore outsourcing as an alternative to in-house copy cataloguing and physical processing of monographs. There were three main objectives at that time. The first goal was to redeploy BDM staff elsewhere in the library system. BDM had a large component of well-trained, skilled library assistant (LA) staff, consisting of 12 LA IVs, 2 LA IIIs, 3 LA IIs, and a supervisor. There was a pressing need for staffing of this caliber elsewhere in the system. The staffing goal for outsourcing was to redeploy as many as four LA IV cataloging positions to reference services and collection development positions. No staff members or positions were to be eliminated. Second, managers wanted to reduce the per-item cataloguing cost for monographs. The final goal was to ensure, as much as possible, that BDM's existing cataloguing standards were maintained.

Outsourcing Project Description

BDM's outsourcing project advanced through four distinct stages. The first stage, begun in May 1994, consisted of planning discussions between cataloguing staff and officials from Information Systems Management/Library Technical Services (ISM/LTS), a division of Information Systems Management (formerly Utlas International Canada), also located in Winnipeg, Manitoba. ISM/LTS's newly created outsourcing service, MARC*ADVANTAGE,* was evaluated at that stage for use by librarians at both the University of Manitoba and the University of Alberta. Both institutions eventually contracted with ISM/LTS.

At the University of Manitoba, no Request for Proposal was issued. Libraries' managers made the decision to enter the pilot project with ISM/LTS based on a long-standing past relationship and on the facts that ISM/LTS is the largest outsourcing vendor in Canada and that the service is located in Winnipeg. Representatives from BDM worked closely with ISM/LTS's staff during this period. They examined local requirements and established routines that would ensure that ISM/LTS's staff received all the necessary information for satisfactory cataloguing of material. This included issuing ISM/LTS's staff a password to access the libraries' online catalogue for any online searching agreed to during the project.

Two areas of the libraries' collection that required special attention by ISM/LTS's staff were Canadian history and literature. During contract negotiations, ISM/LTS's managers agreed, at no extra charge, to classify all Canadian history books in the National Library of Canada (NLC) FC classification schedule, rather than in the Library of Congress (LC) F1000–1140 schedule. Similarly, ISM/LTS's staff agreed to class English-language Canadian literature in the PS8000 range and French-language material in the PS9000 range. Another requirement to which ISM/LTS agreed was to use the current edition of *Canadian Subject Headings* for uniquely Canadian topics.

ISM/LTS's staff were also required to examine call numbers for all Canadian literary authors and to change call numbers that were in conflict with existing holdings in the libraries' catalogue. This problem relates to Cutter numbers for Canadian literary authors, because the University of Manitoba used the PS8000 schedule for Canadian literature before NLC had established its own Cutter numbers or made them available. Because of this conflict, imported records for Canadian literary authors, if not checked against the University of Manitoba Libraries' catalogue, could result in multiple shelving locations for works by individual authors. Non-Canadian authors were less likely to present a problem, due to close adherence to LC call numbers for works by those authors.

For their part, library staff agreed that a vendor-supplied catalogue record that resulted in duplicate call numbers in the libraries' collection would be accepted, with the understanding that, for circulation purposes, barcodes uniquely identify any given item.

Stage Two

The second stage of outsourcing consisted of a trial project begun in October 1994. All approval books and firm-order titles from Blackwell North America, Inc., located in Lake Oswego, Oregon, were shipped by Blackwell directly from their book distribution center in Blackwood, New Jersey, to ISM/LTS. Based on specifications supplied by BDM's staff, ISM/LTS's staff provided copy cataloguing and physical processing for monographs only. Titles in pre-defined problem categories were forwarded to BDM without any processing by ISM/LTS's staff. These problem areas included serial titles, supplements, added copies, added volumes, replacement copies, government documents, rare books, music scores, and Slavic-, Icelandic-, and Asian-language material. In addition, all items designated at the point of order as "Do Not Catalogue" titles were not processed by ISM/LTS's staff.

ISM/LTS's staff processed an average of 450 titles per month during the trial period. This represented approximately 80 percent of the titles routed through ISM/LTS; the other 20 percent fell into one of the problem areas. All materials, including potential problem books, were routed from Blackwell directly to ISM/LTS because it was more efficient to make the decision on whether to proceed with cataloguing at one location, in order to avoid potential confusion.

ISM/LTS's staff catalogued monographs for which they could obtain copy from sources approved by the libraries' staff during contract negotiations. Those sources included LC, NLC, and several Canadian academic libraries. The vendor's staff created descriptive records for titles with no available cataloguing copy from the approved sources. BDM's staff assumed responsibility for classification and subject analysis work on the brief descriptive records.

Physical processing included stamping book edges with an ownership stamp, inserting tattle tape strips for the libraries' security system, spine labeling, and barcoding. Ownership stamps, tattle tape strips, and barcodes were supplied by the libraries as needed. In addition, material shipped directly to ISM/LTS from Blackwell required almost 40 customized bookplates to be applied appropriately. ISM/LTS's staff were supplied with a listing of the gift, grant, and endowment fund numbers that required the application of a bookplate and, possibly, the insertion of a note in the catalogue record. As each book was received by ISM/LTS's staff, related information was entered into their Tracker Program, including the fund number on which it was ordered. This step automatically inserted any required gift note into the catalogue record and generated an internal use note for ISM/LTS's processing staff, indicating which bookplate should be inserted.

Completed bibliographic records were transferred electronically on a daily basis to the libraries' Systems Office, at which point the records were downloaded into the libraries' catalogue. Shipments received by ISM/LTS were stored together and forwarded to BDM's staff as each shipment was completed. This was not accomplished according to any set schedule, but always occurred within the two-week period specified in the libraries' contract. Rush material, however, was processed immediately and sent separately to BDM. BDM's staff reviewed each item processed by ISM/LTS's staff and evaluated the quality of cataloguing and physical processing.

Stage two concluded with a review of the test project, which included input from public services librarians. At that point, there were no major criticisms. The cataloguing error rate, which ranged from 4 percent to 5 percent, was deemed acceptable. An error was defined as anything affecting access, and anything requiring cataloguing or processing steps stipulated in the contract. The turnaround time for new material improved upon the in-house standard, since in-house turnaround time ranged from three to four weeks. ISM/LTS's physical processing was satisfactory, except that spine labels were not adhering properly at the beginning of the project. ISM/LTS's managers responded to this problem and changed to a different clear tape, which was more acceptable to BDM's staff.

Stage Three

Stage three began in April 1995, with a one-year contract for copy cataloguing and physical processing of the same categories of Blackwell material processed during the trial project. In addition to Blackwell orders, similar material from an approval plan with John Coutts Library Services, located in Niagara Falls, Ontario, was also routed directly through ISM/LTS. During this stage, the average number of titles processed by ISM/LTS's staff per month increased to 500. Beginning in stage three, BDM's staff only spot-checked one book per shelf, chosen at random from each shipment, for their quality control evaluation. In addition, it was decided that two entire shipments from ISM/LTS would be randomly chosen for item-by-item evaluation during the one-year contract.

Stage Four

In the middle of stage three, the outsourcing project advanced to a fourth stage more quickly than originally planned. This change resulted from events at both the University of Manitoba Libraries and at ISM/LTS. By fall 1995, BDM's staff were involved full time in the implementation of a new automated library system. The Data Research Associates (DRA) integrated system had been selected to replace the libraries' existing PALS system. During record conversion, the majority of the serials holdings had become scrambled and older, unbarcoded monographic collections appeared without locations. Maintenance work in these areas, along with the process of learning the new system and new procedures, affected the abilities of BDM's staff to keep pace with current cataloguing needs.

At the same time, ISM/LTS hired several professional librarians with experience in original cataloguing and with expertise in Slavic languages and music, among other areas of specialisation. As a result of this factor, the ISM/LTS contract was renegotiated. ISM/LTS's staff began to supply original cataloguing for monographs, as well as cataloguing for Slavic-language material and music scores. All other problem categories of material, identified as exceptions during stage one of outsourcing, were still forwarded to BDM's staff for cataloguing and physical processing. During this stage, the average number of titles processed per month by ISM/LTS's staff increased to over 800.

Outsourcing Results

The goals for outsourcing of cataloguing and physical processing of monographs at the University of Manitoba Libraries were to redeploy cataloguing staff to other areas of the library system, reduce cataloguing costs for monographs, and maintain existing cataloguing standards as much as possible during outsourcing. Within 18 months after initially investigating outsourcing with ISM/LTS, the libraries' managers achieved these goals. The overall success of the initial outsourcing effort also resulted in an extension of the contract with ISM/LTS beyond the one-year time frame established in April 1995.

Staffing

In November 1993, the director of libraries initiated an in-depth internal review of BDM to identify all staff functions. The review was done to assess whether outsourcing would make it feasible for the director to reassign as many as four LA IV positions to other areas of the library system. It was concluded at that time that outsourcing was likely to yield that result. By December 1995, that goal had been met. As a result of the reduced workload for BDM's staff, two LA IVs voluntarily transferred into public services positions in 1995. Two other LA IV positions became vacant when one individual retired at age 65 and when another retired because of poor health. Both of these positions were redeployed to public areas in the system.

Although outsourcing has inevitably left BDM's staff unsettled, the negative impact has been reduced somewhat by several factors. First, staff were requested to do an in-house review and to recommend whether or not positions could be reduced. Second, with the knowledge that two retirements were likely to occur in the forthcoming year, the libraries' managers acted on the Review Committee's recommendation to allow attrition to account for two of the desired positions. Finally, as public services positions at a suitable level became available, those assignments were offered to BDM's staff, if interested. Due to this strategic approach, no staff members had been transferred unwillingly as of July 1996.

Monographic Cataloguing Costs

Before outsourcing, the in-house cost of copy cataloguing was Can$16 per title and, for original cataloguing, Can$40 per title. Both figures include processing costs. These figures were obtained by analyzing all staff time and external resources, as well as the cost of capturing catalogue records from source databases. This total was then divided by the number of monographs processed. Overhead costs for office space, equipment, and supplies were not included in this equation. Library managers are satisfied that anything less than these in-house costs represents a saving and that outsourcing has substantially reduced cataloguing costs.

Another cost savings, as well as a record enrichment factor for the online catalogue, was the availability of tables of contents in the outsourced cataloguing. ISM/LTS's staff were able to add tables of contents notes, supplied from Blackwell's resource file, for an additional charge of US$.75 per title. BDM's policy had been to limit the addition of contents notes as part of an effort to increase all copy cataloguers' output to an average of 20 titles per day. A trial conducted by the copy cataloguing supervisor indicated that adding tables of contents averaged 15 to 20 minutes per book. The reduced rate of production associated with this task was deemed unacceptable.

Although the per-item cost of cataloguing was monitored closely during outsourcing, there were additional costs that were absorbed by the libraries' staff and not analyzed in detail. Because holdings and item record data are not available for outsourced material when books arrive at the libraries, LA IV staff sort each shipment and forward the majority of titles to LA IIs for holdings and item records creation. Reviewing and routing the uncatalogued "problem" titles as they arrive from ISM/LTS are new tasks, which are absorbed by BDM's staff and not factored into the overall cost of outsourcing.

BDM's staff also absorb the cost of correcting errors in ISM/LTS's cataloguing. Corrections are made at the point where a catalogue record is compared with the book in hand. It is more efficient to make the correction at that step than to report the problem to the vendor, because the vendor's staff would have to repeat the same steps. Printouts are made of these mistakes, however, and the error categories, together with examples of errors, are reported to ISM/LTS's supervisors for discussion with their staff.

Maintenance of Cataloguing and Physical Processing Standards

The libraries' cataloguing standards are typical of most North American university libraries. The majority of the collections are arranged by the LC classification. BDM's staff also adhere to the *Anglo-American Cataloguing Rules,* second edition, 1988 revision, and the *Library of Congress Rule Interpretations,* with few exceptions. Each support staff member has desktop access to catalogue records from LC, NLC, and several Canadian academic libraries. LA IVs routinely import, edit, and finish records from these sources, without revision by librarians. For years, the prevailing practice has been to perform minimal editing on imported records.

During the first 18 months of outsourcing, the quality of ISM/LTS's copy cataloguing was equivalent to the quality of copy cataloguing previously performed by BDM's LA IV staff. During the pilot project, when every outsourced record was checked, the error rate was approximately 5 percent. A shipment chosen at random in 1996, which was completely examined for quality, revealed a higher error rate. A significant number of these errors involved series entries, which could have been avoided if the vendor, at a significant cost, had performed copious checking in the libraries' catalogue. However, the libraries' managers still prefer to have this step done in-house.

Other problems in outsourcing quality were also a result of the fact that the vendor's cataloguing is performed without searching the libraries' online catalogue, except in the few categories where this is stipulated in the contract. Because of this, ISM/LTS's staff were not aware of previous editions or additional copies for specific titles. This has had an impact on the quality of catalogue records. Some of these problems had been anticipated; others had not.

Series

As anticipated from the outset, catalogue entries for series have been a problem during outsourcing. ISM/LTS's staff check for form of series entry, but do not check to determine if a series is classed together or classed separately. As records containing series are identified and imported from CATSS, ISM/LTS's bibliographic utility, series are checked against and linked to authorities in CATSS following the same hierarchy of authority sources used by BDM's staff: the University of Manitoba Libraries, NLC, and LC.

If a series title search results in no matches, ISM/LTS's staff establish the series according to the *Anglo-American Cataloguing Rules,* second edition, 1988 revision. By this method, errors related to form of entry are minimized. Treatment, however, remains a problem, since the contract does not require ISM/LTS's staff to check the libraries' catalogue for this information. Even if an NLC or LC series authority record contains treatment information, BDM's staff might not always have followed the same course. No cost-effective way of resolving this problem has been found. Therefore, the cost of examining each book shipment to identify classed-together series, by scanning incoming volumes for numbered series and verifying series treatment in the catalogue, in addition to making all required changes, continues to be absorbed by the libraries' staff.

Binding

Binding procedures have been completely reevaluated, and the workflow modified several times, during outsourcing. At first, an attempt was made to continue the established practice of making binding decisions before books were labeled and barcoded. In the beginning, all paperbacks catalogued by ISM/LTS's staff were shipped to BDM with barcodes and spine labels clipped to each book, rather than having those items applied to each book. The libraries' staff placed all vendor-catalogued paperbacks on specific shelves for bindery decisions by bibliographers. Items that did not require binding were returned to the processing workflow immediately. Items for binding were sent to the bindery and reintroduced into the physical processing workflow at a later date. This procedure proved to be cumbersome and was abandoned for another approach.

After experimentation, the libraries' staff instituted a major change in their binding policy. This change resulted from a reduction in the binding budget, as well as the need to modify binding procedures because of outsourcing. According to the new procedure, ISM/LTS's staff catalogue and complete all physical processing of paperbacks, including the application of spine labels and barcodes. When book shipments arrive at the library, BDM's LA II staff add holdings records, create item records, and forward books directly to individual unit libraries. It is at this point only that each bibliographer now chooses whether to examine paperbacks for binding decisions. In this case, changes in response to outsourcing resulted in the reorganization of monographic binding procedures, which bring them in line with the libraries' established decentralized procedures for periodicals.

Other Impacts of Outsourcing

Adjusting to new arrival schedules for the receipt of ISM/LTS's catalogue records and the receipt of books processed by ISM/LTS's staff presented another challenge during outsourcing. The libraries' staff migrated to a new integrated library system during the course of outsourcing, which also affected the time sequence in which bibliographic record information was available in the catalogue.

The libraries' previous automated system, PALS, indexed access points in newly added titles on a biweekly basis. Consequently, books were often on the shelves before catalogue records were available to the public. In the new DRA system, indexing of all access points occurs in real time, with the exception of daily keyword indexing. Therefore, ISM/LTS's catalogue records, which are received electronically and added by the libraries' Systems Office librarians on a daily basis, are generally available to the libraries' staff and patrons before the books are physically on campus. Public services staff and patrons have learned that the presence or absence of a holdings statement in a given record, which indicates the location and circulation status of an item, is the clue to whether a recently published book is available in the collection. In terms of the overall benefits of outsourcing, this problem has been an acceptable tradeoff.

Problems associated with determining the availability status of new books also resulted from the manner in which the libraries' staff handled invoices in the early stages of outsourcing. Because books were shipped from Blackwell and Coutts via ISM/LTS, and invoices were shipped directly from the booksellers to the libraries, invoice arrival schedules bore no relation to book arrival schedules.

Before outsourcing, the libraries' Acquisitions Department staff had a policy of immediately stamping order forms with a "Received" stamp as corresponding invoices arrived at the library. Order forms with "Received" status were subsequently forwarded to bibliographers and faculty. This procedure presented conflicts during outsourcing, since new books were typically not on campus at the time bibliographers and faculty received notification of their arrival. To remedy this problem, books are now unpacked in the Acquisitions Department and corresponding order forms are inserted in each volume. Books are forwarded to BDM's staff, where the books and order forms stamped "Received" are released simultaneously as processing is completed.

Outsourcing also had an impact on the level of staff required to perform specific tasks. In the November 1993 review of the projected impact of outsourcing, planners had anticipated that an LA II would be able to receive, examine, and route outsourced items, without consulting senior staff for assistance. However, experience has demonstrated that LA II staff often lack the requisite cataloguing background and knowledge of in-house cataloguing policies to make the necessary decisions in the outsourcing evaluation process. It has subsequently been determined that this trouble-shooting responsibility is most efficiently performed by staff at the LA IV level.

A final, unanticipated outcome of outsourcing is the availability of additional LA IV staff time for reallocation to other duties. By outsourcing the cataloguing of new books, LA IV staff have significantly more time for cataloguing of gift material, recataloguing, and resolving complex cataloguing problems. This has increased the workflow to the cataloguing librarians, since material of this nature is given to them for classification and subject analysis more frequently than was the case when LA IVs handled the material that is now outsourced.

It has been increasingly difficult for the librarians to manage this workload, because the librarian-level staffing component for monographic cataloguing decreased to three FTE at the time outsourcing began. This figure is not expected to increase. Furthermore, these three librarians each have a variety of responsibilities in other areas and only the equivalent of one FTE is devoted to monographic cataloguing duties.

Because ISM/LTS's staff now perform original cataloguing, and because the libraries' managers are thinking about routing other categories of incoming acquisitions to ISM/LTS beyond the amount of items already outsourced, it is anticipated that the librarians' workload for the most difficult categories of cataloguing will become more manageable than previously expected. The overall impact of outsourcing, with regard to this issue, remains to be seen.

Conclusion

As of July 1996, the University of Manitoba Libraries' outsourcing project had been operational for 21 months. It will require continued monitoring and modification, and will continue to evolve, because outsourcing is expected to remain as a routine component of the libraries' cataloguing operation.

Now that basic routines have been established, other ways of streamlining cataloguing and physical processing procedures, as well as reducing costs, can be explored. There might be other tasks that can be transferred to ISM/LTS. Although that approach will result in higher outsourcing costs, the net result still might be an acceptable tradeoff within the overall cataloguing budget. Areas of particular concern include: (1) library staff procedures for reviewing and routing incoming books from ISM/LTS; (2) ISM/LTS's procedures for consulting the libraries' catalogue, in cases other than the existing classification review for Canadian literary authors; and (3) procedures for adding holdings and item record data, to investigate the feasibility of obtaining system-generated holdings and item record data at the point where ISM/LTS's records are transmitted to the libraries' catalogue electronically.

As of February 1996, ISM/LTS's staff had successfully catalogued and performed physical processing for approximately 10,000 titles, and were contracted to process an estimated 14,000 titles annually. Plans for the future already include expanding outsourcing to include government publications, Hebrew cataloguing, and item record creation. Outsourcing has resulted in relatively lower overall costs for these services, when compared with previous costs for in-house cataloguing and physical processing. The turnaround time for outsourced material was less than the turnaround time before outsourcing. When the quality of vendor-supplied material was judged by in-house standards, minimal impact on physical processing standards was noted as a result of outsourcing. The number of errors affecting the quality of cataloguing was deemed manageable. In addition, the libraries' managers were able to achieve the goal of redeploying four LA IV positions into public services as a result of outsourcing.

Finally, the potential for reassigning monographic cataloguing staff to temporary projects is another positive outcome of outsourcing. This final point was never made more clear than during the implementation of a new automated library system in the summer and fall of 1995, at which time the established outsourcing structure gave managers the flexibility to utilize cataloguing staff in a manner they otherwise would not have had available to them. The libraries' staff and patrons benefited overall from the impact of outsourcing in that particular experience. Other benefits are expected to be realized as future outsourcing enhancements are made at the University of Manitoba Libraries.

Bibliography

National Library of Canada. 1992. *Canadian Subject Headings.* 3d ed. Edited by Alina Schweitzer. Ottawa: National Library of Canada.

National Library of Canada. 1994. *Class FC: A Classification for Canadian History.* 2d ed. Ottawa: National Library of Canada.

10 Insourcing of Cataloging for a Special Collection: An Alternative to Outsourcing at the University of Nebraska–Lincoln Libraries

Julie Swann and Sandra Herzinger

In 1994, Cataloging Department staff at the University of Nebraska–Lincoln Libraries completed an in-house cataloging project that proved to be a successful alternative to outsourcing. In order to provide timely bibliographic access to the newly acquired Carlton Lowenberg Collection of Emily Dickinson material, catalogers proposed an in-house approach. Cataloging staff were hired to work overtime, and completely processed the collection of 3,200 items within four concentrated six-week sessions. Local cataloging practices that were tailored to the requirements of this special collection were used. As a consequence of insourcing, library administrators successfully met the budgetary constraints and time requirements established for cataloging the collection. This project was also completed without the additional startup costs and time delays that would have resulted from selecting an outside contractor.

The University of Nebraska–Lincoln Libraries acquired the Carlton Lowenberg Collection of Emily Dickinson material in January 1993, as a gift from the University Foundation. In order to cover cataloging costs for the collection, and to ensure timely bibliographic access to the collection's holdings, cataloging funds were also supplied by the University Foundation when the gift was made.

The option of outsourcing the cataloging for this collection was discussed by the libraries' administrators at the time of acquisition. However, in response to a copy cataloger's suggestion at a Cataloging Department meeting, administrators agreed to experiment with insourcing the cataloging of monographs and serials in the collection. Experienced, in-house catalogers, including the cataloger who suggested insourcing, were selected to work overtime to catalog the material. The collection was processed within the established deadlines and budget and was viewed as a successful alternative to outsourcing. Project participants were also rewarded with the knowledge that their insourcing proposal was approved and enacted by the libraries' administrators, and that the project was successfully completed with their involvement.

The Collection

Carlton Lowenberg, a collector and bibliographer, is the author of two works on Emily Dickinson, *Emily Dickinson's Textbooks* and *Musicians Wrestle Everywhere: Emily Dickinson and Music.* For 10 years, Lowenberg collected items that reflect the era and culture in which Dickinson lived. The collection, which includes over 3,000 monograph and serial titles, together with shelves of archival material and musical scores, consists of a broad range of subjects and formats. It includes editions of Dickinson's works, historical information about the region where she lived, works by her friends and relatives, textbooks from the nineteenth century, hymnbooks, serials and songbooks, manuscript items, and musical recordings. For comparison purposes, the estimated time required for cataloging the collection was equal to the time required for about one month of the libraries' routine cataloging workload. However, considerable cataloging expertise was required to process this collection, given the specialized nature of the material and the variety of formats.

Insourcing Objectives

Because funds for cataloging and physical processing were provided when the collection was donated, the libraries' administrators made a commitment to the University Foundation that the collection would be cataloged within one year. The associate dean, with input from the head of cataloging, established the project timetable and budget, basing their projections on compensation rates for copy catalogers, costs for accessing the libraries' online bibliographic utility, and costs for physical processing material.

The head of cataloging and the head of the copy cataloging unit, who was also assigned to manage the cataloging project, were concerned about an outsourcing vendor's ability to meet this cataloging deadline and accomplish the work within the budget framework. In addition, these managers viewed the project as an opportunity to act upon suggestions from their staff to insource this work to existing personnel. There would be fewer startup costs in this kind of cataloging effort, and insourcing would provide cataloging staff with an opportunity to earn extra wages with their skills. The head of cataloging also knew that an insourcing project of this caliber would provide data about the costs and benefits of an in-house overtime project, which would serve as valuable management information for future needs.

Background

In 1992–93, Cataloging Department staff participated in cost and time studies, which resulted in streamlining the departmental workflow. These analyses showed that the libraries' cataloging and processing procedures were managed efficiently. Nonetheless, when the Lowenberg gift was made, cataloging staff understood that the libraries' administrators would consider commercial outsourcing as an option that might offer more efficiencies and less expense than in-house processes. In 1993, the libraries had contracted with the Online Computer Library Center (OCLC) TECHPRO unit to catalog a collection of Czech-language material. Based on that outsourcing experience, staff had a good notion of the procedures involved in outsourcing and a general idea of outsourcing costs. With knowledge gained from this previous experience, and data derived from Cataloging Department time studies, staff believed that the in-house costs of cataloging the Lowenberg material would at least be comparable to outsourcing costs. In that regard, catalogers viewed this project as an opportunity to prove that their skills and services were competitive with the costs and services offered by commercial cataloging agencies.

The libraries' administrators were confident that existing staff were capable of processing the Lowenberg Collection. However, it was apparent that cataloging staff would not be able to complete this project during regular work hours and still meet the established cataloging deadline. When staff expressed a willingness to work overtime, the libraries' administrators, the head of cataloging, and the head of the copy cataloging unit agreed to experiment with an in-house project for a six-week trial period. It was mutually understood and accepted that the in-house procedures and strategic approach were subject to modification at the end of the trial period.

Insourcing Project Description

The libraries' American and British literature bibliographer was responsible for retention and location decisions for the Lowenberg Collection. The goal was to retain items that constituted useful additions to the libraries' general collection, and to forward them to appropriate collection locations. The bibliographer began sorting and evaluating items soon after the collection arrived. Working with an English Department faculty member, she also assigned priorities for processing items. The bibliographer segregated material, separating manuscripts and rare items from other titles that were appropriate for the libraries' general collection. Preservation problems were identified during the sorting process as well. Works were roughly sorted by subject categories. That process enabled other bibliographers to evaluate items in their specific disciplines and make retention decisions on material outside the realm of the libraries' literature collection.

Insourcing Policies and Procedures

While bibliographers continued to assess and sort the collection, the head of cataloging, the head of the copy cataloging unit, and the associate dean for collections and services developed criteria for hiring catalogers on an overtime basis. They also began writing procedures for processing the Lowenberg Collection. It was agreed that only staff with experience in copy cataloging of monographs or serials would be hired as project catalogers. In addition, participants were required to have satisfactory performance evaluations and obtain supervisory permission to participate in the project.

Productivity requirements were also established. Each project cataloger would be expected to catalog a minimum of 10 titles per hour, following established guidelines for copy cataloging that would be tailored to this project. This quota exceeded the performance normally expected of copy catalogers because project participants would be working at a time of day when there were few interruptions and would be expected to concentrate solely on cataloging efforts. Nonetheless, standards for the insourcing project were comparable to procedures established for routine copy cataloging, except that catalogers were instructed to accept minimal-level cataloging if all required elements were present in a record. The project's cataloging would be conducted using the OCLC bibliographic database as the source for catalog copy.

Once those policies were defined, job descriptions for five overtime positions were posted and interviews were scheduled. During the interviews, conducted by the head of the copy cataloging unit, the cataloging quota was explained to candidates. Candidates were also questioned about their abilities to work during specific hours that were tentatively scheduled for the trial period. The temporary nature of the trial project was also discussed. In addition, the fact that a different set of staff members might be hired after the trial period, to replace catalogers from the first phase of the project, was stressed.

The interviewer explained that project participants would be expected to work five hours of overtime per week and would use OCLC during nonprime time, preferably working after 4:00 in the afternoon or on Saturday. Employees would not be allowed to work more than 10 hours on any given day. Separate time records and cataloging statistics would be maintained for work connected with the Lowenberg project. Candidates were also informed that individuals selected for the project would eventually meet with the libraries' associate dean for administration, for details on recording overtime and leave status (vacation time, illness, bereavement leave, and so forth) on time cards.

Staffing for the Insourcing Trial Period

In May 1994, a select group of five staff was hired for the six-week trial period. The head of the copy cataloging unit managed day-to-day operations and was responsible for overseeing the work of all project staff. Three copy catalogers, and two other staff members charged with creating item-level records and performing physical processing, were hired for overtime during the trial period.

A student assistant was also assigned to the project, and an original cataloger served as the project resource person. Records that lacked call numbers, subject headings, and uniform titles, or those that required series decisions, were routed to the original cataloger, as were all other problematic records. The original cataloger, the student assistant, and the head of the copy cataloging unit participated in the project during regular hours, without overtime pay.

Cataloging Activities and Procedures

The student assistant conducted preliminary searches in the libraries' online and card catalogs to locate existing records for all Lowenberg items identified as candidates for addition to the collection. The student assistant forwarded those items from the gift-receiving area to the Cataloging Department. At that point, an orange flag was inserted into each piece, designating that item as part of this special collection. The student also affixed gift bookplates inside the books and placed all items on shelves reserved for Lowenberg Collection material.

Procedural documents were distributed to all staff participating in the project. Catalogers were instructed to adhere to routine copy cataloging practices. Various editions and, in some cases, printings of Dickinson's works were shelflisted by catalogers. However, call numbers in the OCLC records were accepted, unless a call number contained an obvious error.

Series were checked in the local series decision file. Items with series that were not established locally, and were not in the Library of Congress's authority file available on OCLC's database, were routed to the original cataloger for series authority processing. The original cataloger completed local series decision slips and returned items to appropriate copy catalogers who had originally searched for the items. The copy catalogers were responsible for editing OCLC records to reflect local series decisions made by the original cataloger.

For records that lacked call numbers, copy catalogers were instructed to follow routine cataloging procedures and use call numbers from different editions. If different editions with call numbers were not available, those items were also routed to the original cataloger. The original cataloger assigned call numbers, reviewed Cutter numbers against holdings in the libraries' online catalog, and returned completed items to the appropriate copy catalogers.

Because the Cataloging Department supervisors anticipated that several items in the Lowenberg Collection would require uniform titles, copy catalogers were instructed from the outset to monitor those bibliographic fields closely and identify records lacking uniform titles. Catalogers searched OCLC's online authority file for uniform titles. Any authority records that were found, together with the notes for those records, were printed. Printouts were inserted into the items in question and routed to the original cataloger. Items without any authority records were assigned to the original cataloger as well.

When copy catalogers found usable copy in the OCLC database, which included a call number, subject headings, uniform title, and so on, they edited the record according to standard, in-house practices. A local note containing the donor's name was added to each record as well. This note was programmed into a computer keyboard function key, in order to enter this information into each record as quickly and accurately as possible.

Cataloged material was forwarded immediately to the two project participants responsible for marking, labeling, and creating item-level records. Those employees created item records in the libraries' Innovative Interfaces, Inc. online catalog for volumes added to existing titles. Information on added copies was also captured in the local catalog for all duplicate copies requested for retention by the libraries' bibliographers.

Early in the trial period, staff discovered that numerous titles in the Lowenberg Collection had been printed several times over the years, and that various OCLC records existed for different printings. For more efficient searching, catalogers were instructed at that point to qualify all searches with the year of publication. If no records were found for the year of a specific printing, copy catalogers searched for records with other printing dates. When records for different editions only were found, items without matching-edition records were placed on a "Zero OCLC" shelf for processing at a later date.

Before the project began, cataloging supervisors were aware that copy catalogers frequently find only minimal-level records when searching the

OCLC database. The library's regular cataloging procedures stipulate that minimal-level records should be forwarded to an original cataloger for upgrading. For the Lowenberg project, however, copy catalogers were instructed to accept and edit minimal-level records that contained call numbers, subject headings, and uniform titles. Copy catalogers used information from records for other editions to complete minimal-level records with these required data elements.

Because all items in the Lowenberg Collection had been thoroughly searched in the libraries' catalogs before arriving in the Cataloging Department, copy catalogers did not anticipate receiving unwanted added copies for cataloging. Bibliographers were expected to retain a certain number of duplicate copies for processing, but those items were to have been identified as acceptable duplicates during the pre-catalog search. Nevertheless, copy catalogers did encounter duplicates that were not identified by bibliographers as added copies. In those instances, duplicate copies from the Lowenberg Collection were compared with the libraries' existing copies. Items in the best physical condition were retained.

Insourcing Results

After the six-week insourcing trial period, pre-catalog searching of 609 items and cataloging for 578 titles had been completed. Nineteen items, for which no available OCLC copy was found, were placed on the "Zero OCLC" shelf. Forty-one copies were added to the collection as replacements for items already held, and 12 items were identified as copies that would not be added to the collection.

Everyone involved in the trial project agreed that it had been a success, although some participants had a difficult time completing their overtime hours because of illness and other complications. Schedules varied for personal reasons. Some staff in the trial session also chose not to continue in the ensuing sessions, because they found the overtime work to be too exhausting. It is important to emphasize, however, that participants had known in advance that they were expected to complete their regular 40-hour schedule in addition to the overtime, and that overall productivity in regular hours should not decline as a result of work on the insourcing project. Overall, no significant scheduling problems were associated with this project.

In July 1994, the libraries' administrators decided to continue the in-house cataloging and physical processing activities for other titles in the Lowenberg Collection. In all, four, six-week processing sessions were conducted over a period of five months until the project was completed. By the end of the project, the workload of titles, which had been assigned location decisions and had received preservation treatment in preparation for cataloging, had decreased. As a result, the number of participants was reduced to three.

Overall, the project participants cataloged and completed physical processing for 2,753 monographic titles. Copy catalogers worked a total of 600 overtime hours. In the last phase of the project, a Serials Department copy cataloger, in consultation with a serials librarian, processed 24 serials titles. An additional 252 "Zero OCLC" items, which had been stored in the Cataloging Department because of the lack of OCLC records, were processed as well. Working closely with the original cataloger assigned to this project, a high-level, monographic copy cataloger handled the "Zero OCLC" titles.

Although the majority of work for this project was performed during overtime hours by copy cataloging staff, members of the Cataloging Department's authority control unit were involved to some degree. In spite of the copy catalogers' efforts to identify records that needed uniform titles, 30 percent of the items requiring uniform titles were not identified at the point of cataloging. These problems were not addressed until they were later observed by staff in the authority control unit. In hindsight, it would have been advisable if lists of uniform-title problems had been generated by the copy catalogers and used as the basis for an overtime project by a member of the authority control unit. Instead, employees from the authority control unit resolved these problems along with their normal assignments, and did not receive overtime compensation. The weekly impact of this workload was not significant, but other authority work with a lower priority was postponed.

The time required by staff in the authority control unit, by the original cataloger assigned to the project, and by the head of the copy cataloging unit was absorbed in the libraries' regular budget. All staff overtime connected with the four different phases of cataloging activity was charged against the project budget. In the end, the Lowenberg Collection was fully cataloged within the budget and deadline established at the time the libraries received the collection. Project funds were also made available for the purchase of material needed to process and store archival material in the collection.

Evaluation of Insourcing

There were numerous benefits from insourcing the cataloging for the Lowenberg Collection. Because the collection was processed in-house, bibliographers were able to make location decisions over a more extended period of time than might have been available if the collection had been shipped off-site for processing. Because of this flexibility, bibliographers were able to examine material and determine which items should be retained

in their areas in a manner that did not severely affect their regular schedules. If the collection had been packaged immediately for shipment to a
commercial cataloging service, the bibliographers might have had more
difficulty evaluating the collection in a limited time frame.

The turnaround time for processing individual collection items was
also reduced, since cataloged and processed material could be released
from the Cataloging Department and forwarded to the libraries' stacks on
a daily basis. If these pieces had been outsourced, they would have been
batched for shipment to a vendor. All items in each batch would have been
unavailable until the entire batch had been returned from the commercial
cataloging service.

The libraries' administrators were also fairly certain about the level of
quality they would receive by using in-house cataloging staff for this project. Although cataloging records for this collection were not randomly
checked for errors, the long-established accuracy rate of the catalogers who
participated in the project is between 95 percent and 98 percent. Moreover, in-house processing of the collection facilitated adherence to local
procedures. Catalogers could maintain consistency in using the local series
authority file. They could also easily check call numbers for original cataloging against holdings in the local database, and assign Cutter numbers
that best fit the shelflist for the existing collection.

Another benefit of in-house processing was the ability to address preservation problems as they were identified by catalogers. Although the most
serious preservation problems were noticed by the libraries' bibliographers
during the initial examination of items, some problems were less notice-
able at that time. As the copy catalogers worked with individual books,
they noted items with mold and mildew damage, and forwarded that material immediately to the libraries' preservation librarian for treatment.

The libraries' copy catalogers discovered that participating in the project was a welcome challenge, although it was difficult for them to meet the
established quota in the beginning. It required discipline on everyone's part
to work the required overtime within the assigned time schedules. They also
had to modify their OCLC search strategies to fit the peculiarities of the
items in this special collection. Nevertheless, the cataloging skills these
staff members possess enabled them to earn additional income in this endeavor. Their initiative in proposing this project was also rewarded when
the work was done successfully.

Conclusion

This insourcing project satisfied the objectives of the libraries' administrators and staff. Catalogers demonstrated the quality and efficiency of their

work. The collection was cataloged within the established time frame and budget. Surplus funds were used to process, preserve, and store archival items from the collection that were not included in this project. Because the collection was processed in-house, material was readily accessible to bibliographers. Library patrons had access to individual items immediately after they were processed. In addition, local policies and established cataloging standards were followed in a manner consistent with routine technical services operations.

There were also innumerable benefits for staff morale, as team members worked together to complete the project that they had initially proposed to the libraries' administrators. No serious, adverse consequences resulted from the amount of overtime hours required by staff for this effort. Staff members were also able to earn additional income while providing the libraries with high-quality work and a high level of productivity. The project not only proved to be a successful alternative to outsourcing in this particular instance, but also yielded a wealth of information about the costs and benefits of managing an insourcing operation at the University of Nebraska–Lincoln Libraries.

Bibliography

Lowenberg, Carlton. 1986. *Emily Dickinson's Textbooks*. Lafayette, Calif.: C. Lowenberg.

Lowenberg, Carlton. 1992. *Musicians Wrestle Everywhere: Emily Dickinson and Music*. Berkeley, Calif.: Fallen Leaf Press.

Chapter 11

Leveraging Value from the J. Hugh Jackson Library's Collections: Outsourcing Document Delivery and Tables of Contents Services at Stanford University's Graduate School of Business Library

Robert E. Mayer, Paul Reist, and Suzanne Sweeney

In 1991, managers at Stanford University's J. Hugh Jackson Library, housed in the Graduate School of Business, developed a new focus on service output. A major reconfiguration of library operations, coupled with establishment of a Faculty Document Retrieval and Delivery Service, revitalized user services and increased service demand. Managers responded to this situation by leveraging value from their collections through outsourcing document retrieval and delivery services to Information Express, located in Palo Alto, California. The infrastructure made available by this business partnership enabled library managers to meet increasing document delivery demands, redirect staff into core research support, and move toward a more comprehensive virtual library. Outsourcing helped blend tables of contents and document delivery services, as well as interlibrary loan and journal collection development, into a more seamless process.

The Stanford University Graduate School of Business (GSB) was founded in 1926, and has maintained a library since 1933. The J. Hugh Jackson Library is funded and managed solely by the GSB and is not a branch of Stanford University Libraries. Among its varied collections, Jackson Library has over 425,000 volumes in the classified collection, hundreds of thou-

The authors wish to thank Jackson Library staff member, Nora Richardson, for technical assistance in compiling this chapter.

sands of corporate reports, 2,000 periodical subscriptions, and dozens of electronic business resources. Library staff serve a primary clientele of 110 faculty, 730 students in a Master of Business Administration (MBA) program, 95 doctoral students, 125 administrative staff, and a corresponding Stanford-wide community of 20,000.

Background

Until 1991, the Jackson Library was fundamentally a resource-centered organization. Faculty outreach services, as distinct from traditional in-house services, were concentrated in two main activities emanating from the library's Technical Services Division. A bimonthly publication, *Selected Additions to the J. Hugh Jackson Library,* constituted a reader's alert service with lists of recent library acquisitions. Copies of this list were distributed to individual GSB faculty, as notification of new material that could potentially be of interest to them. The Faculty Tables of Contents Service consisted of photocopied tables of contents from individual issues of journals, based on a profile of Jackson Library subscriptions created for individual faculty members. There was no delivery mechanism to retrieve or deliver desired items to faculty.

In conjunction with managerial and organizational changes in June 1991, a number of new library service initiatives were begun. These included the establishment of an in-house Faculty Document Retrieval and Delivery Service, and development of a separate Faculty Research Service. The Faculty Document Retrieval and Delivery Service, as expected, was an immediate success. By March 1992, library staff delivered over 200 articles and books per month to faculty. Service was expanded to GSB administrative staff as well, although most requests still emanated from faculty.

The success of the Faculty Document Retrieval and Delivery Service led to the examination, on the part of library managers, of the potential for an outsourcing arrangement. The outsourcing of the library's photocopy services and several of the library's cataloging processes to commercial vendors was already part of the library's overall outsourcing strategy. In examining the possibility of outsourcing document retrieval and delivery processes, library managers concluded that research libraries, such as Jackson Library, constitute substantial information infrastructures, whose value to host institutions and others, including commercial brokers, has not been fully tapped. Evidence of this exists in the fact that these facilities and resources have long been exploited for profit by individuals at information brokerage firms.

Because information brokers have interests that are complementary to those of librarians, Jackson Library's staff saw this as an opportunity to view information brokers not merely as resource consumers, but as potential players in the information enterprise. Library staff envisioned an outsourcing arrangement that might actually expedite a broker's ability to use the library's resources for the broker's own purposes. In exchange, the information broker would be expected to make a commitment to return a definable amount of service to the library for support of its academic research mission.

Implementation of Outsourcing

In 1994, library managers engaged in the necessary steps to make the concept of partnering with a commercial information broker a reality. When legal issues surrounding this concept were resolved with the university's legal office to the satisfaction of the GSB's administrators, the path was cleared for implementation of outsourcing. A small task force was formed consisting of the library's head public services librarian, the library systems manager, the reference librarian with document delivery oversight responsibility, and the operational manager of the in-house document delivery system. Members of this group were experienced in the document delivery processes, had demonstrated leadership in faculty research support, and possessed strong computing skills. In concert with the university's procurement office staff, the project progressed from the identification of interested vendors to specifications development, proposal evaluations, and contract negotiation.

An agreement was signed in May 1994 with Information Express (IE), a Palo Alto–based document retrieval and delivery company. Founded in 1985 by Bruce Antelman, an entrepreneurial Stanford graduate, IE's staff developed mechanisms for the rapid retrieval and delivery of technical articles for all industries. IE's staff provide full-service document delivery through various document sources, ranging from on-site holdings to publishers, authors, associations, and other libraries and vendors.

After a six-month trial period, during which staff evaluated the results of the agreement, the partnership became a valued and ongoing part of the library's information infrastructure in November 1994. The main components of the outsourcing agreement with IE are summarized as follows:

- A small, on-site office for IE's staff is available within the library.
- IE's staff provide personnel and equipment to fulfill the library's document delivery requests, using Jackson Library and IE's other California resources.
- On the basis of an annual maximum quota, IE's staff provide library staff with document delivery articles at no cost.
- IE's library access is limited to hours when the library is closed, in order to eliminate any negative impact on the library staff's service to its clientele.

- All items photocopied by IE's staff are reshelved by their staff after use.
- IE's personnel have access to all nonrestricted resources in Jackson Library, in order to fill IE's own commercially based document needs.
- IE's staff are obliged to follow all appropriate copyright laws and regulations in fulfilling Jackson Library's document delivery requests and IE's own document needs in the Jackson Library.
- IE's internal tracking system is used to provide monthly management reports detailing the number of copies and orders filled for Jackson Library and for IE's other clients, which includes the sources used, turnaround time, and related data.
- IE's personnel agree not to use any name or mark of the GSB or the Jackson Library in any advertising or publicity, without explicit permission.

The operational processes devised as a result of this agreement between IE's managers and the library's managers are summarized as follows:

- Incoming document delivery requests from GSB faculty or staff are evaluated by the library's designated support staff.
- Requests with reasonably clear citations are transmitted to IE's headquarters via a fax machine, where they are entered into an automated tracking system.
- IE's staff fill the library's requests by using either their own California resources or those of the Jackson Library.
- IE's runners bring requests that are to be filled by Jackson Library's resources to the library overnight and fill them from their on-site center, using their own photocopy equipment. They fill their own document needs from other clients at this time as well.
- Filled requests are delivered daily to the library's Access Services Desk.
- Unfilled requests are returned to the library's Document Delivery Service staff for fulfillment through other means.
- Quality control and other operational issues are resolved by returns and direct discussion.

Outsourcing Results

One result of outsourcing was the transfer of document delivery tasks to individuals for whom these tasks represent core competencies. Before library staff began providing document delivery services to GSB faculty, these tasks were performed by GSB faculty, faculty support staff, and research assistants, the latter of whom are usually doctoral students. Verifying bibliographic citations, locating library material, and photocopying and borrowing publications are important academic skills, but they do not represent the core competencies of those staff groups. The transfer of these tasks to the library's staff in June 1991 marked an initial realignment of these duties.

The transfer of these tasks to library staff, and subsequently to IE's staff, also resulted in tremendous growth in the number of faculty document delivery requests. The increase in volume of requests filled by library staff from June 1991 to mid-1994 is illustrated in Exhibit 11.1. As also indicated by Exhibit 11.1, the volume of filled requests continued to rise after IE's staff began participating in this service program in June 1994. During March 1996, the service peaked at over 900 transactions per month.

Although significant peaks and valleys have occurred in the volume of requests filled on a monthly basis, the general trend has been toward increased demand for this service from GSB clients. One major decline in the fulfillment rate took place in May 1994, because of procedural realignments as outsourcing was implemented. Other peaks correspond to in-

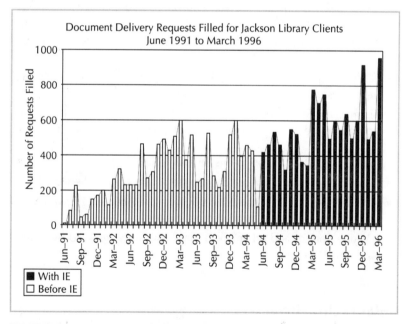

EXHIBIT 11.1 Document Delivery Requests Filled for Jackson Library Clients, June 1991 to March 1996. The volume of monthly document delivery transactions resulting in filled requests is indicated in this chart. The period from June 1994 to March 1996 represents the time frame in which the bulk of this activity was outsourced to Information Express.

creased demand during periods of academic course development and preparation of course readers.

Since June 1994, IE's staff have provided the majority of the library's document delivery services. The volume of requests filled by IE's staff after June 1994 is compared in Exhibit 11.2 to the total volume of filled requests after that date. The decrease in the amount of requests filled by the library's staff from January 1994 to March 1996 is apparent from the data presented in that exhibit.

The document delivery requests that continue to be filled by library staff, after outsourcing with IE, include rush requests, material that is circulated to faculty (for example, books, videos, corporate reports, working papers), and material not obtainable by IE's staff. Some of the increase in the number of requests filled by library staff after June 1995 can be attributed to the transfer of the GSB's video collection to the library during that summer, at which time library staff assumed responsibility for delivering videos to GSB faculty.

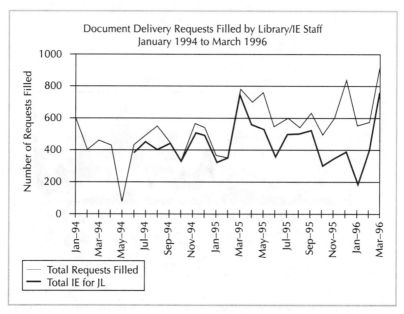

EXHIBIT 11.2 Jackson Library (JL) Document Delivery Requests Filled by Library and IE Staff, January 1994 to March 1996. The total volume of requests filled by IE's staff is compared to the total volume of filled requests. Beginning in June 1994, IE's staff began to provide the majority of document delivery services for the library.

Outsourcing versus Interlibrary Loan

Another result of outsourcing is evident in the impact of this activity on the library's interlibrary loan operation. In addition to absorbing most of the photocopying of articles in the library's collection for GSB faculty and staff, IE's staff also provide an allowance each year for articles obtained from sources other than Jackson Library. These sources include IE's own holdings and material in other libraries used by IE's staff. Without IE's services, material in these other source categories would have been requested via interlibrary loan (ILL) or from commercial sources.

The sources used for filling document delivery requests from January 1993 to March 1996 are identified in Exhibit 11.3. There are four source categories: ILL articles, Jackson Library titles or other Stanford University holdings, IE's holdings, and IE-supplied material from other libraries. Data for the volume of ILL borrowing, and the Jackson Library and Stanford University document delivery material prior to outsourcing, are included in this exhibit as a baseline. The number of requests filled by ILL, together with the number of document delivery requests filled by IE's staff from other sources, are shown in Exhibit 11.3.

As indicated in Exhibit 11.3, there has been a slight overall decrease in the number of ILL requests for journal articles, despite the overall growth

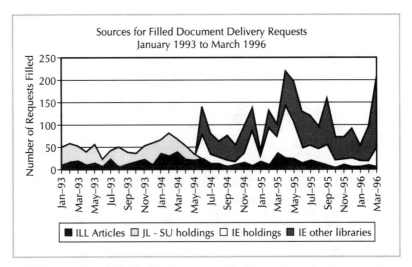

EXHIBIT 11.3 Sources for Filled Document Delivery Requests, January 1993 to March 1996. This illustration includes four categories of sources used for filling document delivery requests: interlibrary loan (ILL) articles, Jackson Library (JL) titles or other Stanford University (SU) holdings, Information Express (IE) holdings, and IE-supplied material from other libraries. The category for documents supplied by IE via the "other libraries" includes material obtained from Jackson Library or other Stanford libraries, or acquired directly from authors or publishers.

in document delivery requests. It is important to note that some documents supplied by IE via the "other libraries" category in this exhibit include material available in Jackson Library or other Stanford libraries, or items acquired directly from an author or publisher. Nevertheless, the increased volume of document delivery requests in the mid-1990s indicates that library staff would have had to rely on ILL as a source much more often. Outsourcing with IE and access to IE's holdings and material available in other libraries are viewed as main factors that enabled library staff to maintain a relatively steady volume of ILL borrowing.

Impact of Outsourcing on Library Collection Use

One concern connected with access to library collections by an outside document delivery supplier relates to the cost of wear and tear on library material, which results from increased use of collections. The fact that IE's staff are trained to exercise care in photocopying and reshelving material has helped to alleviate part of this concern. In addition, use of the collection by IE's staff has been limited, in relation to use of the collection by all patrons and library staff. From June 1994 to January 1996, IE staff's use of the collection for their own clients averaged less than 10 percent of the collection's total use, as is illustrated in Exhibit 11.4.

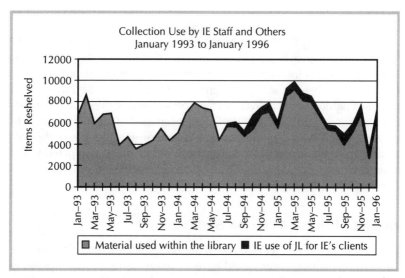

EXHIBIT 11.4 Jackson Library (JL) Collection Use by Information Express (IE) Staff and Others, January 1993 to January 1996. Data on in-house use of JL material, based on statistics of items reshelved in the collection, are illustrated here. The increased collection use by IE's staff, in fulfilling document delivery requests for the GSB and IE's other clients, was significantly less than use of JL material by all library patrons.

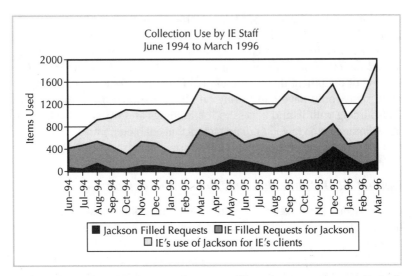

EXHIBIT 11.5 Jackson Library Collection Use by Information Express (IE) Staff, June 1994 to March 1996. The number of collection items used by IE's staff in filling document delivery requests for the GSB faculty is compared in this chart to the number of items used by IE's staff for their other clients' needs. Document delivery requests for the GSB, which were filled by in-house library staff, are also illustrated here to indicate the total amount of collection use relating to GSB document delivery requests.

As revealed by the data in Exhibit 11.4, access to Jackson Library's collections by IE's staff has increased overall utilization of the collections. However, the total increase resulting from IE's collection use for their other clients has not been much more significant than the increased use related to providing document delivery to the GSB's clients. Collection use statistics from June 1994 to March 1996 were examined to identify the ways in which IE's staff have used the library's resources. IE's staff use of the collections for their other clients during this time period, as compared to the amount of use for delivery of documents to GSB faculty, is illustrated in Exhibit 11.5.

Impact of Outsourcing on Staffing

In addition to the impact of outsourcing on stabilizing the volume of ILL transactions, which likely would have increased with the corresponding growth in document delivery requests during the mid-1990s, outsourcing also enabled the library's managers to minimize the amount of staff assigned to document delivery. Before outsourcing, part-time student employees performed the majority of document delivery tasks. However, a paraprofessional reference and information specialist was assigned to over-see the work of these students. To identify the impact of outsourcing on student staffing, the utilization of student assistants was tracked on the basis of average hours per day from November 1991 until the IE contract began in June 1994. The time spent both by librarians and by other staff members in fulfilling rush requests for document delivery, resolving questions pertaining to problematic citations, and retrieving or delivering requests or items was not measured during this study.

Using data extrapolated from the reported average hours per day gathered during the study period, an estimate was made of the projected number of student hours per month that would have been required to support the in-house document delivery program through March 1996. The calculation of this quantity of staff hours is illustrated in Exhibit 11.6. The actual number of student hours used after outsourcing is captured in Exhibit 11.6 as well.

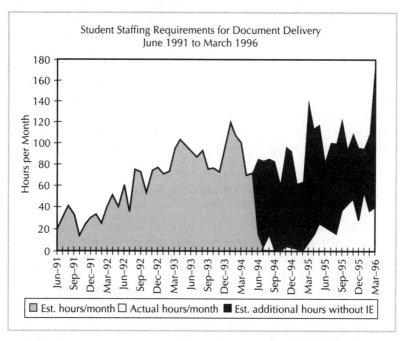

EXHIBIT 11.6 Student Staffing Requirements for Document Delivery Service, June 1991 to March 1996. The estimated in-house student hours required per month for document delivery service are illustrated here, based on an extrapolation of data for actual hours gathered during a study from November 1991 through June 1994. An estimated additional number of staff hours that would have been required to keep pace with the increased demand for document delivery, if part of this service had not been outsourced to Information Express (IE), is also represented in this chart to reflect the estimated staff savings from outsourcing.

Online TOC Services

The development of a comprehensive, electronic tables of contents and document delivery service, utilizing IE's World Wide Web (Web) document delivery system, was identified as the next step for streamlining these processes within the Jackson Library. This change occurred in the summer of 1996. The transition from a paper-based and manually operated system to an interactive, online process on the Web, managed largely by end users, should increase direct faculty access to journal contents and documents to an extent substantially beyond the library staff's former capabilities. Furthermore, because the Web-based system is supported by a large journal contents database, the system enables patrons to receive tables of contents directly by electronic mail. This feature permits patrons to order articles directly by electronic-mail reply as well.

Although IE's Web-based service is independently maintained by IE's staff, the GSB gateway to this service, via the GSB's own Web site, has been customized in such a way as to make it appear to users as a fully integrated Jackson Library service. The implementation of this kind of service eliminates the library staff's role in supplying tables of contents pages to users, because electronic pages are directly available to end users through the customized IE front end. Library staff act as delivery agents only for paper copies of documents that are not available in electronic format from the online service. As a result, substantial document delivery staff time will become increasingly available for reallocation to other public services needs.

Lessons and Benefits of Outsourcing

Several lessons were learned from outsourcing document retrieval and delivery at Jackson Library. The first lesson pertains to the way in which internal operations of special academic libraries, including Jackson Library and others, are managed. The second relates to the role of this kind of special library in a local academic setting. The third lesson is connected with the level of contribution the library's staff offer their parent school, within both the current and future national academic landscapes. There is, however, a limit to how widely the lessons learned in this case can be applied to all libraries, since several unique properties associated with this library organization are not universally applicable. Jackson Library contains a highly specialized, graduate-level collection, and is located within a top-tier academic professional graduate school at a top-tier university.

Perhaps the most valuable lesson learned by library staff from this outsourcing effort is the critical importance of selecting the right vendor or partner. Preferably, an ideal vendor might be willing to forgo immediate obvious financial reward, both for the sake of building a long-term alliance and for deriving insights for its own business strategy. In this case, the fruits of this commitment were demonstrated in the willingness of IE's managers to view this outsourcing project as an experiment, without numerous preset boundaries. The personal commitment to this effort on the part of IE's founder was doubtless a significant component in this mix.

Mutual trust formed another key success factor, which was viewed in retrospect as conducive to the positive outcome of this experiment. For the library's staff, there were elements of risk in this entire venture. With that realization in mind, IE's managers were willing to commit significant resources to ensure the success of this endeavor. The library's managers, in turn, abandoned certain internal controls and released staff time for other purposes. These actions alleviated some of the psychological stress on the part of library staff during implementation and development of the outsourcing project.

Finally, the constructive, flexible environment in which this outsourcing activity was launched contributed to the success of the program. Flexibility on the part of both the library's staff and IE's staff permitted adjustments in delivery modes and material handling, which allowed the process to refine itself over time.

Paradigm Shifts in the Jackson Library

Much has been written on the notion of a paradigm shift in various settings. Certainly, a fundamental shift has occurred within the Jackson Library during the 1990s. Outsourcing, among other factors, has provided a framework for library staff to transcend a traditional service model and assume the role of a more aggressive service provider to its primary clients, the GSB faculty. It has already been noted how the outsourcing relationship with IE affected the library's internal restructuring and enabled staff to expand client service levels. It is also important to note that the library's professional librarians are increasingly being engaged as quasi-researchers, in a role that releases faculty time for more innovative and intensive pursuits.

External pressures associated with the larger academic community, including heightened budgetary consciousness, have impacted on library staff and their perception of themselves within the GSB. There is an increasing conviction on the part of library managers and staff that individuals within the library, who traditionally were more passive participants in the university, must strive toward more prominence in the university's teaching and research support arm. This participation should be commensurate with the fiscal resources consumed by the library organization.

As the demand for customer service to GSB faculty has grown since 1991, the imperative for redirection and increased efficiency of limited intellectual resources has assumed greater intensity. Paraprofessional-level resources were redirected as document delivery and interlibrary loan staff alike discovered time for cross-training, which ensured more support coverage. Librarians, who were often called upon to assist in these searches, are no longer needed for document delivery support and have more opportunities to concentrate on research commitments to faculty. In this manner, library staff are positioning themselves as indispensable players in the academic and research environment at Stanford University. In times of financial stress, even libraries may be expendable. Document delivery and the outsourcing effort, as well as TQM (Total Quality Management) and other customer-motivated strategies, have become pieces in the overall strategy to secure for the library a lasting place in the new academic environment.

Leveraging the Academic Library

Another lesson from this outsourcing program pertains to the Jackson Library staff's responsibilities to their parent institution, the GSB, as the school competes for students and economic survival in the competitive world of higher education. Through an outsourcing partnership, the GSB's administrators can offer the library's resources, traditionally regarded as strictly an in-house treasure, as a negotiating chip in developing alliances outside the university that can provide cost-effective resources to faculty. In negotiating alliances with information vendors, library staff may well be able to leverage the library's resources in a way that will reap substantial benefits for the GSB. In this case, a beneficial relationship was built with the managers of IE, who also recognized the power of Jackson Library's collections for the GSB's own business ends.

Conclusion

Outsourcing has provided Jackson Library's staff, and administrators at Stanford University's Graduate School of Business, with an opportunity to develop use of the school's intellectual resources beyond the customary level. The net result for these institutions was a superior advantage in today's academic environment. This outsourcing endeavor has been judged a success by both library staff and their faculty clients. It also demonstrates how staff in a traditional library teamed with a commercial vendor to produce a dynamic synergy, which benefited the staff and clients of both organizations.

Bibliography

Cain, Mark. 1995. Periodical access in an era of change: Characteristics and a model. *Journal of Academic Librarianship* 21, no. 5: 365–70.

Coons, Bill, and Retar McDonald. 1995. Implications of commercial document delivery. *College & Research Libraries News* 56, no. 9: 626–31.

Criteria for selecting document delivery suppliers. 1994. *Online Libraries and Microcomputers* 12, no. 5: 1–5.

Eiblum, Paula. 1995. The coming of age of document delivery. *American Society for Information Science Bulletin* 21, no. 3: 21–22.

The Emerging Virtual Research Library. 1992. Washington, D.C.: Association of Research Libraries, Office of Management Services.

Fueseler, Elizabeth A. 1994. Providing access to journals: Just in time or just in case? *College & Research Libraries News* 55, 3: 130–32, 148.

Gassaway, Laura N. 1994. Document delivery: Increasing demand and decreasing funding spurs new attention to copyright implications. *Computers in Libraries* 14, no. 5: 25–32.

Higginbotham, Barbara Buckner, and Sally Bowdoin. 1993. *Access versus Assets: A Comprehensive Guide to Resource Sharing for Academic Librarians.* Chicago: American Library Association.

Jackson, Mary E. 1994. Dissecting document delivery. *Information Today* 11, no. 10: 44–45.

Jackson, Mary E., and Karen Croneis. 1994. *Uses of Document Delivery Services.* Washington, D.C.: Association of Research Libraries, Office of Management Services.

Journal of Interlibrary Loan, Document Delivery & Information Supply. 1993– . Binghamton, N.Y.: Haworth Press.

Kaser, Dick, ed. 1995. *Document Delivery in an Electronic Age: A Collection of Views and Viewpoints.* Philadelphia, Pa.: National Federation of Abstracting and Information Services.

Key elements in an advanced document delivery and ILL system. 1994. *Online Libraries and Microcomputers* 12, no. 1: 1–4.

Kinnucan, Mark T. 1993. Demand for document delivery and interlibrary loan in academic settings. *Library & Information Science Research* 15, no. 4: 355–74.

Kurosman, Kathleen, and Barbara Ammerman Durniak. 1994. Document delivery: A comparison of commercial document suppliers and interlibrary loan services. *College & Research Libraries* 55, no. 2: 129–40.

Leach, Ronald, and Judith Tribble. 1993. Electronic document delivery: New options for libraries. *Journal of Academic Librarianship* 18, no. 6: 359–64.

Mancini, Alice Duhon. 1996. Evaluating commercial document suppliers: Improving access to current journal literature. *College & Research Libraries* 57, no. 2: 123–31.

Mitchell, Eleanor, and Sheila A. Walters. 1995. *Document Delivery: Issues and Answers.* Medford, N.J.: Information Today.

Selected Additions to the J. Hugh Jackson Library. 1958– . Stanford, Calif.: Stanford University, Graduate School of Business.

Turner, Fay. 1995. Document ordering standards: The ILL protocol and Z39.50 item order. *Library Hi Tech* 13, no. 3: 25.

Walters, Sheila. 1994. Document delivery. *Computers in Libraries* 14, no. 9: 14–17.

Part Two

Public Libraries

Opening-Day Collections and Current Acquisitions: Outsourcing Item Record Creation and Physical Processing for the Albuquerque/ Bernalillo County Public Library System

Patricia Haber

Albuquerque/Bernalillo County Public Library System has outsourced selected item record creation and physical processing activities with Baker & Taylor, Inc. (B&T) since 1992. B&T ordered and supplied shelf-ready books for three opening-day collections, each with a total of 35,000 volumes. Upon examining more than 10,000 volumes during an initial pilot project, library staff found only six cataloging and physical processing errors. B&T's services were used for two other outsourcing programs as well: (1) a one-year collection-expansion effort resulting from special funding allocations, and (2) ongoing cataloging and physical processing services for current acquisitions. Less than 1 percent of books processed by the vendor for the collection-expansion program required revision by library staff. In 1996, outsourcing for current acquisitions enabled the library's managers to transfer two full-time staff members from the physical processing department to other service areas.

Staff at the Albuquerque/Bernalillo County Public Library System (ABCPLS) have outsourced selected item record creation and physical processing activities with Baker & Taylor, Inc. (B&T) since early 1992. Outsourcing began as an effort to establish opening-day collections for three new branches, but was later expanded to encompass current programs for each of the system's 16 branch libraries. B&T's services have included physical processing for shelf-ready books, item record creation, barcode attachment to bibliographic records, individualized drop shipments of material directly to all branch locations, and centralized invoicing for the customized shipping program.

Background

Although ABCPLS's managers and staff were experienced in creating opening-day collections, having established seven branches from 1982 to 1992, they determined that the challenge of opening three new branches in 1994 alone required an innovative and improved strategy. The best option appeared to be for a vendor to supply shelf-ready books with item records linked to the library's catalog records. Library staff were confident about a vendor's ability to perform physical processing in that manner. However, uncertainty existed about the degree to which barcode data links for bibliographic records in the library's catalog could be achieved successfully by a vendor. Library managers concluded that a pilot project would be conducted to explore this new approach.

In early 1992, ABCPLS's managers entered into negotiations with staff at B&T's Opening Day Collection (ODC) Division, located in Commerce, Georgia, for an outsourcing pilot project. The project was designed to allow the library's staff an opportunity to assess the feasibility of the outsourcing concept and evaluate the vendor's performance. ABCPLS's staff established the following objectives when the initial pilot project and potential long-term outsourcing program began:

- Evaluate the vendor's performance on a pilot-project basis before full-scale outsourcing.
- Acquire shelf-ready material for three new branches in one year, with a total of 35,000 books for each branch.
- Prove to funding officials that the library's managers could expend increased collection budget allocations for new material with existing staff.
- Make titles available to the library's patrons more quickly.
- Reduce technical services costs for physical processing of material.
- Reduce the amount of material handled by local system staff.
- Reduce the number of on-the-job injuries among technical services staff caused by Repetitive Motion Syndrome.

Pilot Project and Outsourcing for Opening-Day Collections

The first task was establishing an electronic connection to link the library's database to the vendor's facility. More than six months were required to complete the communications link between the data center at B&T's ODC Division and ABCPLS's GEAC Glis computer system. ODC's staff used a Digital Equipment Corporation VT 220 terminal and a dedicated, analog-telephone line, with a 9600-baud modem multiplexer, to connect directly to ABCPLS's catalog.

To acquire a selection of shelf-ready material that could be evaluated for processing quality, the library's staff ordered one copy of each title in *Children's Catalog.* These titles formed the core children's collections for two of the new county-funded branches. *Children's Catalog* was chosen as the selection tool because it had been a standard resource in children's literature at ABCPLS for many years. B&T also had this resource available in their database and could generate all book orders electronically. With a single telephone call, the library's staff placed orders for approximately 5,000 titles per branch.

In addition to the availability of the *Children's Catalog* titles in the vendor's database, library staff believed that those titles were already in ABC-PLS's catalog. Because catalog records should have been available in the library's database from the previous purchase of most titles in that source, staff assumed that B&T's staff would only have to process added copies for the majority of titles. Library staff thought that this would reduce the number of bibliographic records that would need to be created during the pilot project.

The vendor was instructed to order the pilot-project titles, complete physical processing for each volume in the library's catalog, link the barcodes for individual volumes to records in ABCPLS's database, forward uncataloged titles for full cataloging and processing by the library's staff, and ship the material in specially marked boxes. The shipping procedure was designed to make it easier for the library's staff to identify items in the pilot project once the boxes arrived at the library's Bibliographic Services Department (BSD) for routine cataloging and physical processing operations. During the project, all shipments were sent to the central Acquisitions Department, where the library's staff inventoried and monitored the processing quality of every volume.

Outsourcing Results for the Pilot Project and Opening-Day Collections

The assumptions about using *Children's Catalog* for the selection of titles in the pilot project proved to be valid. B&T's staff were able to attach barcodes for over 97 percent of the items to an existing bibliographic record in ABCPLS's database. New catalog records had to be created by the library's staff for only the remaining 3 percent of titles. Those titles, from more current supplements of *Children's Catalog,* had not yet been ordered for any branches.

After examining more than 10,000 volumes, the library's staff found only six problems: one damaged book, two books without internal labels, and one typographical error on a call number label. Two other books had been processed correctly, but the wrong branch locations were entered in the catalog. The library's staff were able to correct those errors easily. Minor changes in labeling procedures were also made during the project, to prevent potential problems that might have resulted from the initial guidelines to the vendor. Communication between the library's staff and B&T's staff was ongoing during the project, resulting in a minimal amount of outsourcing difficulties.

ABCPLS's managers were immensely satisfied with the quality of processing in the initial pilot project. Shortly thereafter, they expanded the ordering process for the two new branches. The next phase included the purchase of books from a locally developed core list of approximately 2,000 titles in adult fiction. To supplement the children's collection, multiple copies of specific "easy" picture books in *Children's Catalog* were acquired. Other picture books, which were not in *Children's Catalog,* were ordered as well. Most of those acquisitions represented added copies for titles already in the library's catalog.

It became evident at one point that the opening date for the third new branch was to be accelerated in the overall schedule. One telephone call to B&T and the mailing of property stamps to the vendor were all that was required to have an additional 9,000 volumes of core titles prepared for the third branch.

Outsourcing the processing for these opening-day collections was a tremendous success. Because B&T personnel were responsible for ordering the core collections, as well as cataloging and physical processing, the library's selectors and BSD's staff were able to focus on customizing the remainder of the three collections to fit the individual needs of the different neighborhoods. The library's managers also successfully achieved their goal of opening all three branches, each with an average of 35,000 books, in February, May, and November of 1994.

Collection-Expansion Program Outsourcing

While in the process of completing the opening-day collections in 1994, ABCPLS's staff also faced the unexpected challenge of a system-wide expansion of the collection. The cooperative and innovative Connections 21 program, designed to increase resource sharing between the library system and Albuquerque's public schools, was expanding. The library system received a funding increase that permitted staff to purchase 60,000 children's books that year, an increase of 70 percent from the previous year.

Library managers determined that in-house processing of the collection-expansion titles would have resulted in a 52 percent increase in the BSD staff's workload. Because the library's managers were not able to hire additional staff, and wanted to process material for public access as quickly as possible, preprocessing options were explored. Based on the success of the opening-day collections' outsourcing program, the library's managers elected to outsource with B&T for processing of the collection-expansion titles as well.

Several factors had to be considered in devising outsourcing procedures for the collection-expansion program. This outsourcing varied from the pilot project in that it did not constitute an opening-day collection. The quantity of titles to be ordered also increased to 16 copies—one for each branch location. It was acknowledged at the outset that the purchase of that quantity of multiple copies would increase the amount of sorting and the number of locations in Albuquerque to which books would need to be shipped.

In the opening-day outsourcing program, 97 percent of the acquisitions were duplicate copies of titles previously cataloged by ABCPLS's staff. Because the collection-expansion program involved the acquisition of titles that were not yet available within ABCPLS, either a vendor or the library's staff would be required to supply new catalog records for the library system's database. The library's technical services staff had concerns about the quality of records that would be supplied by a vendor in this mode. The library's staff also wanted the expansion material to have call numbers that would be consistent with local, customized practices.

In the process of designing outsourcing procedures, BSD's staff concluded that the amount of time required to catalog one title would be minimal, compared to the amount of time needed for physical processing of 16 copies. It was believed that the library's managers could achieve a larger cost savings by outsourcing physical processing, rather than by outsourcing cataloging. In addition, the library's systems support staff were concerned about lead time to devise a procedure for the electronic download of a vendor's bibliographic records if titles were cataloged by a vendor rather than by local staff.

With those factors in mind, ABCPLS's managers elected to order only one copy of each title from B&T for the initial phase of the collection-expansion program. Each title was cataloged by BSD's staff and a record was created in the local database. At that point, multiple copies of the same titles were ordered from B&T, using one of the following formulas: (1) one copy for each branch library, yielding a total of 16 copies per title; or (2) one copy for each branch library, and added copies for branches with high children's circulation, yielding a total of 22 copies per title.

Added copies were drop shipped directly to appropriate branch libraries. Because books were not shipped to a central point for verification of receipt, employees in each branch were responsible for supplying staff in the central Acquisitions Department with the number of books received. Consolidated invoices for all books were mailed directly to the Acquisitions Department.

Because the library's staff had established a catalog record for each title in advance of ordering the multiple copies, the vendor's staff only had to enter added copies on the initial record before completing the physical processing on all multiple copies. To eliminate potential problems with items requiring unique processing treatment, the library's staff identified those titles at the point of order and completed all processing for those items in-house. One example of these exceptional items is a title for which the library acquires both reference and circulating copies.

Outsourcing Results for the Collection-Expansion Program

B&T's staff entered added-copy information for the collection-expansion volumes into the library's catalog and performed physical processing for 22,056 children's books for ABCPLS during FY 1994. Through outsourcing and drop shipping items to 16 different branches, the library's staff reduced processing time and delivered new books to patrons in the most expeditious manner possible. Without outsourcing, a processing backlog would have developed for a large portion of this material. Fewer than 1 percent of the books processed by the vendor required revision by ABCPLS's technical services staff. Those problems included spine label omissions, improper location stamping, or improper location listings in the library's catalog.

Shipping problems were minimal. Approximately seven books purchased by another library system were sent to Albuquerque in error. About 20 books were shipped to the wrong location within ABCPLS and rerouted, using an inter-branch courier service. Staff who received an incorrect item immediately notified employees at the proper branch about the error, so that the daily inventory of B&T material arriving at each branch would be correct. The average amount of time from the date of order for each title to the date of arrival at an individual branch library was seven weeks. That turnaround time was viewed as acceptable for children's books, but was thought to be too slow for popular adult titles.

The major problem with the outsourcing strategy in the collection-expansion program was the duplication of effort required to order each title twice: once for initial cataloging and again for the acquisition of multiple copies. Because of the time delay in duplicate ordering, there were also occasions when B&T no longer had available copies of requested titles and could not acquire additional copies by the time the second orders for multiple copies were placed. Approximately 7 percent of titles fell into this problem category.

Because the library's staff were able to find other vendors with available copies of the books that B&T could not supply, communication with B&T's staff on this fill-rate problem was not pursued to the degree that it could have been. There was concern about the accuracy of B&T's records on the availability status for those specific titles. However, there could have been several reasons for this problem, including the fact that B&T's computer system was upgraded during the one-year project. This singular problem, however, meant that the library's staff not only had to order 7 percent of the titles a third time from different vendors, but that BSD's staff also had to perform physical processing on all the multiple copies. Although this re-sulted in an increased workload for local staff, outsourcing 93 percent of the processing for multiple copies enabled staff to complete the collection-expansion program in a timely manner. No significant processing backlog was associated with the 70 percent increase in book acquisitions during 1994. Furthermore, there was no need to hire additional staff for the collection-expansion effort.

Outsourcing Obstacles

On two occasions during outsourcing, the library's managers were not able to achieve their goals. In 1995, the library's staff investigated the possibil-ity of acquiring vendor-supplied catalog records for ABCPLS and the Rio Grande Valley Library System (RGVLS). RGVLS is a consortium of several public libraries in the Albuquerque metropolitan area. One of RGVLS's li-braries received a collection budget increase and was in need of assistance with book cataloging and physical processing.

On behalf of RGVLS, staff at ABCPLS began working with B&T on a project to provide vendor-supplied catalog records for both library organi-zations. Catalogers from each system prepared two 20-page profiles of cat-aloging preferences for their specific processing centers. B&T's staff generated a test tape for loading into ABCPLS's database. Although there were no problems with loading the tape, the lack of an Online Computer Library Center (OCLC) control number in B&T's records meant that the li-brary's staff could not perform a duplicate record check as the records were loaded. Although the library's staff considered using either an International Standard Book Number (ISBN) or Library of Congress (LC) number as the duplicate search key, rather than an OCLC number, there was still concern about the need to rewrite local programs and incur additional charges in that process. Instead, ABCPLS's staff decided to reconsider this option at a later date, after migrating to a new UNIX-based system planned for 1997.

The only other significant drawback of outsourcing, which still affects the library's staff, is the manner in which trade paperbacks were handled by B&T's staff during the opening-day collections' pilot project. B&T's staff were instructed to bind all trade paperback titles. The vendor shipped material to a bindery, which added about eight weeks to the processing turn-around time. The vendor's ability to meet the binding requirement was excellent. However, the library's staff were not as pleased with the binding quality as they had anticipated.

Consequently, a decision was made to place trade paperback orders with other vendors who could supply a more acceptable level of bindery service for that category of material. As of 1996, ABCPLS's staff continued to catalog and process trade paperbacks in-house because of the binding issue. However, library staff with collections that do not require such durability in their trade paperbacks may not find this issue as problematic as it has been for ABCPLS's staff.

Outsourcing Cataloging, Item Record Creation, and Physical Processing for Current Acquisitions

In September 1995, ABCPLS's managers successfully expanded the B&T outsourcing program a second time for selected, ongoing acquisitions. This outsourcing enhancement was limited to current-year publications of children's books and adult nonfiction. All cataloging and physical processing for other new material was still handled in-house during this experiment.

The ultimate goal of this outsourcing phase was to eliminate the duplicate ordering procedure for new titles, which had been established during the collection-expansion segment of ABCPLS's outsourcing program. Instead of having ABCPLS's staff acquire the first copy of each new title and catalog it in-house, the library's staff were willing to experiment with accepting matched bibliographic records from an outside vendor at the point of order. This experiment was viewed as an interim step toward obtaining vendor-supplied records from B&T.

Library managers decided that bibliographic records from the OCLC database would be matched during the order process, using ISBNs as the search key. Using this approach, B&T's staff could attach item records to the OCLC bibliographic records as books were processed by the vendor. The remaining procedures for this outsourcing experiment were relatively easy to complete. B&T's staff were authorized to have read-only electronic access to the acquisitions module of ABCPLS's database. The library's staff submitted paper orders for specified quantities of titles to B&T. Books were collected at B&T's Commerce, Georgia, warehouse and forwarded to ODC's staff in the same building. After establishing online access to ABCPLS's acquisitions module, ODC's staff matched titles and added item records for copies, according to ABCPLS's branch distribution information.

Outsourcing Results for the Current Acquisitions Program

This outsourcing experiment permitted the library's staff to place a single order with B&T for all copies of selected new titles, instead of the previous practice of placing two orders for every title. Using matched OCLC bibliographic records also enabled the library's staff to avoid the difficulties associated with tape loading of bibliographic records from B&T. In addition, the library's staff retained the options of editing records and customizing call numbers.

On average, it takes about two weeks to initiate book orders and to receive corresponding bibliographic records in the library's catalog. Once orders are forwarded to B&T, an average of seven weeks elapse before books are received at different branches. Because ABCPLS's staff do not accept partial shipments, B&T's staff have to wait for their suppliers to fill certain orders. That factor has a definite impact on turnaround time. Libraries without requirements for shipping of complete orders might experience faster turnaround times for this process. Nevertheless, this outsourcing time frame is an improvement over the time usually required by ABCPLS's technical services staff to process new material in-house. ABCPLS's average turnaround time, from point of order to delivery of books to branches, is approximately 15 weeks.

There was one obstacle to the procedures in this phase of the outsourcing program. In the beginning, library managers thought that current-year publications of children's books and adult nonfiction would be the easiest categories of material for matching of order and bibliographic records in the OCLC database. However, an evaluation of the OCLC bibliographic records selected in this manner revealed that not all catalog records matched the order data. In the library's study, about 3 percent of the titles differed in OCLC records from their appearance in book review literature. Because those titles had the same ISBNs, however, the library's staff were able to verify that the titles captured in the match process were accurate. B&T's staff have correctly resolved all but two of these discrepancies on their own.

Conclusion

As a result of outsourcing, three new opening-day collections were acquired and shipped shelf ready in one year, with high quality standards and minimal impact on routine library operations. In addition, the library's staff proved to funding officials that they could expend increased collection budget funds without having to acquire additional technical services staff. There are hopes that this success may result in the special allocation of additional collection resources in future years.

Other goals established at the beginning of the outsourcing program were also met. Although the number of volumes within the entire system has increased significantly, the amount of material handled by ABCPLS's staff and internal delivery system personnel has decreased substantially now that B&T's staff handle approximately 20,000 to 30,000 books. The number of on-the-job injuries has also been reduced. Most important, new acquisitions have been made available to the public in a more timely manner than would have occurred if outsourcing had not been deployed.

Outsourcing for current acquisitions has allowed the library's managers to reduce the overall cost of adding new material to all branches in the system. Processing costs for each book have dropped. In 1996, the library's managers were also able to reallocate two full-time clerical technical services positions from the physical processing area to other service areas. As a result of outsourcing, the library's managers and staff have been able to maintain a cost-effective, efficient, and well-managed technical services operation. Best of all, the library's patrons have benefited from outsourcing by having substantially better and larger collections now available within the Albuquerque community.

Bibliography

Children's Catalog. 1909– . New York: H. W. Wilson.

13 From Selection to Shelf: Outsourcing Book Selection, Copy Cataloging, and Physical Processing at Fort Worth Public Library

Catherine A. Dixon and
Frances G. Bordonaro

In FY 1992/93, a 66 percent reduction in staffing occurred in the Catalog Unit at Fort Worth Public Library. Physical processing staff were also reduced by approximately 50 percent. Since that year, library staff have used five different vendors for over five different outsourcing programs. Technical services operations provided by outside contractors have included copy cataloging and label creation for monographic firm orders and gifts, as well as cataloging and physical processing for shelf-ready books and audiovisual material. Selection, cataloging, and physical processing of best-sellers and children's collections have also been among the library's outsourcing programs. By the mid-1990s, Brodart Company, located in Williamsport, Pennsylvania, and Professional Media Service Corporation, in Gardena, California, were established as the primary vendors. Multivendor outsourcing enabled library staff to provide essential collection development and public services programs, while downsizing and enduring years of budgetary challenges.

In FY 1995/96, the acquisitions budget for all 11 branches in the Fort Worth Public Library system was $1,281,368. Over 35,500 volumes and 17,000 audiovisual items, including about 11,700 audiocassettes, 4,700 video-

This chapter is based on a presentation made by Catherine A. Dixon at the Association for Library Collections and Technical Services' Commercial Technical Services Committee's program, Outsourcing from Selection to Shelf: How? When? Why? in Portland, Oregon, March 29, 1996.

cassettes, 1,700 compact discs, and 1,000 other items, were acquired that year. Approximately 60 percent of technical services activities for these collections were outsourced that year, including nearly 100 percent of the selection, cataloging, and physical processing of new children's books and between 40 percent and 45 percent of processes for audiovisual material.

Multivendor outsourcing within technical services began at Fort Worth Public Library in FY 1992/93. During preceding budget years, libraries in this system faced reductions in staffing and hours of service. Due to the poor state of the economy in Texas, librarians at Fort Worth Public Library endured serious reductions in the library materials budget in the early 1990s. Vacant positions in public services areas had also remained unfilled during that period. During FY 1992/93, library administrators identified the need for reductions in technical services and targeted several operations for outsourcing. In the end, technical services outsourcing enabled additional economies in staffing, while retaining 70 percent of the materials budget. However, copy and original cataloging, physical processing for shelf-ready books and audiovisual material, and book selection for best-sellers and children's books were privatized.

At the beginning of the FY 1992/93 fiscal year, the Catalog Unit's staffing was reduced from six to two positions. The Processing Unit was reduced from nine to five staff members. Online database connections were canceled for two of the Catalog Unit's three Online Computer Library Center (OCLC) workstations. The Collection Development Unit was downsized from four to two positions. All these changes occurred between May and September 1992. In addition, the position of support services coordinator was eliminated upon the retirement of the incumbent in January 1993. From fall 1992 through summer 1993, Support Services Division staff were cross-trained and coached in functioning as a self-directed team.

Although technical services positions were eliminated in FY 1992/93, there were no staff layoffs as a result of outsourcing. Technical services staff affected by this downsizing were transferred to vacant public services jobs. Because of the rapid pace with which staffing reductions occurred, however, there was an urgent need to select vendors for ongoing processing immediately thereafter. Library administrators and staff were not afforded much time for thorough preparation of detailed specifications or a comprehensive vendor selection process prior to outsourcing in the midst of the rapid redeployment of staff.

Initial Outsourcing Projects

As a consequence of staff downsizing, five outsourcing contracts were established in FY 1992/93. Vendor A was selected for copy cataloging of titles purchased by direct orders with publishers and monographic gifts. That vendor also supplied spine and pocket labels for books. Vendor B was awarded three individual contracts: (1) acquisitions, cataloging, and physical processing services for adult books; (2) acquisitions, cataloging, and physical processing for audiovisual material; and (3) selection, cataloging, and physical processing of fiction best-sellers. Vendor C provided selection for children's collections and shelf-ready books. Contracts with these vendors have since been canceled for various reasons, including poor performance. Although services by these vendors might have improved since the early 1990s, their names are omitted here in compliance with policy regulations established for the Fort Worth Public Library system.

Copy Cataloging (Vendor A)

Copy cataloging of direct-order titles and gifts was contracted to a vendor who provided MARC (machine-readable cataloging) records for $.17 each. This cost was less than OCLC's per-record charge. Spine and pocket labels for books were supplied at a cost of $.06 per label. MARC records were ordered electronically by cataloging staff, using either an International Standard Book Number (ISBN) or Library of Congress Card Number (LCCN) as the match keys. On a weekly basis, a library staff member entered standard numbers into a computer file, using vendor-supplied software, and transmitted data to the vendor's computer via dial access. The vendor's catalog records were supplied on magnetic tape and loaded into the library's Dynix automated system from Ameritech Library Systems in Provo, Utah.

Eventually, this endeavor was abandoned because of unanticipated problems. Catalog records were not available for direct-ordered audiovisual media, foreign-language material, or pre-1968 titles lacking ISBNs. Cataloging-in-Publication (CIP) records from the Library of Congress (LC), which were supplied by the vendor, also had to be upgraded in-house because the vendor could not provide upgrading. Most new acquisitions forwarded to the Catalog Unit during FY 1992/93 and FY 1993/94 fell into one or more of the preceding categories. The Catalog Unit's staff devoted nearly as much time to quality control monitoring of vendor records and preparation of additional copy cataloging records as had been required for in-house processing before outsourcing.

Processing Unit staff also continued to create labels during this time, because the vendor could not provide labels with full Dewey Decimal Classification numbers to match fully extended call numbers in the 099 local call number field used in the library's cataloging. Because of a combination of cataloging and physical processing problems, the library's catalogers resumed in-house copy cataloging operations for direct orders and gifts in summer 1995.

Shelf-Ready Books (Vendor B)

The initial contract for shelf-ready books was also awarded in FY 1992/93, following vendor responses to the library's Request for Proposal (RFP). Books, acquired on the basis of firm orders placed by library staff, were supplied with full MARC cataloging and full physical processing. Dewey Decimal Classification numbers were entered in the 099 field, per the library's specifications. The vendor was also asked to create holdings records using the 949 field.

Catalog records were provided on magnetic tape for loading into the library's Dynix catalog, using the 035 field as a match point to overlay online order records. The library's specifications required the vendor to input the bibliographic number for Dynix order records in the 035 field. This was done to ensure the replacement of the order record, with attached patron-hold requests, by a full-MARC bibliographic record in the record-overlay process.

As with the outsourcing of copy cataloging, technical services staff devoted considerable time to monitoring the vendor's quality and upgrading CIP records. In this case, staff had to check both the vendor's cataloging and physical processing services. The CIP requirement, vital in hindsight, had been omitted from contract specifications. Due to that oversight, the library's catalogers revised titles and subtitles for CIP records, which included mostly new fiction. However, for expediency, 300 field data were not supplied.

Incorrect overlay of order records was a significant problem as the vendor's catalog records were loaded into the Dynix database. Records were received either without the required 035 field or with incorrect numbers in that field. For records received without 035 fields, a manual record merge by the library's staff resolved the problem. When the wrong number was input in the 035 field, however, existing catalog records were incorrectly replaced by nonmatching vendor-supplied records during the overlay step. The percentage of errors was low, but resolving the resultant problems was time-consuming. Quality control monitoring and problem resolution for this conflict consumed a significant percentage of time for the library's two remaining catalogers.

In addition, the 949 field requirement for holdings information was discontinued after a trial period. Library staff discovered that the vendor's holdings records did not automatically replace the generic barcodes generated as part of order records within the Dynix system, as had been assured. Some Dynix clients indicated that Dynix had developed customized programs for replacement of on-order holdings in this manner, but Dynix's staff were not able to locate them and make them available to Fort Worth's staff. For a number of reasons, it was not feasible for in-house systems staff to write a program for this need. Consequently, holdings records were input by Processing Unit personnel.

Although full Dewey Decimal Classification numbers were supplied on catalog records, classification numbers were truncated on spine and pocket labels by the vendor's label-production program. The net result was that call numbers on catalog records did not match call numbers on books. Because this problem could not be rectified, the library's staff had to prepare and apply new labels with fully extended Dewey numbers to a considerable volume of material.

Cataloging and Physical Processing of Audiovisual Media (Vendor B)

The FY 1992/93 contract for cataloging and physical processing of audiovisual media was awarded to the same vendor who received the FY 1992/93 shelf-ready books contract. Outsourcing results for audiovisual material paralleled the problems experienced with shelf-ready books. Records were initially supplied with 949 holdings data, but that feature was discontinued because of difficulties with replacement of order-record holdings in the overlay process. Missing or incorrect 035 data resulted in overlay problems for audiovisual titles as well. Because LC's CIP program does not include audiovisual media, the vendor also was unable to supply CIP records for this category of material. If full-level MARC records were unavailable for specific titles, library staff often did not receive catalog records for those items when material was examined upon receipt. In addition to these issues, however, the major obstacle in audiovisual media outsourcing was the vendor's inability to supply popular videos and sound recordings in a timely manner.

Book Selection

Historically, librarians at Fort Worth Public Library had been responsible for selection processes since the library was founded in 1905. Selection decisions for new material had traditionally been made by librarians in branches and service units throughout the system. This process was centralized in 1987, however, following a recommendation from an in-house task force.

In FY 1991/92, staff in the centralized Materials Collection Development Unit selected new books from primary review journals for the system's 11 branches. That unit consisted of an adult materials coordinator, a children's materials coordinator, and two support staff. Despite this centralization, selectors in branches and other service units were still responsible for choosing audiovisual material, new books from specialized journals, and duplicate and replacement titles.

Outsourcing of book selection in FY 1992/93 was initiated entirely for budgetary reasons, as was the case for privatization of cataloging and physical processing of books and audiovisual material. Library administrators, including the adult materials coordinator and the children's materials coordinator, had conducted several brainstorming sessions to identify additional budget savings. A proposal to outsource selection for certain categories of library material was implemented. That plan resulted in reduction of the Materials Collection Development Unit's staff from four to two. Only one materials coordinator and a library aide remained after that point.

Selection of Best-Sellers (Vendor B)

Selection, cataloging, and physical processing of best-sellers was also outsourced in FY 1992/93. Because selection of best-sellers is based primarily upon demand for popular material, as opposed to literary merit or long-term value to the collection as a whole, preparation of written specifications for vendor selection of this material was relatively easy. Selection decisions were based on author popularity, publisher advertising budgets, and the volume of first printings for books. The best-sellers program consisted solely of fiction titles. Specific authors who had been perennially popular in Fort Worth were also identified for the vendor, since material by several of those authors was not expected to appear on national best-seller lists.

Although cataloging and physical processing services were included in the contract, they were budgeted separately and were not covered by adult book budget funds. This outsourcing program was successful, but library managers later determined that this activity could be reabsorbed by in-house staff, because the number of vendor-processed items supplied in FY 1994/95 totaled only about 160 titles. Consequently, the best-sellers selection contract was discontinued in October 1995.

Selection of Children's Books (Vendor C)

Children's book selection was identified as another area for outsourcing in FY 1992/93. A Request for Information (RFI) was issued in 1992 to identify vendors' abilities in this arena. Library staff received a wide range of responses to the RFI, including vendors who elected not to provide the service, vendors who suggested submitting lists of book titles for review and selection by in-house staff, and vendors who were willing to provide selection. Because this was a new concept, some vendors were not prepared to implement selection at that time. However, because the children's materials coordinator position had been eliminated during downsizing, in-house selection of material was not a viable option.

In contrast to selection profiles for adult book collections, which vary widely by branch, children's book collections are more homogeneous from branch to branch. The major differences among branches lie in specific cultural and language needs. Variations in the amount of collection funds in the budget for each branch also account for diversity in collection expenditures. Nevertheless, titles by Arnold Lobel and Mercer Mayer are popular throughout the library system, as are books in the Dr. Seuss and Berenstain Bears series. All branches also include books in the following categories: the (John) Newbery Medal, the (Randolph) Caldecott Medal, the Coretta Scott King Awards, the Texas Bluebonnet Award, and the Texas Lone Star Reading Award.

The library's administrators wrote specifications for vendor selection of children's books, which were designed to reflect existing selection policies for children's collections. Among other factors, the selection criteria included titles of publications from which selection would be conducted, specific categories of titles required for purchase, age groups for which material would be selected, and binding requirements. A complete list of requirements for the vendor's selection of children's books is included in appendix A at the end of this chapter.

Individual collection profiles were constructed for each children's collection in all branch libraries, to enable the vendor to become familiar with selection practices for each branch. All branch profiles included the size of the children's book budget, a per-item cost limit, and a budget breakdown for various categories of books. Children's librarians specified the percentages of each branch's funds that should be devoted to picture books, fiction for grades three to five, or six to eight, as well as allocations for each major category in the Dewey Decimal Classification. The profiles also included lists of authors, illustrators, and popular series that were to be purchased, regardless of the availability or quality of book reviews. An example of a children's collection profile for one Fort Worth Public Library branch is included in appendix B at the end of this chapter.

Summary Results of Initial Outsourcing Contracts

The multivendor outsourcing contracts established in FY 1992/93 included one vendor contract for copy cataloging and labels for monographic direct orders and gifts; multiple contracts with another vendor for shelf-ready books, cataloging and physical processing of audiovisual media, and selection of best-sellers; and a contract with a third vendor for outsourcing selection of children's books. By the summer of 1995, the contract for copy cataloging and physical processing of direct orders and gifts had been canceled. The contract for outsourcing of best-sellers was canceled in October 1995. Those activities were resumed by in-house staff. A half-time cataloger as well as two processing positions were added. Also, a half-time librarian was added to the Collection Development Unit. The initial outsourcing contract for cataloging and physical processing of audiovisual media and the contract for selection of children's books were not renewed after FY 1992/93.

During the first year of outsourcing, Fort Worth Public Library's support services team prepared new bid specifications for outsourcing services. By that point, the team's leaders had gained experience in this area and were able to revise outsourcing contract specifications. A contract with Brodart Company and a contract with Professional Media Service Corporation resulted from the rebidding processes.

Outsourcing with Brodart Company for Shelf-Ready Books

Since FY 1993/94, Brodart has provided cataloging and physical processing of adult and children's books, as well as selection of children's books. Brodart's staff supply popular reading and general technical books. Although the majority of the library's new titles are now acquired solely from Brodart, items that are not available from this vendor, including works in popular series, continue to be ordered from publishers. Cataloging and physical processing for direct orders are performed by in-house library staff. Upon completion of the vendor-selection process, Brodart's managers were required to send representatives to Fort Worth for an all-day meeting with the support services team leaders responsible for managing outsourcing contracts. Brodart also assigned a contract supervisor for the library's account and designated vendor liaisons for cataloging and physical processing.

Children's Book Selection

Brodart's selector benefited from using the selection profiles established in FY 1992/93, and encouraged the library's children's librarians to revise those specifications on an ongoing basis. In spite of the usefulness of these profiles, however, problems have occasionally risen with their day-to-day use. Unless enough excellent children's science books are published in a given year, for example, Brodart's selector is unable to choose $400 worth of science books to meet the budget expectations for a particular branch. In other cases, where branch budgets are minimal, the overall budget structure and corresponding collection profile have more impact on the purchase of new material than any decisions made by the selector.

During the second year of outsourcing with Brodart, branch collection profiles were expanded to include a patron profile component as well.

These patron profiles describe the children in each neighborhood, contain demographic information, and provide details about specific reading preferences. An example of a patron profile appears in the children's collection profile for one of Fort Worth's branch libraries in appendix B.

The library system's materials coordinator has stated emphatically that the children's book selection performed by Brodart's staff is exceptionally good and is certainly comparable to previous in-house standards. Nevertheless, reactions to outsourcing by the library's children's librarians have been mixed. Specific staff members believe they have lost that part of a librarian's role that is critical in tailoring a collection to fit the unique needs of its patrons. However, satisfaction with the quality of Brodart's selection service, as well as the ability to devote more time to selecting specialized acquisitions for individual collections, have been viewed as acceptable trade-offs in the outsourcing scheme. In addition, as a result of outsourcing, children's librarians have more time to address outreach and programming concerns.

Turnaround Time

The major obstacle at the outset of the Brodart contract was turnaround time for shipment of books. During the FY 1993/94 startup period, a considerable amount of time was devoted to establishing procedures with the new vendor during the all-day, on-site visit by Brodart's staff. Unfortunately, new children's books did not arrive in Fort Worth until January 1994, four months into the contract. Although there was concern about the time period required for implementation, it should be noted that selection was an entirely new service offered by Brodart that year.

In FY 1994/95, another problem resulted from the library staff's delay in submitting revised budget figures to the vendor. Specifications for monthly vendor selections, with book shipments every two weeks, proved difficult to meet. Turnaround time improved in FY 1995/96, largely because of cooperative efforts by both Brodart's representatives and the library's support services team.

Cataloging and Physical Processing for Children's Books

From a technical services standpoint, outsourcing the selection, cataloging, and physical processing of children's books streamlined operations in the library's Acquisitions, Cataloging, and Processing units. Book orders are no longer created, although Brodart's biweekly status reports enable children's librarians and other staff to monitor the status of each title from the initial selection stage until a book is shipped. As weekly shipments arrive, all items are reviewed for quality control and forwarded to children's units in about two days.

Corresponding magnetic tapes of MARC bibliographic records with 949 holdings field information are shipped separately from books. Tapes usually arrive on Monday and book shipments arrive later in the week. MARC records are available for all children's books supplied by Brodart. Occasionally, staff receive fully processed adult books without MARC records. Brodart's cataloging liaison has made arrangements to add missing records to a later tape.

Because order records for Brodart-selected titles do not exist in the library's catalog, MARC records are matched by ISBNs. Furthermore, because not all copies of a title arrive in one shipment, a duplicate MARC record with matching holdings is supplied when additional copies are shipped. The ISBN match merges the two records. Library-selected titles supplied by Brodart contain Dynix bibliographic numbers in the 035 field for matching of MARC records in the overlay process.

In FY 1995/96, library staff budgeted $99,000 for Brodart-selected books and $216,000 for adult books ordered from Brodart by library staff. Brodart's quality of book cataloging and physical processing has met contractual expectations. Books and MARC records are received on a timely basis, and problems with mislabeled books or incorrectly overlaid records have occurred with no more than 2 percent of items. This outsourcing experience enabled library staff to understand and appreciate the importance of detailed contract specifications, ongoing quality assurance, and good day-to-day communication with vendors.

Outsourcing with Professional Media Service Corporation

In FY 1993/94, the second contract for outsourcing full cataloging and physical processing for audiovisual media was awarded to Professional Media Service Corporation, located in Gardena, California. Professional's representatives were willing to work with the library's support services staff on every detail of cataloging and processing specifications. Nevertheless, some audiovisual material, such as audiobooks from certain publishers, is still acquired by direct-order purchases. Consequently, the percentage of in-house cataloging for audiovisual media at Fort Worth Public Library exceeds the percentage of ongoing in-house book cataloging.

Professional's staff have supplied shelf-ready videos and sound recordings for the library, following detailed specifications for physical processing of audiovisual material. Labels include a collection code abbreviation based on format (for example, SCS for sound cassettes and VCS for videocassettes). Dewey Decimal Classification numbers are used for nonfiction titles. The appropriate branch library is indicated on the outside of the container as well. Each item in a package is barcoded and labeled individually. The vendor is required to add the last four digits of the barcode(s) to the label on the outside of the container and to indicate the total number of pieces in each container. Additional warning labels are attached as needed, including labels with the following messages: "Keep Away From Heat," "Please Be Kind & Rewind," "Damage May Occur If Placed Near Magnetic Field," and "Do Not Put In Book Drop." Children's videos are prominently labeled "Child."

In addition to supplying full-MARC cataloging with format-appropriate tagging, the audiovisual media vendor is also required to add eight specific headings in 650 fields for videorecordings (for example, "Western films" and "Foreign films"). Furthermore, the vendor adds 650 fields indicating a film's language, as appropriate for foreign-language material. These headings were identified by public services librarians as useful in fulfilling patron requests for specific categories of audiovisual material.

Conclusion

Outsourcing of cataloging, physical processing, and material selection at Fort Worth Public Library has been implemented successfully. Initially, outsourcing of cataloging and processing for shelf-ready books and audiovisual media required a considerable amount of the library staff's time for quality control monitoring. The rapid pace of staff reductions that necessitated outsourcing contributed to this problem, because careful planning and implementation could not be done. When outsourcing specifications were revised, and contracts were established with new vendors at the end of the first year, the subsequent contracts resulted in improved services and less in-house effort for management of outsourcing. Furthermore, as a result of outsourcing selected processes, including copy cataloging of gifts and direct orders, library staff found that those activities could be more efficiently handled by in-house staff.

The initial contract for combined selection, cataloging, and physical processing of the children's book collections provided the greatest challenge, but outsourcing of these processes has become part of mainstream operations. Outsourcing of cataloging and physical processing for both audiovisual media and adult books has worked well. The key elements to success have been the development of thoughtfully written, detailed outsourcing specifications and constant vigilance on the part of the library's staff to ensure that all aspects of the outsourcing program function effectively.

During the years since outsourcing began, library staff have been able to maintain high levels of productivity, and no backlogs have developed. The high quality of cataloging provided by the library's current vendors has also enabled the library's cataloging staff to maintain good overall cataloging standards. Although all the library's local-cataloging practices are not performed by the vendors with the same level of customization that library staff had provided in the past, standardization of those aspects of technical services processing are viewed as acceptable tradeoffs of outsourcing.

Another example of the benefit of outsourcing at Fort Worth Public Library occurred in fall 1996, when the East Regional Library, one of the system's larger branch libraries, opened with a collection obtained largely through outsourced services provided by Brodart Company and Professional Media Service Corporation. This opening-day collection represents another way in which the library's staff have been able to provide additional technical services support with fewer staff.

Although large-scale outsourcing in a multivendor environment might not be appropriate for every organization, it was the best solution for Fort Worth Public Library's administrators when they were forced to address a funding crisis that led to drastic reassessment and reevaluation of the library's programs. Without the extensive training received by support staff services team members in working as a self-directed team, this project might have failed. Staff with strong commitments to library service, and vendors willing to work with the library's staff to develop new avenues for book selection and technical services, were the essential elements that contributed to the success of these outsourcing efforts. These elements of success also contributed to the library staff's overall ability to continue providing library material and ongoing services to patrons during a period of fiscal crisis and staff downsizing.

Bibliography

Booklist. 1969– . Chicago: American Library Association.

Children's Books. 1964– . Washington, D.C.: Library of Congress.

Horn Book Magazine. 1945– . Boston, Mass.: Horn Book.

Kirkus Reviews. 1933– . New York: Kirkus Service.

School Library Journal. 1961– . New York: R. R. Bowker.

Appendix A

Requirements Established for Vendor's Selection of Children's Books

1. Select according to the profile for each branch.

2. Begin contract selection with titles reviewed in October journals, which coincide with the beginning of the library's fiscal year. (That date established both an implementation date for the vendor and a cessation date for the library's selectors of children's books.)

3. Select books for children and young adults. Children are defined as newborns through 14 years of age, or 8th grade. Young adults are defined as 15 through 17 years of age, or grades 9 through 12.

4. Select from *School Library Journal, Booklist,* and *Kirkus Reviews.* Fort Worth's librarians will continue to select from journals specific to Texas. In-house staff will also make selections from *Horn Book* and *Children's Books,* both of which review titles well after publication and might contain titles with out-of-stock or out-of-print status.

5. Choose books with positive reviews in all three above-specified, required journals. Reviews identified with a star in *Booklist* are also required for selection. Since library staff no longer collect fairy tales and folktales, however, those titles are selected only when they are award winners.

6. Choose new imprints, not reprints or re-issues of previously published titles.

7. Provide copies of all ALA Notable Books and all titles for the (John) Newbery Medal, the (Randolph) Caldecott Medal, the Coretta Scott King Awards, and the Texas Lone Star Reading Award, if those titles have not been previously selected under the above criteria.

8. Provide copies of all titles on the Texas Bluebonnet Award's master list, which were reviewed after the contract began.

9. Exclude from selection all pop-up books, books with movable parts, book and toy combinations, cloth books, vinyl or plastic books, and books smaller than 4-by-4 inches.

10. Supply titles of a regional nature, including books about Texas and the Southwest, and Spanish-language and bilingual Spanish-English titles issued by American publishers.

11. Provide books in publisher's library binding whenever available. Trade or single-reinforced bindings are acceptable, but only if publisher's library binding is unavailable for a particular title.

Appendix B

Example of a Children's Collection Profile for a Fort Worth Public Library Branch

Fort Worth Public Library
Facility Selection Profile
Facility Name: _____ Branch Library
Address: Fort Worth Public Library
          300 Taylor Street
          Fort Worth, Texas 76102

1. Facility budget for the year: $10,000.00.

2. Cost limit per title: $75.00.

3. Reprints and reissues will not be accepted. Titles will be limited to 1994 and later copyrights.

4. Selections in all categories will be based on positive reviews and should be representative of the best, as well as the most popular books, the industry has to offer during the contract period. Exceptions are listed below in #5.

5. Percentages listed indicate approximate allocation of funds per category/genre.

   36% Picture books: See attached list of authors/illustrators

   low demand: Picture books with many words

   high demand: Popular authors and illustrators, books with fewer words

   13% Easy readers: Especially beginning readers, rookie readers

   1% Board books

   5% Fiction, Grades 3 to 5: See attached list of authors/illustrators

   low demand: Problem novels, historical novels

   high demand: Popular authors, mysteries, adventure, romance

   3% Fiction, Grades 6 to 8: See attached list of authors/illustrators

   low demand: Problem novels, historical novels

   high demand: Popular authors, mysteries, adventure, romance

   2% Young Adult Fiction, Grades 9 to 12:

   low demand: Historical novels

   high demand: Popular authors, romance, mysteries

   0% Foreign language; language?_____

1% 000s:

> *low demand:* Computers, libraries
>
> *high demand:* Monsters, UFOs

2% 100s:

> *low demand:* Feelings
>
> *high demand:* Ghosts, supernatural, witches

1% 200s:

> *low demand:* Different religions
>
> *high demand:* Mythology

5% 300s:

> *low demand:* Immigration, coping skills
>
> *high demand:* Ghost stories, pollution, airplanes, military, holidays

1% 400s:

> *low demand:* Dictionaries
>
> *high demand:* Phonics

10% 500s:

> *low demand:* Genetics, general science
>
> *high demand:* Ecology, animals, ocean, dinosaurs, astronomy, insects, weather, individual animals, reptiles

6% 600s:

> *low demand:* Gardening, robots
>
> *high demand:* Body, illness, pets, technology

4% 700s:

> *low demand:* Art, architecture, song books
>
> *high demand:* Drawing, how to draw, sports how to, martial arts

2% 800s:

> *low demand:* Plays, general anthologies
>
> *high demand:* Collections of poems on themes

8% 900s:

> *low demand:* Flags, sports biographies
>
> *high demand:* Texas, Black, Hispanic, Asian and Native Americans, wars, other countries and areas of the world

6. These authors' works will be purchased regardless of reviews: See list.

7. These illustrators' works will be purchased regardless of reviews: See list.

8. Titles in these series will be purchased regardless of reviews: See list.

9. Other criteria/requirements

AUTHORS' WORKS TO PURCHASE
NO MATTER WHAT THE REVIEWS

Ahlberg, Allen and Janet
Ames, Lee J.
Asch, Frank
Avi
Bang, Molly
Blume, Judy
Bond, Felicia
Brown, Marc
Brown, Marcia
Brown, Ruth
Browne, Anthony
Byars, Betsy
Carle, Eric
Carlson, Nancy
Cleary, Beverly
Cole, Babette
Cole, Joanna
Cooper, Ilene
Coville, Bruce
Crews, Donald
Dahl, Roald
DeClements, Barthe
Ehlert, Lois
Fleming, Denise
Fritz, Jean
Hahn, Mary Downing
Hamilton, Virginia
Henkes, Kevin
Hoberman, Mary Anne
Hughes, Shirley
Hutchins, Pat
Isadora, Rachel
Jonas, Ann
Kellogg, Steven
Lowry, Lois
MacLachlan, Patricia

Marshall, James
Martin, Bill, Jr.
Mayer, Mercer
McPhail, David
Merriam, Eve
Myers, Walter Dean
Naylor, Phyllis Reynolds
Nixon, Joan Lowery
Ormerod, Jan
Paulsen, Gary
Polacco, Patricia
Prelutsky, Jack
Reid-Banks, Lynne
Rockwell, Anne
Ross, Tony
Rylant, Cynthia
Sacher, Louis
Sendak, Maurice
Seuss, Dr.
Silverstein, Shel
Simon, Seymour
Soto, Gary
Spier, Peter
Spinelli, Jerry
Van Allsburg, Chris
Viorst, Judith
Wallace, Bill
Walter, Mildred
Wells, Rosemary
Willard, Nancy
Williams, Vera
Wisniewski, David
Wood, Don and Audrey
Wright, Betty Renn
Yolen, Jane
Zolotow, Charlotte

ILLUSTRATORS TO PURCHASE NO MATTER WHAT THE REVIEWS

Aliki

Dillon, Leo and Diane

Ernst, Lisa

Foreman, Michael

Galdone, Paul

Hubbard, Woodleigh

Say, Allan

Tafuri, Nancy

Young, Ed

NEW TITLES IN THE FOLLOWING SERIES SHOULD BE PURCHASED

Banks Street ready-to-read

Berenstain bears

Creatures all around us

Eyewitness books

Eyewitness juniors

Eyewitness visual dictionaries

Hello reading

Let's-read-and-find-out science books

New true books

Rookie readers

Spot stories

Step into reading

_____ BRANCH LIBRARY PATRON PROFILE

Patrons: Patrons range from upper middle class to very poor. The majority are middle class to lower middle class. Approximately one-third are white, one-third are African American, and one-third are Asian and Hispanic. There are a number of home-schooled children, largely in the elementary grades.

Collections: Picture books constitute almost one half of the circulation. Easy readers circulate well. Nonfiction books with color pictures circulate well. One-third of juvenile fiction should be for reluctant readers.

14 Outsourcing Three Technical Services Operations: Physical Processing, Copy Cataloging, and Authority Control at Houston Public Library

Gene Rollins

In the early 1990s, Houston Public Library's staff faced the dilemma of accommodating an expansion of services, without a corresponding increase in personnel. Incorporating outsourcing into three technical services workflows proved to be a viable solution to this predicament. Physical processing and item record maintenance of added copies for monographs were outsourced to Baker & Taylor, Inc. (B&T). B&T's turnaround time averages less than one month from point of order to delivery of shelf-ready books, compared with previous turnaround times ranging from four months to two years. Outsourcing of copy cataloging and matching authority record delivery for federal depository items to MARCIVE Inc. has resulted in the availability of bibliographic access to this collection as well as dramatically increased collection use. A contract for retrospective and ongoing authority control for all material except government documents was awarded to Blackwell North America, Inc. Among the improvements from this effort was a reduction of 49 forms of name entry for Leo Tolstoy in the library's catalog to a single entry with appropriate cross-references. All three outsourcing programs have become an integral part of the overall technical services operation.

This chapter is based on a presentation made by Gene Rollins at the Association for Library Collections and Technical Services' Commercial Technical Services Committee's program, Outsourcing from Selection to Shelf: How? When? Why? in Portland, Oregon, March 29, 1996.

Houston Public Library (HPL) in Texas consists of a large central facility and 36 branches. A major issue facing library administrators in the late 1980s was the challenge of expanding service levels without increasing staff. With the implementation of the CARL online system in 1991, improving access to bibliographic records and increasing the accuracy of holdings and item status information were also high priorities. The availability of remote bibliographic access to the collection made it essential for uncataloged collections, including government publications, to be captured in the online catalog as well. Before outsourcing, bibliographic access to these documents was available only by in-house consultation of the *Monthly Catalog of United States Government Publications.*

One means of addressing bibliographic access issues at HPL was outsourcing with different vendors in the following technical services areas:

1. Physical processing of monographs: Baker & Taylor, Inc. (B&T).

2. Copy cataloging and authority control for Government Printing Office (GPO) depository publications: MARCIVE Inc.

3. Retrospective and ongoing Library of Congress (LC) authority control for all records, except GPO material: Blackwell North America, Inc.

Background

HPL's staff use the CARL online system for their online public access catalog (OPAC), circulation control, and serials control. A separate Innovative Interfaces, Inc. system is used for acquisitions. The Online Computer Library Center (OCLC) database is the primary source for bibliographic records, although the Research Libraries Information Network (RLIN) serves as a secondary resource. HPL's primary vendor for library material is B&T.

A major challenge for HPL's administrators in the 1990s has been a rapidly increasing demand for services without a corresponding increase in resources. The number of active registered borrowers increased from 300,000 in 1983 to nearly 900,000 in 1995. At the same time, the library's staff size and operating budget remained almost unchanged. In June 1996, there were approximately 670 FTE library employees, a figure almost equivalent to the number of staff in the early 1980s. During the past decade, several new branches were also opened. Because HPL's hours of service were not reduced, a significant portion of staffing for new facilities resulted from reallocation of technical services personnel to branch services. HPL's administrators were forced to maximize available resources in this manner to avoid service reductions.

Outsourcing Philosophy and Strategic Planning

The establishment of an outsourcing philosophy was a key factor in strategic planning and in ensuring the eventual success of this endeavor. This approach to outsourcing was to improve turnaround time for book processing, provide bibliographic access to uncataloged government documents, and improve the overall quality of HPL's bibliographic database. An essential ingredient of this approach was a commitment to maintaining a significant degree of intellectual control over both the outsourcing process and the vendors' products. This philosophy stems from a conservative institutional culture that exists because of necessity. HPL receives as many as 40,000 books each month. With this volume of activity, a minor modification in acquisitions, cataloging, or processing procedures can produce far-reaching consequences.

Copy cataloging of non-GPO material and all original cataloging were specifically excluded from outsourcing. This tactic was used because HPL possesses a high level of staff expertise in the Catalog Department. Their long-standing practices in modifying cataloging records to meet the needs of local customers was a highly regarded feature that HPL's administrators did not want to abandon. Tailoring of catalog records was deemed to be of particular importance for fiction classics, picture books, easy readers, and literary criticism. Outsourcing of physical processing for books also was restricted to added copies, which in-house staff had already cataloged and classified.

The outsourcing program was carefully planned, as HPL's staff addressed the following basic questions:

1. What operations existed before outsourcing and how effective were those processes?
2. What could be outsourced and what were the desired results?
3. How could the desired results be accomplished from a technical standpoint, and how would vendor performance be evaluated?

HPL's managers decided to outsource physical processing, which was not being done effectively in terms of quality and quantity; to outsource GPO cataloging, for which remote bibliographic access was not available; and to outsource authority control, which was not being done at all.

Outsourcing of Physical Processing

The vendor-selection phase for outsourcing physical processing for books was initiated in 1989, when the library's administrators issued a Request for

Proposal (RFP). Technical services managers developed quality and quantity benchmarks for staff and used that information to establish standards for a vendor. A manual with step-by-step documentation of procedures also was developed for submission with the RFP. The manual contained examples of finished products, including photocopies of each type of spine label for different sizes of books. This document was used for subsequent training of new library employees and vendor staff. B&T was selected as the vendor for this program.

Technical Considerations

The technical approach to accomplishing the outsourcing task was determined by the capabilities of the library's CARL system and B&T's response to the RFP. Because the goal was to receive shelf-ready material, the book processing performed by library staff and the processing done by the vendor's staff needed to be identical. To achieve parallel processing for shelf-ready material, B&T's staff created CARL item records and linked barcodes to bibliographic records. Two options existed for accomplishing this: (1) obtain either 949 or 966 item fields in bibliographic records supplied on tape by the vendor; or (2) have the vendor's staff update CARL records online, via a remote connection to HPL's database. Because keying of item and barcode data for tape loading into CARL would have been time-consuming and prone to error, the online option was chosen.

Pricing

HPL's full physical processing rate from B&T is $3.69 per book and includes the following services: application of barcodes, security system targets, book pockets, and dust jackets; property stamping; application of dot labels in assorted colors for different collection locations; creation and application of call number and book labels; indication of "in process" status in the online record; and completion of online item record conversion. HPL's partial-processing cost is $.55 for hardback books and trade paperbacks. Partial processing includes property stamping, dust jackets, book pockets, and security targets. Minimal processing for mass market paperbacks, which consists of only a property stamp and book pocket, is priced at $.30 per item.

Physical Processing Workflow

HPL's cataloging staff conduct pre-order searching on OCLC and download bibliographic information into Innovative's acquisitions module. Pre-cataloging is performed on appropriate titles before ordering, which results in an automatic download of OCLC records into the CARL OPAC as well as identification of items for physical processing by B&T. Orders for precataloged titles that are canceled are deleted from the CARL and OCLC databases by cataloging staff.

Based on decisions made by cataloging staff, acquisitions staff place electronic orders against either a B&T full-processing or partial-processing account. The electronic orders are followed by paper confirmations, which indicate library identification and designate location distribution for each copy (for example, reference or circulating). Acquisitions staff notify cataloging staff when titles marked for full processing are canceled. Acquisitions staff also segregate the partially processed and full-processed books when the books arrive.

B&T's staff perform physical processing, based on account data and the detailed order grids supplied with orders. After affixing item barcode labels, item conversion is performed online via the dedicated telecommunications line between the vendor's processing facility and HPL's CARL database. The item status is established as "in process" at this time as well. The "in process" code is used because outsourced material is delivered to Houston via ground transportation from B&T's facility in Georgia. This status prevents holds from being placed on books during the one-to-two weeks when items are in transit.

HPL's Materials Processing Department staff assign CARL system passwords to B&T's staff and provide CARL training material. They also monitor the quality of items received from B&T, distribute books for delivery to branch libraries, and report physical processing errors to the vendor. The errors are corrected by library processing staff, who also notify B&T's staff and HPL's staff on procedural changes and distribute updates to HPL's processing manual.

As new items are circulated to the public, the "in process" status is automatically changed to "shelf" status. However, Automation Department staff also execute a monthly program to change status codes for all items that have not circulated within a specific time frame. This final step in the outsourcing process ensures that the "in process" status for noncirculating reference collection and other special collections material is updated in the CARL system.

Impact of Physical Processing Outsourcing on In-House Operations

An unexpected benefit of outsourcing was the reorganization of in-house operations for greater efficiencies. During the workflow analysis done before outsourcing, it was apparent that some technical services areas could be reorganized to improve internal operations. Staff in the Acquisitions,

Cataloging, and Materials Processing departments were reallocated in this process. One FTE devoted to catalog searching and three FTEs from item conversion were reallocated to the Materials Processing Department.

Several policy and organizational changes were implemented during outsourcing as well, to maximize the number of added copies ordered from B&T and to increase the volume of the vendor's physical processing. When outsourcing began in 1990, the library received full physical processing for less than 15 percent of all volumes supplied by B&T. At that time, the vendor handled only those titles that were added copies for the same edition of a previously ordered and fully cataloged title. In 1992, library staff began cataloging review copies of all children's books, immediately after titles were placed on selection lists for system-wide ordering. This practice ensured that most children's books ordered beyond that point were added copies.

After 1993, all Cataloging-in-Publication (CIP) fiction titles were precataloged before order. In 1994, staff began precataloging all non-CIP nonfiction for which OCLC records with Dewey Classification numbers were available. After 1994, precataloging of CIP nonfiction was restricted to use of LC records only. Because HPL's staff frequently order added copies, they discovered that using only LC-supplied Dewey Classification numbers ensured that the call numbers on all added copies matched the call number on the first copy. The use of OCLC-member records in 1994 revealed call number variations among member libraries and resulted in added copies with different call numbers. These in-house policy changes more than doubled the amount of material with full processing from B&T. The volume of material supplied by B&T, and the annual increases in B&T's physical processing rates, from 23 percent in 1992 to 34 percent in 1995, are listed in Exhibit 14.1.

Physical Processing Services from B&T			
Year	Volumes from B&T	Volumes with Full Processing	
1992	283,323	6,314	23%
1993	223,207	59,712	27%
1994	270,829	106,166	39%
1995	199,104	66,977	34%

EXHIBIT 14.1 Physical Processing Services from Baker & Taylor, Inc. (B&T). The total number of volumes supplied to Houston Public Library by B&T, from 1992 to 1995, as well as the total amount and percentage of volumes with full physical processing, is itemized in this table.

Another in-house organizational change was the transfer of pre-order searching from the Acquisitions Department to the Cataloging Department. This change simplified precataloging and allowed bibliographic records for added copies to be downloaded into Innovative's acquisitions module after they were produced on OCLC. The call number and other elements in a book's MARC (machine-readable cataloging) record are used to determine the account on which a book is ordered. As a result of this change, acquisitions staff were trained in interpreting MARC format and understanding catalogers' output.

In order to precatalog titles for maximum outsourcing of physical processing, library staff adopted use of the *Anglo-American Cataloguing Rules,* second edition, 1988 revision, with minimal exceptions. For the same reason, staff decided to adopt the current version of the *Dewey Decimal Classification and Relative Index,* even if books on similar subjects were likely to appear in different shelf locations as classification numbers changed between editions. Cataloging staff also had to cope with new pressures associated with fiscal year schedules—pre-order searching must be finished before orders are placed, items are received, and funds are expended.

In order to ensure that the quality of in-house processes is equivalent to the quality of similar work performed by B&T's staff, responsibilities for creating item records and editing holdings data at HPL were centralized in the Materials Processing Department. As a result of outsourcing, staffing for in-house physical processing also has been reduced from 18 positions to 13. The positions were moved to public services and there have been no staff layoffs.

Initially, HPL's processing staff resisted the outsourcing concept, because of concern about the in-house productivity and accuracy goals established in conjunction with outsourcing. These goals were originally perceived as quotas, despite the fact that performance levels from previous years were used for development of the benchmarks for in-house staff and the vendor's staff. As reports of in-house production rates and accuracy have been used since then, in employee evaluation processes, trust has been established that the same standards are being applied to all departmental staff. Library staff also realize that attainment of these benchmarks will not result in arbitrary justification for increasing production goals or demanding more accuracy than might be feasible.

From a public services standpoint, outsourcing has increased the number of bibliographic records without holdings in the CARL system. This is due to the delay between precataloging and receipt of material. Because the turnaround time from order to receipt averages less than one month, however, this issue creates serious problems only when titles are delayed in publication or backordered by the vendor. Ultimately, a direct link between the library's Innovative acquisitions system and the CARL OPAC will resolve this problem.

Results of Outsourcing Physical Processing

By 1996, B&T's staff were responsible for physical processing of 33 percent of HPL's annual processing activity. The accuracy rate for combined vendor and in-house processing has increased to an overall range of 95 percent to 98 percent. No comparable data for in-house accuracy rates are available, because this was not tracked before outsourcing. There is no physical processing backlog, and turnaround time for new material has been reduced significantly. Before outsourcing, an average turnaround time of four months was required for processing multiple copies. Single-order titles often required as much as two years for processing. In 1996, the turnaround time from point of order to availability of material on library shelves averaged less than one month.

From 1990 to 1994, the number of terminals used by B&T's staff to access HPL's OPAC increased from one to three. Each one of B&T's staff members assigned to HPL's program is issued a separate password that can be used to track errors and identify personnel who may need additional training. For most shipments, B&T's physical processing error rate ranges from 2 percent to 5 percent.

Based on in-house copy cataloging volume, HPL's managers should allocate approximately 4 percent of the library's collections budget for outsourced physical processing of this material category. This percentage amount is a rule of thumb, based on experience at HPL, and fluctuates depending on standards for acceptable cataloging copy. In 1996, that percentage amounted to approximately $225,000 annually, which was funded by staff savings in the Materials Processing Department and savings in processing supplies.

Copy Cataloging of Government Publications

In 1992, HPL's staff contracted with MARCIVE Inc. for copy cataloging and matching authority records for approximately 200,000 GPO depository titles, as well as cataloging and authority records for ongoing acquisitions. HPL is a selective depository for GPO publications and acquires approximately 80 percent of GPO items available for distribution. Depository material does not circulate and is housed in closed stacks. Before acquiring MARCIVE's catalog records, the collection was underutilized, because bibliographic access was limited to staff and patrons using the central library.

Because depository items do not circulate, a generic barcode is added to each MARC record in a 949 field. The 949 fields automatically generate item records as the vendor's file is loaded into the CARL OPAC. This feature creates precise branch, location, and status information in the OPAC. It also distinguishes purchased government documents, which circulate for outside use, from noncirculating titles received on deposit.

Retrospective Government Documents Cataloging Project

The depository program's structure simplified the plan for outsourcing copy cataloging. GPO routinely issues item selection cards for new publications, and HPL's staff return selection cards for items they wish to receive. Staff have traditionally maintained a file of item selection cards that were not returned to GPO. By eliminating items not represented in the collection from a total file of GPO publications, the process of capturing a comprehensive list of HPL's holdings was relatively easy. That process assumes, of course, that the library received everything requested. MARCIVE's personnel supplied HPL's staff with a list of GPO items for which catalog records exist (that is, since July 1976), and in-house staff identified titles not acquired from GPO.

HPL's staff elected to receive both bibliographic and authority records from MARCIVE. The cost was $.08 per record, including $.07 for the basic selective extraction of records and $.01 for authority records. The authority records' cost did not cover processing of bibliographic records through authority control. With miscellaneous tape charges and implementation fees, the total retrospective cataloging and authority record costs were approximately $20,000.

The completed retrospective file consisted of approximately 200,000 new bibliographic records. Based on random spot-checking by the cataloging staff as the tapes were loaded, the records were deemed to be of high quality. One unforeseen aspect of loading this file, however, was that these records were, on average, between 20 percent and 30 percent larger than the standard bibliographic records in HPL's database. There were obvious disk storage implications associated with increasing the library's database by this magnitude, and more hardware was added to the system to accommodate the files.

Ongoing Government Documents Cataloging Program

In 1996, HPL's staff received approximately 800 bibliographic records for new documents each month from MARCIVE. The vendor's ongoing service charges are based on a subscription rate, rather than a per-record basis, because it is impossible to predict GPO publishing output. HPL's subscription cost is $2,200 per year, with an additional annual fee of $1,500 for authority records. Cost studies were not conducted to compare in-house versus outsourcing costs.

Results of Outsourcing GPO Copy Cataloging

Use of the documents collection after outsourcing, as measured by retrievals from closed stacks, has increased. In 1993, 400 titles were retrieved from the stacks. By 1995, there was a fivefold increase, as 1,965 titles were retrieved. With increased requests for titles in the collection, however, reference staff have discovered cases where selected GPO items were not received. In these cases, titles are deleted from both the bibliographic database and the library's MARCIVE profile. A regular audit of the MARCIVE GPO profiles is planned.

A welcome and unanticipated benefit of outsourcing was experienced by collection development staff. Because documents records are now available in the CARL OPAC, they are routinely captured with books each time the database is searched. Searches in numerous subject areas have revealed that HPL's collection includes only government publications in selected subject fields. Selectors have been able to use this information in making decisions on new purchases, in order to enhance the quality of the library's overall collection.

Outsourcing of Authority Control

HPL's technical services area is an extremely production-oriented operation, cataloging between 1,500 and 2,500 titles monthly. Approximately 20,000 to 40,000 items are handled each month as well. Historically, there was inadequate staff to manage the authority control requirements for ongoing cataloging or to complete retrospective authority processing. Attempts to perform in-house authority work proved unsuccessful because of the workload.

Retrospective Authority Control

In 1993, HPL's staff issued an RFP for retrospective and ongoing authority control. Based on an evaluation of bid responses, Blackwell North America, Inc. was selected as the vendor. At that time, HPL's non-GPO titles database contained approximately 570,000 bibliographic records. The first step in this project was to download the entire bibliographic database of non-GPO records. Unique CARL bibliographic identification numbers were included in this tape output, because they would be used to match and overlay bibliographic records after authority processing.

Blackwell performed the project in two phases. The first phase included preprocessing, a filing-indicator review, and LC automated matching and updating. In the preprocessing step, common abbreviations were expanded, spelling errors and typographical mistakes were corrected, obsolete subject headings were deleted, dates were added to period subdivisions, direct geographic headings were updated and changed, tagging errors were corrected, and occurrences of the "‡w" subfield were removed. Other file cleanup was completed as well. Updated bibliographic records for approximately 570,000 titles were delivered upon completion of processing in this first phase. Approximately 21 business days were required to complete the first phase.

The second phase consisted of manual review and editing of non-matched and partially matched headings by Blackwell's staff. The output consisted of a file of only bibliographic records modified during the manual editing, along with files containing 306,398 collection-specific LC name and subject authority records.

HPL's staff specified custom requirements in the RFP for handling names for fiction authors. HPL uses the author's surname on title pages to create fiction call numbers (for example, the call number for William Faulkner is FAULK). However, before 1960, the call number was F. Given these discrepancies, it was important for bibliographic records to match author-name information in call numbers. Blackwell's staff compared the LC updated record to the author's name for all fiction works. Updates were made only if the first letter of the author's surname would not be changed. According to HPL's specifications, "Plaidy, jean. 1906– " could be updated to "Plaidy, Jean, 1906– ." This was possible whether the call number was P or PLAI. However, "Plaidy, jean. 1906– " could not be changed to "Holt, Victoria, 1906- ." If the LC update would have changed Plaidy to Holt, the proposed update was written to a report instead of executed. HPL's staff used these reports to change spine labels on books and to correct headings in OPAC records manually.

Automated matching, including the custom requirement, was priced at $.06 per bibliographic record. Manual review was an additional $.05 per record. The overall match rate for names and subjects against the LC authority files was 93.7 percent. At a cost of $.11 per record, the total cost of retrospective authority control for approximately 570,000 titles was $62,700.

Ongoing Authority Control

HPL's staff elected to receive both ongoing authority work for new cataloging, as well as changes to HPL's collection-specific LC authority records. During the retrospective authority control project, Blackwell built a history file of the library's collection-specific authority records. Using Blackwell's Notification Service, a quarterly file of changed authority records is supplied to HPL.

At least once each year, HPL's staff generate a tape of new or changed records for LC authority control by Blackwell's staff, following specifications for machine match and manual review used in the retrospective project. Changed bibliographic records, together with matching authority records, are delivered by the vendor. HPL's staff use a standard loader to enter records into CARL for the match process, rather than solely using CARL bibliographic identification numbers as match points. The difference in match points between retrospective and ongoing authority control is caused by the operational difficulty of maintaining a nonstandard loader on a continuous basis.

Results of Authority Control Outsourcing

Before outsourcing, the lack of authority control was dramatically evident. In the author index, there were 28 variants of Barbara Cartland's name and 49 versions of Leo Tolstoy's name. After authority processing was completed, variant forms of Cartland's name were reduced to two. There should have been one form only, but there appears to be some disagreement about Cartland's date of birth. The 49 versions of Tolstoy's name were standardized to a single form, with appropriate cross-references. The impact of authority control processing on misspellings and outdated LC subject headings was equally spectacular.

Based on HPL's database size and updating frequency, the annual cost for Blackwell's quarterly Notification Service to maintain records in the existing CARL OPAC is $2,288. The volume of authority control processing requirements for ongoing cataloging activity is estimated to range between 30,000 and 40,000 added or changed records annually. Blackwell's authority control processing cost for this range of titles is between $3,500 and $4,500 per year.

The manager of HPL's Catalog Department estimated that it would require two full-time catalogers to maintain HPL's database if this same work were performed in-house. Estimated in-house costs would range between $70,000 and $90,000 per year, depending on levels of staff experience. The cost benefit of outsourcing this category of authority control to Blackwell for approximately $7,000 per year has been a major advantage for HPL's managers.

Nevertheless, HPL's long-range staffing plan calls for hiring an additional full-time professional cataloger to work half-time on authority control, once the CARL authority module is operational. Duties for the new position will include managing quality control for the outsourcing contract and performing in-house editing for locally assigned subject headings.

Conclusion

Outsourcing of selected technical services operations has been highly effective for Houston Public Library's staff. Outsourcing physical processing for added copies reduced costs, increased output, and improved accuracy. The outsourcing of copy cataloging for GPO publications and authority control processing of the entire database resulted in the provision of better service, without a substantial increase in ongoing costs. In fact, there were no alternatives to outsourcing, because personnel budgets have not been, and are not likely to be, increased in the 1990s. The municipal budget has not maintained pace with inflation either.

HPL's staff have learned that there are three main components to successful outsourcing. As a first step, developing an institutional philosophy, with regard to what is appropriate for outsourcing and why outsourcing is appropriate, is essential. Engaging in the necessary measures to ensure that all staff understand and appreciate this philosophy is important. Staff need to recognize that a high degree of customization is not feasible, but that the benefits of outsourcing outweigh this factor. This strategic approach also provides a framework for decision making as outsourcing projects evolve. It is also critical to develop a solid plan for achieving the desired result. During the implementation planning phase, it is important to be realistic about what library staff can and cannot do. Determining the vendor's capabilities, as well as what is technically possible, are equally important in this phase.

Finally, proactive management of the outsourcing contract is a key ingredient. Library managers need to understand the details of the contract and share this knowledge with their staff and the vendor's staff. Vendor personnel should be viewed as extensions of library staff and should be kept apprised of changes in policies, procedures, and practices. It is helpful to have one staff member serve as the key vendor contact and vice versa. Ideally, the library and vendor contacts should make on-site visits as well. The more knowledge each partner has, the more successful outsourcing will be. In this case, the strength of relationships that library staff, located in Texas, established with three different vendor teams, located in Georgia, Texas, and Oregon, was a major factor that contributed to the positive outcome of HPL's various outsourcing programs.

Bibliography

Monthly Catalog of United States Government Publications. 1895– . Washington, D.C.: Cataloging Branch, Library Division, Library Programs Service, Superintendent of Documents, U.S. Government Printing Office.

Part Three

Special Libraries

The Outsourcing Solution for Cataloging and Database Maintenance at the Chubb Law & Business Library

Aimee Ruzicka

Until 1990, the collection for the Chubb Law & Business Library, located in Warren, New Jersey, was uncataloged. After examining options for creating the library's first catalog, as well as acquiring continued database maintenance, the library manager elected to outsource the entire technical services operation to Cassidy Cataloguing Services, Inc. of Harrison, New Jersey. Cassidy's staff performed cataloging and physical processing for over 1,200 titles in the 7,500-volume collection. Following this initial project, Cassidy has continued to function as the library's cataloging department. As this client/consultant relationship has evolved over time, Cassidy's staff have offered both cataloging expertise and a value-added component of advice and advocacy to Chubb's library manager.

Until 1990, the legal and business collection of the Chubb Law & Business Library, located in Warren, New Jersey, was uncataloged. Over the years, sporadic attempts had been made to catalog the collection, using a combination of home-grown classification schemes and the Library of Congress Classification. However, none of those efforts resulted in an accurate or thorough book, card, or automated catalog of the library's holdings.

In the process of confronting this problem in 1989, it was determined that outsourcing the library's entire technical services operation was the best solution to accomplish the corporate goal of acquiring bibliographic access to the library's collection. Cassidy Cataloguing Services, Inc., located in Harrison, New Jersey, was subsequently selected as the outsourcing vendor for cataloging and physical processing of the existing collection and ongoing processing of new acquisitions. All database maintenance was outsourced to Cassidy as well.

Background

The Chubb Law & Business Library was formed in the 1960s as the Law Library for the General Counsel Department of Chubb & Son Inc., the operating company of the Chubb Corporation. Chubb is a major property/casualty insurer, which has operations worldwide and employs approximately 10,000 people. In 1983, the law library and all other corporate and administrative staff were consolidated and relocated to the Chubb Corporation's headquarters in Warren, New Jersey.

During the 1980s, the law library's collection consisted of selected reporters, texts, and treatises covering insurance topics, and the National Insurance Laws (NILS) publications. The NILS collection is a staple for any legal department dealing primarily with statutory and regulatory insurance matters. Although no reliable statistical information is available for the size of the collection at that time, it is estimated to have ranged from 6,500 to 9,000 volumes.

With a staff of only one law librarian, who also served as library manager, and limited part-time, temporary clerical assistants, there had never been enough staff or time to catalog the entire collection. Technical services functions were secondary in importance, when compared with the librarian's reference service and administrative responsibilities. Although the desire existed to create and maintain accurate holdings records for the library's collection, the time and expertise were not available to accomplish that goal.

Nevertheless, staff members in the General Counsel Department were not as frustrated with this lack of bibliographic access as might have been expected. One reason was that the large, multivolume legal reporter series and NILS book sets were easily distinguishable by their consistent size and binding. It was relatively simple to find those major titles in a visual sweep of the library. Furthermore, other unique titles were loosely arranged into approximately 10 subject categories. Library patrons and staff had memorized the exact location for many of those items and could usually locate titles with little searching. On those occasions in which books could not be found, the librarian typically conducted a book-by-book search for requested material.

This scenario became increasingly unacceptable over time, as newly hired legal staff frequently were unable to identify holdings or locate material in the collection. The lack of procedures for handling new acquisitions was also a problem for library staff. In addition, the desire to offer reference service to nonlegal staff had emerged as a long-range corporate goal. The lack of bibliographic access to the collection, however, rendered that service concept infeasible until the cataloging problem was addressed.

In early 1989, a new library manager was hired and assigned the tasks of employing a records management staff member and reconfiguring the library's collection within the existing office space. Although each of those responsibilities presented challenges for the new librarian, the most pressing problem was the lack of bibliographic access to the collection. The perception was, and continues to be, that the library's collection is an important and expensive capital investment for Chubb. Therefore, the best possible access to this resource is desired by its employees.

Given those factors, the library manager immediately reviewed options for acquiring both a fully cataloged collection in the near term and continuing technical services support for the future. The following options were identified in that analysis:

1. Hire a cataloger and obtain access to an online bibliographic utility, in order to perform cataloging in-house.
2. Purchase cataloging software intended for a small collection and have the library manager do all cataloging in-house, in addition to performing all managerial and reference responsibilities.
3. Outsource the entire cataloging for the existing collection and all future acquisitions.

The first two options were quickly eliminated. Hiring the requisite staff was out of the question. Because the library manager did not possess cataloging expertise, and did not have time for a project of this magnitude and complexity, relying on that individual for the cataloging work was also not a viable option. Consequently, outsourcing the entire cataloging project and ongoing database maintenance was selected as the best alternative for creating and maintaining the catalog.

Implementation of Outsourcing

In 1989, a proposal was developed by the library manager for outsourcing the library's cataloging and database maintenance. The proposal was submitted for consideration and approval by the General Counsel Department's senior staff and the company's financial officer. The library manager also lobbied appropriate administrative staff to promote the outsourcing concept. The goal of those efforts was twofold: (1) to convince Chubb's administrators and staff of the necessity for establishing bibliographic control over the collection as soon as possible; and (2) to emphasize the need to adopt the Library of Congress (LC) cataloging and classification practices as processing standards for the collection.

In preparation for the eventual cataloging activity, library staff weeded the collection to make it easier to manage. After weeding, the collection contained approximately 7,500 volumes. About 1,200 volumes represented unique titles for cataloging. The few records that existed from previous cataloging attempts were not used.

While the outsourcing proposal was being reviewed, initial efforts were made to identify contractors for this project. Because competitive bidding was not strictly required, the library manager interviewed individuals from two companies regarding their pricing structures and strategies for handling this project. Cassidy Cataloguing Services, Inc. was selected as the lead vendor, because of their staff's expertise in handling legal and business collections exclusively and because of their competitive price structure. Cassidy's estimate for online catalog software, as well as the retrospective cataloging, was $22,000. Their bid for ongoing cataloging, whether it was copy or original cataloging, and maintenance for any new titles, was $20 per title.

These costs were inclusive; that is, Cassidy's staff would perform all work involved in collecting bibliographic information, copying records from their own database of approximately 100,000 records, creating original cataloging, and adding all records to the online catalog supplied by Cassidy. Cassidy would also print labels, and supply circulation cards and other physical processing products. Cassidy's staff would perform all physical processing for the collection as well. It was not necessary to barcode the collection, because circulation is based on an honor system.

In December 1989, the outsourcing proposal was accepted and funded. Because library staff finally had received the unique opportunity to develop the library's first comprehensive catalog, a decision was made to create a state-of-the-art online catalog and bypass the traditional book or card catalog formats. The software initially supplied by Cassidy was MOLEhill, a customized version of Nutshell Plus II.

Cataloging of the retrospective collection began in early 1990. Cassidy's clerical staff made on-site visits to photocopy title pages and versos of the library's volumes. The books were reshelved by Cassidy's staff until processing could be completed. Professional catalogers and computer staff completed other portions of the project off-site. Within the first quarter of 1991, catalog records for approximately 1,200 titles and over 7,500 volumes had been entered into personal computers in the library and the cataloged books were retrieved by Cassidy's staff to be labeled and reshelved in call number order. The library's staff were able to establish a simple circulation system, using book cards provided by Cassidy.

At this point, the project moved into its next phase, maintenance of the existing database and cataloging of new acquisitions. Cassidy's staff continued to make on-site visits to photocopy title pages and versos, and later returned to finish the physical processing of books. Monthly updates to the catalog are made on-site by Cassidy's staff as well.

Outsourcing Goals

There were several goals in this outsourcing program. The immediate goal was to create an online catalog and resolve the problem with lack of bibliographic control of the collection. A parallel goal was to accomplish this task without utilizing the library's limited staff, as they had no expertise in this area and no time for this activity. Long-range goals involved setting a standard within the company for future cataloging projects, obtaining timely upgrades to the catalog, and enabling efficient migrations to future cataloging software. There was also a desire to offer Chubb's employees an online catalog that could be distributed throughout the building via a local area network (LAN).

A companywide cataloging standard was needed because acquisitions were decentralized. Small library collections had developed throughout Chubb's headquarters over the years, as individuals in various business departments purchased reference volumes for day-to-day use. Managers of the smaller collections, however, faced the same problem with the lack of bibliographic access as did staff in the Law & Business Library. The other libraries also had no reliable circulation systems. Consequently, the main library's outsourcing project had the potential for serving as a model for the departmental libraries, if decisions were made later to contract out the cataloging and database maintenance for those collections.

Evaluation of Outsourcing

By 1996, the library's outsourcing arrangement had reached its sixth year of existence and had accomplished more than the original goals. The results of outsourcing fall into two clearly defined areas: the technical aspect, and the interpersonal or client/consultant relationship. The technical aspect involves the abilities of the outsourcing company's staff to accomplish the contractual task of providing bibliographic access to the collection and maintaining the library's database. The benefit of the interpersonal or client/consultant relationship was added value to the project, which in many ways was not anticipated at the outset.

Technical Aspect

On the technical side, the library staff's primary outsourcing goals were met with the completion of cataloging for the retrospective collection and the availability of an online catalog for the library's holdings. In addition, procedures were developed by the library's staff and Cassidy's staff for handling new acquisitions, title changes, and other aspects of the continuing maintenance of the database and collection. The turnaround time is two weeks or less and there is a 24-hour rush service for requested titles. The library's staff relied on Cassidy's quality control measures to catch potential problems; no in-house monitoring was done. In accordance with the original outsourcing plan, the entire technical services operation was contracted to an outside vendor. The volume of fully cataloged and processed titles ranged from 30 to 35 per month and the annual cost was about $10,000.

The presence of Cassidy's staff in the library during the cataloging effort for the retrospective collection and beyond was positive. The library's clerical staff depended on Cassidy's professional staff to answer questions concerning the handling and processing of material. Of equal importance, the library manager relied on Cassidy's staff as cataloging experts who consistently offered sound judgment and constructive opinions.

Another project goal was met because the outsourcing arrangement enabled the library's staff to focus on reference, research, and other administrative projects. The library's outsourcing project also established a standard for the other departmental libraries at Chubb. Three departments joined the catalog outsourcing project, and their collections are processed by Cassidy's staff in the same manner as the Law & Business Library's collection has been managed. In addition, because unique location identifiers are attached to each record in Chubb's union online catalog, patrons are able to determine where a specific title is held among the different cataloged collections within the company's headquarters.

From the beginning, Cassidy's staff maintained the library's records in LC MARC (machine-readable cataloging) format, a factor that at first appeared to be desirable, but not strictly necessary. Library staff quickly gained an appreciation for the importance of the LC MARC standard, as the online catalog migrated through three unique software packages in five years. The software migrations did not create extra work for the library's staff, because there was no need to correct or modify catalog records before loading them into the new software programs. In all instances, Cassidy's staff generated an updated snapshot of the library's LC MARC file for uploading to the new software. It is expected that future software changes will be handled in the same manner.

Since the inception of this outsourcing project in 1990, disaster planning for companies and libraries has been stressed in the professional literature. The general recommendation is for libraries to store up-to-date tape copies of their catalogs off-site for insurance and reconstruction purposes. A bonus of this library's outsourcing arrangement is that Cassidy's staff maintain and update the catalog database off-site, automatically satisfying the company's disaster recovery plan.

Client/Consultant Relationship

The long-term outsourcing relationship with Cassidy has been beneficial in providing the library's staff with cataloging expertise, as well as advice and advocacy on various administrative and operational matters. Because Cassidy's staff are familiar with the library's physical layout, they are able to understand the library staff's questions and offer alternative suggestions for placement of selected material. Additionally, the vendor's staff have advised the library manager on catalog database management software selections, as decisions in this area needed to be made.

Cassidy's managers have served as an interface to software vendors in several ways throughout the relationship. One of these efforts pertained to the issue of providing access to the library's catalog on Chubb's LAN. Cassidy's managers attempted to persuade the vendor of MOLEhill, the library's first database management system, to make that product compatible with a network environment. When that failed, Cassidy's staff advised the library manager in the choice of LAP's Assistant, the second database management system, which enabled library staff and Chubb's departmental staff to access the catalog from a LAN server.

In another instance, after the LAP's Assistant product was acquired by Data Trek, Cassidy's staff again acted as an advocate on the library's behalf. In the library's agreement with the previous vendor, there was no charge for record conversion during software migration. Cassidy's managers successfully lobbied to maintain this term in the Data Trek agreement. Consequently, a new, updated tape of the library's database was supplied to Data Trek for software migration at no charge.

An outsourcing vendor can provide added value to the outsourcing contract, as in these examples of interfacing with software vendors, throughout the life of a long-term relationship with a special library. A large number of special libraries consist of one-person operations, in terms of their professional staffing, and that individual's expertise often does not fall into the technical services area. By outsourcing technical services activities in these settings, the vendor becomes responsible for ensuring the orderly processing of new material and the quality of a library's catalog. Outsourcing all aspects of the cataloging operation, including ongoing maintenance of the catalog database, also releases time for library staff to concentrate on research and administrative details.

Organizational Changes
and New Developments

Two significant operational changes occurred since the outsourcing program was established. The library's name changed during the last quarter of 1991 to the Chubb Law & Business Library, with a concurrent new mission to provide resources and services to Chubb's business staff, as well as to the company's legal staff. The library's staffing formula also stabilized, with a total of four (1 FTE) employees. One part-time professionally trained business librarian and two part-time clerical staff were added. Each of these staff members was hired before 1994. In spite of the staffing increase, however, the library's staff have not had time for technical services work. The increased amount of reference and research projects, as a result of the library's new focus, required as much public-service time and resources as when the smaller staff served only the General Counsel Department.

Modification of the Outsourcing Program

In 1994, the library manager was informed that the outsourcing budget had to be severely reduced or eliminated, as part of an overall drive to curtail departmental expenses. The perception among Chubb's administrative staff was that the library's staff should be able to maintain the library's catalog database in-house. With regard to the small, departmental libraries elsewhere in the firm, the expectation was that these collections would be maintained independently.

The library manager was seriously concerned about preserving the integrity and continuity of the existing catalog database and wanted to continue to use Cassidy's staff for database maintenance only. A compromise was reached in which the annual outsourcing expense would not exceed $3,000. This budgetary limitation required library staff to reduce the amount of work performed by Cassidy's staff by approximately $7,000 per year. The small, departmental libraries are being handled by Cassidy's staff either on a full-service or a reduced service basis, depending on the direct negotiations between those department managers and Cassidy.

To accomplish this goal, library staff in 1994 assumed responsibility for all physical processing of new material and all labeling and physical maintenance of older material. Cassidy's staff continue to perform cataloging and database maintenance as part of this new agreement. The immediate impact of this contract modification was the elimination of the full-service aspect of the outsourcing arrangement, which had been in place since the inception of outsourcing.

As is the nature of compromises, there are disadvantages in the new outsourcing scheme. The library's clerical staff member now responsible for physical processing can no longer perform as many public services tasks. The library manager has also been required to devote time to technical services issues on a regular basis, in order to advise the clerical assistant on certain matters. The new budgetary restrictions do not provide adequate funds for cataloging all new material as it arrives, requiring the library manager to decide which titles require priority handling and which can be held for later processing.

A backlog developed immediately following the contract modification with Cassidy, since a certain amount of new material has remained uncataloged in order to hold outsourcing costs at fixed monthly allocations. This backlog, consisting of 25 percent to 30 percent of the new and revised titles, has not disappeared since 1994.

The reduced level of outsourcing services also required that a new circulation procedure be established for uncataloged material, since those purchases were often requested by staff who wanted access to the material immediately after it arrived in the library. Uncataloged titles are kept in a staff area and an order file is maintained. If a patron wants to check out an uncataloged title, a photocopy is made of the title page, the patron's name is noted on it, and the photocopy takes the place of the book on the shelf. Maintaining a reliable record is paramount.

Although overall service to patrons has not declined in this backlog environment, the level of frustration about the backlog on the part of library staff has increased. On a positive note, cataloging and database maintenance remain in the hands of fully qualified catalogers, and the integrity of the catalog and cataloging standards have been maintained.

Conclusion

Library staff have experienced a successful and ongoing relationship with the outsourcing contractor, Cassidy Cataloguing Services, Inc. From a business perspective, the library staff's need for an up-to-date catalog of its holdings, without requiring time from existing staff responsibilities for this effort, has been met. Cataloging standards were established for the library and were adopted by other participating departmental libraries within the company's headquarters as well. The library's catalog is available on Chubb's LAN, and migrations through several software database management systems have been completed with ease. Library staff also operate in full compliance with Chubb's disaster recovery requirements, in terms of maintaining a current machine-readable copy of their catalog database at an off-site facility. Furthermore, outsourcing costs for current cataloging have been contained by training library staff to perform physical processing duties, which were formerly managed as part of the full-service arrangement with Cassidy.

The library's outsourcing program began in 1990. Four years later, in 1994, the American Association of Law Libraries' Private Law Libraries Special Interest Section published cataloging guidelines for law libraries. One of those guidelines stated that "the cataloging function in small, medium and large libraries should be performed or managed by an on-staff degreed librarian *or* [emphasis added] through a qualified cataloging service" (AALL 1994, 195). To its credit, the Chubb Law & Business Library was already in full compliance with this guideline and had been for some time, as a consequence of its outsourcing program with Cassidy.

Work Cited

American Association of Law Libraries (AALL). Private Law Libraries Special Interest Section. 1995. Guidelines for technical services in private law libraries: Text, survey, results, commentary. In *Managing the Private Law Library 1995: Affecting the Bottom Line.* New York: Practising Law Institute, 193–210.

16 Outsourcing Becomes Insourcing: Cataloging Ephemeral Trade Literature at the Indiana Historical Society Library

Ellen Crosby

Staff at the William Henry Smith Memorial Library of the Indiana Historical Society (IHS) have used two outsourcing methods for cataloging their collection of trade literature pamphlets published by Indiana businesses. A short-term arrangement for off-site original cataloging of over 250 pamphlets was completed in 1995 by the Indiana Cooperative Library Services Authority (INCOLSA). Also in 1995, library staff hired a local cataloger on a part-time, temporary basis, for on-site cataloging. INCOLSA's staff provided original cataloging and physical processing services at a rate of slightly less than 30 minutes per title. The temporary cataloger performed cataloging alone at a rate of slightly more than 30 minutes per title. The quality of cataloging from both sources fully met the library's standards. Among the advantages of using the second approach, however, was that the in-house cataloger was able to produce significantly more titles per month than INCOLSA's staff could. Outsourcing and insourcing demonstrated the value of using contractors for technical services work on a project-oriented basis. The net result was additional funding for ongoing support of the part-time, temporary position.

During the 1990s, staff at the William Henry Smith Memorial Library of the Indiana Historical Society (IHS), located in Indianapolis, Indiana, have concentrated on developing their collection of trade literature published by Indiana businesses. As a historical resource, according to the library's curator of printed collections, "trade catalogs are indispensable not only to the study of business, but also to research in other areas, such as consumerism, artifact study and dating, architectural history, and fashion history" (Darbee 1996, 1). These pamphlets constitute a significant intellectual and historical resource. However, only a portion of the collection was cataloged by 1994, because the rate of acquisition had far outpaced the rate of cataloging over the years.

When surplus funds were available in the library's budget at the end of FY 1993/94, library staff used that money in 1995 to contract for original cataloging and physical processing of pamphlets with Indiana's state-supported library service provider. Although this initial project had advantages and disadvantages, library staff acquired valuable experience in outsourcing, which was applied toward a second, in-house contract cataloging project in 1995. The result was that outsourcing, and the subsequent insourcing program, reduced the pamphlet cataloging backlog by 1,051 items as of June 1996.

Background

The Indiana Historical Society is a private, nonprofit, educational organization with a mission to collect, preserve, interpret, and disseminate material pertaining to the history of Indiana and the Old Northwest. The library's collection includes approximately 65,000 print items; 3,500 manuscript and archival collections; 1.5 million photographs; and several thousand maps, broadsides, videorecordings, microfilms, and artifacts.

Collection development librarians have targeted the business history of the state as a focal point, and curators have acquired corporate archives and ephemeral publications as part of this plan. While some libraries have only uncataloged, vertical-file access to trade literature, the policy at Smith Library is to provide full cataloging for each item, with authority control over corporate names and subject headings. Because few libraries have acquired or cataloged this material, almost every item requires original cataloging. Because of the cataloging backlog, however, much of Indiana's business and industrial history remains inaccessible to researchers.

Smith Library does not have an online catalog. Catalog cards are purchased from the Online Library Computer Center (OCLC) and are filed in a standard dictionary catalog, as well as in specialized files. One example of a specialized file is the library's printer/publisher catalog. In order to document the history of printing and publishing in Indiana, a separate catalog houses cards with the names of all Indiana entities that have been responsible for publishing or printing material represented in the library's collection.

The library's pamphlet collection consists of material in all shapes and sizes. To maintain items in the best possible physical condition, each item is encased in a sleeve made of acid-free, 10-point card stock. The sleeve protects the item from abrasion when it is placed in a larger, acid-free storage envelope. Each envelope is labeled with an item's call number, author, and title. Envelopes are stored flat inside one of three sizes of shallow, covered boxes, depending on the size of each item. Items are arranged in call-number sequence.

The Cataloging Department has one full-time cataloger for print material, a half-time cataloger for manuscripts, a three-quarter-time clerical assistant, and the head of cataloging. Approximately 25 percent of the head of cataloging's time is devoted to cataloging special-format items, including maps, photographs, and microfilm. In 1994–95, staff prepared 923 original cataloging records and processed 1,435 copy cataloging records. By mid-1996, Cataloging Department staff had also nearly completed a retrospective conversion project for approximately 11,000 titles, using the OCLC database, while simultaneously reclassifying from the Dewey Decimal Classification to Library of Congress Classification.

The library's staffing budget has not benefited from the addition of any new positions during the 1990s, and efforts to increase part-time positions to full time have met with little success. Therefore, when an unexpected year-end budget surplus occurred in September 1994, the head of cataloging made a proposal to use the funds to reduce the pamphlet collection's cataloging backlog.

Outsourcing Project with INCOLSA

At the outset, library staff were uncertain of the best strategy for cataloging pamphlets in the backlog. Outsourcing with OCLC's TECHPRO service was considered, but either original material or surrogates would have to be shipped to Dublin, Ohio, for cataloging. Because the library's curator of printed collections was reluctant to ship pamphlets out of the state, surrogates seemed the only option. The pamphlets are quite fragile, however, and photocopying them to create surrogates was not an acceptable solution.

Another alternative was to contract with an agency closer to home. The Indiana Cooperative Library Services Authority (INCOLSA), also located in Indianapolis, was identified as a local source for cataloging and processing services. The head of cataloging developed a detailed proposal for outsourcing pamphlet cataloging to INCOLSA and submitted it to the library's director and IHS's administrative director.

Outsourcing Objectives

The outsourcing project proposal contained the following objectives:

- Use off-site contract catalogers for selected material, allowing more time for the library's staff to catalog items that could not leave the premises.

- Secure cataloging quality from INCOLSA's catalogers that would meet the high standards of accuracy expected of the library's in-house catalogers.

- Have INCOLSA's catalogers use IHS's OCLC identification number, to ensure that original catalog records added by INCOLSA's staff to the OCLC database would be credited to Smith Library's OCLC account and reduce the library's overall cataloging costs. This cost savings was later viewed by IHS's administrators as an asset, since the library would receive credit from OCLC for each original record input by INCOLSA's staff.

Contractual Agreement

The proposal for the outsourcing project was not without potential disadvantages. Nevertheless, the head of cataloging was able to identify a contractual agreement or reasonable tradeoff for each of the following disadvantages or problems:

- Library material would be stored and handled off-site for cataloging. After an on-site evaluation of INCOLSA's facilities by library staff, the curator of printed collections and the library's Conservation Department staff concluded that INCOLSA's staff would be able to provide acceptable security and an appropriate environment for storage of in-process material. The curator and IHS's conservator agreed that only pamphlets that were in stable physical condition would be shipped off-site for cataloging. In addition, INCOLSA's catalogers were willing to be trained in safe handling practices for rare and fragile material.

- Because Smith Library's staff use a card catalog, INCOLSA's catalogers did not have online access to the library's shelflist file and there was no easy way to verify if call numbers were unique. It was initially thought that communication via the Internet or OCLC's Save File could be used to verify the accuracy of newly assigned call numbers before records were produced.

- When spine and pocket labels are typed at the library for pamphlet storage envelopes, a list of new pamphlets also is created for the Conservation Department staff's use in their condition-survey database.

This survey documents the physical condition of each item that is added to the library's collection. INCOLSA's catalogers used surplus OCLC labels to create the condition-survey list, thereby satisfying that requirement as well.

Once these issues were resolved, a letter of agreement, a budget, and an outsourcing evaluation plan were developed for project implementation. It was agreed that Cataloging Department staff would supply INCOLSA's staff with pamphlets that required original cataloging only, based on pre-catalog searches of the OCLC database before each shipment. Cataloging staff were scheduled to deliver 25 to 50 pamphlets per month to INCOLSA. Although no monthly quotas or turnaround time standards were established, the contract specified that INCOLSA's staff would attempt to catalog one pamphlet per hour. Because both parties anticipated that this production rate might be difficult to achieve, it was also agreed that quality of cataloging was a higher priority than speed.

In order to expend the surplus funds before the end of FY 1993/94, the funds were transferred to a deposit account established with INCOLSA. INCOLSA's managers agreed to provide regular statements of the balance remaining in the deposit account. The outsourcing budget was designed to cover 1,000 hours of cataloging, equal to an estimated total of 1,000 pamphlets, at the rate of $10.20 per hour. Funds were also designated for 1,000 label sets, at the rate of $.14 per set. Each set contained two envelope labels and a label for the conservation list. The budget also included mileage reimbursement funds for automobile transportation costs that would be incurred while transporting pamphlets to INCOLSA.

Outsourcing Project Implementation

The library's Conservation Department staff identified pamphlets stable enough for off-site use and trained INCOLSA's catalogers in handling this material. A precise inventory was maintained of items shipped to INCOLSA, and the library's staff prepared a list of accession numbers and pamphlet titles for inclusion in each shipment. INCOLSA's catalogers later supplied corresponding call numbers and the dates on which OCLC catalog cards were produced, by adding that information in appropriate places on the inventory sheets.

Cataloging staff provided INCOLSA's catalogers with the Smith Library's cataloging policy and procedure manual. The manual explains the various added-entry procedures required for creating extra cards for the different catalogs, as well as local practices for selecting call numbers and subject headings. Catalogers at both agencies agreed that the second level of cataloging description in the *Anglo-American Cataloguing Rules* (second edition, 1988 revision) would suffice. From the outset, the library's staff decided to monitor catalog records, in case additional subject headings might be warranted.

The initial negotiation specified that there would be frequent communication between the library's staff and INCOLSA's staff, in order to identify and resolve any policy or procedural questions and problems. After experimenting with various means of communicating about in-process records, the catalogers concluded that placing a telephone call was the easiest and most effective method of resolving problems.

A standard cataloging routine was developed by INCOLSA's staff. The INCOLSA cataloger would log on to OCLC, using the Smith Library's authorization and password, and enter new records in the IHS Save File. When a batch of records was ready, the cataloger would telephone the library's print material cataloger and supply the Save File numbers. The print material cataloger would verify that the call numbers assigned off-site did not conflict with records in the library's shelflist. Cuttering required close coordination, since staff at both locations were working on advertisements for the Studebaker Company. As a shelflisting tool, a holding card was filed in the browsing file (a classified catalog for all subjects, without regard to shelving location) to reserve each call number assigned to particular categories of publications. By consulting the browsing file, in-house catalogers could ensure that all Studebaker publications of different sizes and in different collection locations were classified consistently.

INCOLSA's catalogers produced catalog cards, prepared labels for pamphlet envelopes, completed accession sheets, and entered call numbers in pencil on the first page of each pamphlet. The extra label for each pamphlet was placed on a separate sheet of paper to create the condition-survey database. As cataloged pamphlets were returned to Smith Library, the cataloging assistant evaluated the accuracy of the physical processing at the same time as call numbers were checked. Catalog cards shipped from OCLC were filed according to standard procedures. The cards usually arrived before the books, but this sequence varied throughout the project.

Productivity

Cataloging production rates proved to be the most significant problem in the project. The initial contract specified that INCOLSA's staff would attempt to catalog one pamphlet per hour, but the actual cataloging rate averaged two pamphlets per hour. INCOLSA's staff were able to perform cataloging and physical processing for 21 pamphlets within 10.5 hours. For a variety of reasons unrelated to this project, however, INCOLSA's managers were not able to devote as many catalogers or hours to the project as had been expected during contract negotiations. Although the eventual productivity rate exceeded one pamphlet per hour, INCOLSA's staff were able to devote only six and one-half hours per week to this project. Consequently, the first shipment of 25 pamphlets was not completed for two months.

After five months of outsourcing at this production rate, it was obvious that INCOLSA's staff would not be able to catalog 1,000 pamphlets and expend the deposit funds before the end of FY 1994/95. Because IHS's administrators expressed concern about the status of the deposit account, the head of cataloging requested a partial refund and left only enough funds to cover work that was expected to be done by September 1995.

Outsourcing Results

The following results were achieved during the INCOLSA outsourcing project:

- *Productivity and Turnaround Time:* From January to September 1995, 253 original cataloging records and label sets for pamphlets were created in 117 hours. The average amount of time devoted to cataloging was 13 hours per month. Because this production rate was only half the amount of time expected for the project, the cataloging turnaround time was twice that anticipated by the library's staff.
- *Cataloging Quality:* Records produced by INCOLSA's catalogers fully met the standards established in the library's policy and procedure manual. Corrections were needed only for minor, specialized details in the library's cataloging and physical processing routines. In one case, this meant producing an extra card for Indiana imprints, even when there was no need for an added entry for the printer or publisher. No statistical data were collected for the number of changes made by library staff, because the few changes did not reflect negative performance by the vendor.
- *Impact on Library Operations and Staffing:* For each shipment of pamphlets to INCOLSA, the cataloging assistant had to select titles or subjects that would be easy to catalog as a single shipment. This process required the cataloging assistant to sort and identify like categories of material, including several years of advertising from the same company or catalogs from several product manufacturers in the same industry. The library's printed material cataloger also devoted approximately two hours per week to the task of verifying INCOLSA's call numbers.
- *Budget:* The INCOLSA project did not overrun the outsourcing budget, but the deposit account funds were not spent as quickly or as fully as expected.

- *Other Issues:* No significant problems occurred with regard to material loss, labeling, accession records, or shelflist and subject heading conflicts. Conservation staff also were satisfied with the ways in which fragile material was handled and the condition-survey database was maintained.

By the end of FY 1994/95, sizable funds remained on deposit with IN-COLSA, because their catalogers were not able to maintain the productivity level anticipated for the project. In the interim, library staff established an insourcing project with a contract cataloger, which showed more promise than the off-site INCOLSA project. Consequently, the INCOLSA effort ceased in September 1995, at which time the surplus deposit was returned to the library.

Outsourcing Becomes Insourcing

The surplus funds from the 1993–94 budget, refunded from INCOLSA's deposit account in September 1995, were used to fund a different pamphlet cataloging project at the same time as INCOLSA's staff were under contract. In this alternate approach to reducing the pamphlet cataloging backlog, a former library employee, with experience in pamphlet cataloging, was hired on an insourcing contract to catalog pamphlets on-site. A second round of negotiations between the library's staff and IHS's administration ensued with this proposal, because IHS's personnel guidelines did not permit this type of contract employment arrangement. Eventually, it was agreed that the contract cataloger could be hired as a part-time, temporary employee at 15 hours per week.

The most difficult challenge with this staffing configuration was identifying a work space in the library for the new cataloger. Because of the fragile nature of pamphlet material, it was not feasible for that individual to process the collection off-site. The cataloger also would not have been able to access cataloging tools, unless the work was performed at the library. To resolve this problem, a table in the library's public reading room was commandeered and reconfigured as a cataloging workstation.

Workflow procedures for the contract cataloger differed from those of the outsourcing agreement with INCOLSA. The library's cataloging assistant was required to perform OCLC searching and input new catalog records in the database, instead of having the contract cataloger perform those tasks. In addition, the Cataloging Department staff assumed responsibility for preparing labels and performing more physical processing work than was done for material outsourced to INCOLSA. As a tradeoff, the contract cataloger verified subject and name headings, as well as call numbers, since, unlike INCOLSA's staff, that individual had access to the library's browsing file and card catalog.

In addition to cataloging pamphlets, the contract cataloger participated in NACO (Name Authority Cooperative) training with other cataloging staff. Although this training enhanced the contract cataloger's authority work skills, the library's managers recognized that this activity could not easily have been added to the workload of an off-site contract cataloger.

Insourcing Results

The following results were achieved during the insourcing project:

- *Productivity and Turnaround Time:* From June to September 1995, the contract cataloger produced 360 original cataloging records, without label sets, in 203 hours. This contribution of approximately 90 original catalog records per month effectively doubled the library's Cataloging Department production rate. The contract cataloger completed the cataloging work only in slightly more than 30 minutes per title, whereas INCOLSA's staff required less than 30 minutes to produce a catalog record and label sets for one title. Although the contract cataloger was not as productive in terms of per-title processing time, the total time devoted to pamphlets cataloging increased to an average of 60 hours per month. INCOLSA's average monthly rate of cataloging time was only 13 hours. The contract cataloger's overall output was significantly higher within a relative time frame, because of this increased weekly cataloging activity.

- *Cataloging Quality:* Records produced by the contract cataloger fully met the standards established in the library's policy and procedure manual.

- *Impact on Library Operations and Staffing:* The high volume of cataloging produced by the contract cataloger dramatically increased the cataloging assistant's workload. There were more catalog cards to file each month, because of the larger output of work by the contract cataloger. Permanent staff also had to devote more time to searching and inputting OCLC records, as well as typing labels. More than four months were required to recover from the filing backlog and other backlogs that developed from June to September 1995, because of added work created by the contract cataloger.

- *Budget:* There was no difficulty expending the budget for the insourcing project. The contract cataloger maintained a steady work schedule, which enabled the library's staff to manage the insourcing budget effectively.

In addition to the contract cataloger's ability to maintain a high standard of cataloging while processing the pamphlet collection backlog, library staff benefited from having this work performed by an individual who had experience with the library's multiple files and procedures. The contract cataloger also had the advantage of ready access to reference tools and resources in the Smith Library and the Indiana State Library while performing authority work. The contract cataloging arrangement was a valuable contribution to the library as a whole as well. Library and IHS's administrators observed the value of appropriating money to hire outside staff for specific cataloging projects.

Due to the success of insourcing, the 15-hours-per-week temporary position was retained and funded in the 1995–96 budget. On the basis of a collection inventory conducted in June 1996, it is estimated that this cataloger could eliminate the pamphlet cataloging backlog by June 1998. The library's administrators are optimistic that funding will be available for this purpose.

In order to remedy the additional workload problems for permanent staff, which resulted from the high production rate of the contract cataloger during the initial contract, the Cataloging Department's workflow was evaluated in fall 1995. Work was redistributed among staff for better management of the increased volume of OCLC searching and inputting and catalog card filing generated by insourcing. Permanent staff absorbed the additional workload, thereby increasing the level of productivity among the entire cataloging staff.

Conclusion

For staff at the Smith Library, outsourcing and insourcing provided models for improving in-house work processes. The ongoing insourcing project with the contract cataloger has reduced the backlog of pamphlets for cataloging, and has provided an opportunity to redesign processing routines for increased efficiencies. Permanent staff are more productive as a consequence of insourcing. A small library also has benefited from the addition of a skilled and thoughtful employee who provides valuable perspectives on cataloging.

The insourcing cataloger now has more experience in applying NACO principles than other staff do, because her assignment requires establishing new corporate names on a regular basis. In May 1996, this cataloger was designated as the in-house NACO reviewer, with responsibility for reviewing other catalogers' records for accuracy before they are submitted for formal review.

Although outsourcing with INCOLSA was limited to a specific time frame and was not wholly successful, their catalogers' contributions decreased the pamphlet cataloging backlog to some degree. In addition, the library staff's opportunity to acquire experience in managing the INCOLSA outsourcing program was invaluable. The benefits of outsourcing as a management approach for addressing the pamphlet cataloging backlog also were successfully conveyed to administrators of the Indiana Historical Society during the INCOLSA project.

By using both INCOLSA's catalogers and the contract cataloger, library staff were able to expend the total technical services budget for 1993–94 for their own area. The outsourcing and insourcing proposals made it possible to use those funds for cataloging, when they might otherwise have been used by default to purchase equipment or furniture for other areas. In addition, a part-time, temporary position was retained for cataloging work after the initial year-end surplus funding for outsourcing activities was depleted. Most likely, this incremental increase in the staffing budget would not have been feasible without the achievements of the outsourcing and insourcing projects.

Work Cited

Darbee, Leigh. 1996. Business as usual: Trade literature as historical resource. *The Bridge: A Newsletter of the Indiana Historical Society* 2, no. 2: 1–2.

WORKS REFERENCED FREQUENTLY

The following standard tools are cited frequently in this book as key resources referenced by librarians in outsourcing proposals and contracts.

Dewey, Melvil. 1989. *Dewey Decimal Classification and Relative Index.* 20th ed. Edited by John P. Comaromi and assistant eds. Julianne Beall, Winton E. Matthews Jr., and Gregory R. New. Albany, N.Y.: Forest Press.

Gorman, Michael, and Paul Winkler, eds. 1967. *Anglo-American Cataloging Rules.* Chicago: American Library Association.

Gorman, Michael, and Paul Winkler, eds. 1988. *Anglo-American Cataloguing Rules.* 2d ed., revised. Prepared under the direction of the Joint Steering Committee for the Revision of AACR, a committee of the American Library Association, the Australian Committee on Cataloguing, the British Library, the Canadian Committee on Cataloguing, the Library Association, and the Library of Congress. Chicago: American Library Association.

Library of Congress. Subject Cataloging Division. *Library of Congress Classification.* Washington, D.C.: Cataloging Distribution Service, Library of Congress.

Library of Congress Rule Interpretations. 2d ed. 1989– . Washington, D.C.: Cataloging Distribution Service.

National Library of Canada. 1992. *Canadian Subject Headings.* 3d ed. Edited by Alina Schweitzer. Ottawa: National Library of Canada.

Marylou Colver

Checklists, Manuals, and Surveys

See also Library Case Studies for Ohio State University

American Library Association. Association for Library Collections and Technical Services. Commercial Technical Services Committee. 1995. *Outsourcing Cataloging, Authority Work, and Physical Processing: A Checklist of Considerations.* Edited by Marie A. Kascus and Dawn Hale. Chicago: American Library Association.

> This checklist is designed to assist librarians in collecting data to analyze their own situations, in order to make informed decisions about the options that best meet their individual needs. The list covers cataloging, authority processing, and physical processing, within the framework of the financial, partnership, and staff ramifications.

Ashley, Lowell. 1994. Outsourcing, cataloging costs, value of cataloging. AUTOCAT [autocat@ubvm.cc.buffalo.edu], January 25.

> Administrators need to weigh several factors before deciding how cataloging should be done in their own institutions. This article lists many considerations relating to the cost of cataloging, the value of cataloging, and approaches to cataloging, including outsourcing.

Bush, Carmel C., Margo Sasse, and Patricia Smith. 1994. Toward a new world order: A survey of outsourcing capabilities of vendors for acquisitions, cataloging and collection development services. *Library Acquisitions: Practice & Theory* 18, no. 4: 397–416.

> This spring 1994 survey of materials jobbers, cataloging agents, and library consortia discusses existing outsourcing capabilities, as well as those in development, to perform acquisition, cataloging, and collection development functions. Survey responses were synthesized into summaries for each type of outsourced service from each source. A copy of the survey is provided as an appendix.

Hirshon, Arnold, and Barbara A. Winters. 1996. *Outsourcing Library Technical Services: A How-to-Do-It Manual for Librarians.* New York: Neal-Schuman.

> Firsthand experience with outsourcing is shared by the authors. They used lessons acquired in outsourcing at Wright State University to formulate a how-to manual. This approach begins with process reengineering and proceeds through decision making, cost analysis, the RFP process, contract writing, and compliance monitoring. One chapter is devoted to the human factors involved in a decision to outsource. A diskette containing RFP specifications is also available.

Tan, Wendy. 1996. Resources guide for outsourcing cataloging. AUTOCAT [autocat@ubvm.cc.buffalo.edu], March 1.

> This resource guide covers cataloging agencies and book jobbers. Some background is provided for the cataloging agencies that have been included. The book jobber section lists only selected companies; no background or information on their services is furnished. The guide is not comprehensive, but this information is a useful starting point.

General Articles

Alley, Brian. 1993. Reengineering, outsourcing, downsizing, and perfect timing. *Technicalities* 13, no. 11: 1, 8.

> Prompted by Wright State University's decision to contract for all cataloging of approximately 21,000 new titles a year, this editorial applauds the decision as one whose time has come. The convergence of reduced library budgets, advances in telecommunications, and OCLC's (Online Computer Library Center) capabilities have created a climate that is right for outsourcing.

Baker, Barry B. 1997. Outsourcing and technical services. In *Computers in Libraries '97. Proceedings.* Medford, N.J.: Information Today.

> The business world has used reengineering and outsourcing as tools for some time and, without always using the same terminology, so have libraries. In the 1990s, as libraries struggle with limited resources, they need to design improved workflows—or reengineer. Also, further curtailing of resources is causing libraries to look to outsourcing solutions. Baker urges librarians to focus on goals but to be creative and open to other approaches when dealing with limited resources.

Berry, John, Susan DiMattia, and Wilda Williams. 1995. Outsourced, downsized, and gun shy. *Library Journal* 120, no. 13: 42–43.

> This report from the Special Library Association Conference in June 1995 notes that special libraries are faced with both internal downsizing and outsourcing of library services. In response, librarians are reexamining what they do, plus how to market and promote their services internally.

CannCasciato, Daniel. 1994. Tepid water for everyone? The future OLUC, cat-alogers, and outsourcing. *OCLC Systems and Services* 10, no. 1: 5–8.

If all library managers were to follow Wright State University's lead to outsource all cataloging, there would not be any catalogers to contribute to and maintain the OCLC database. The author's solution to this dilemma is for librarians to outsource all copy cataloging to OCLC and then to con-centrate cataloging staff's efforts on maintaining the OCLC database and contributing original cataloging to OCLC.

Dunkle, Clare B. 1996. Outsourcing the catalog department: A meditation in-spired by the business and library literature. *Journal of Academic Librari-anship* 22, no. 1: 33–44.

Outsourcing of business information systems (IS) and outsourcing of cataloging in libraries have many similarities. Based on the literature of both worlds, parallels between the two are drawn and explored. Both IS and cataloging are, arguably, viewed as non-core activities and precisely the typical candidates for outsourcing. The distinction is made between to-tal and selective outsourcing. Selective outsourcing has been, and will most likely continue to be, a useful tool. Total outsourcing is a major step with long-term ramifications that managers must weigh carefully.

Dwyer, Jim. 1995. From PromptCat to recat, or, you only catalog twice. *Tech-nicalities* 15, no. 5: 4.

One outsourcing alternative, OCLC's PromptCat, is discussed with emphasis on the need for Cataloging-in-Publication (CIP) data to be com-pleted by book vendors to make PromptCat a viable service. If librarians need to upgrade 50 percent to 80 percent of records they receive, it de-feats the advantages of the product.

Dwyer, Jim. 1994. Does outsourcing mean "you're out?" *Technicalities* 14, no. 6: 1, 6.

In this reaction to Intner's article, "Outsourcing: What Does It Mean for Technical Services," (see below) Dwyer argues for outsourcing of se-lective drudgery, such as book processing and cataloging of approval books. This allows more time for higher-level tasks, such as authority con-trol, catalog cleanup, and public services. Dwyer notes that outsourcing can be a means to improve the everyday life of library staff.

Epstein, Susan Baerg. 1991. Streamlining costs with technology. *Library Journal* 116, no. 9: 62–63.

Library funding has always been cyclical. When funding is restricted, there are opportunities to examine what and how library operations are performed. Technical services is an easy target for study, because the ac-tivity is quantifiable. Costs, however, should be examined across the li-brary. Decisions resulting from these studies must be made with the ultimate goal, access to information, in mind. Last, the author states that it does not make sense to do something well, if it should not be done at all.

Fecko, Mary Beth. 1996. The changing face of cataloging: The impact of tech-
nology on copy cataloging, part II: A report of the ALCTS Copy Cataloging
Discussion Group Meeting. American Library Association Conference,
Chicago, June 1995. *Technical Services Quarterly* 13 (3/4): 109–15.

Representatives from Colorado State University, Central Michigan
University, and the University of Virginia addressed the impact of technology on copy cataloging operations. In all three situations, the copy cataloging process was examined from the standpoint of staffing, cost,
workflow, quality control, and timeliness. The unanimous conclusion was
to reevaluate the copy cataloging status quo to achieve improved results.

Gorman, Michael. 1995. The corruption of cataloging. *Library Journal* 120, no.
15: 32–34.

Gorman issues a plea against the current outsourcing target: the trend
to dismantle catalog departments and eliminate catalogers. Catalogers, as
bibliographic controllers and mappers, are viewed as essential to the *rai-
son d'être* of libraries—access to information. Outsourcing produces dam-
aging results not only within the library, but also within the general library
community, threatening progress toward universal bibliographic control.
The ones who could make this a reality are being dismissed. We are also
cheating the future out of those best qualified to organize access to the
wealth of unruly information on the Internet.

Gorman, Michael. 1994. Innocent pleasures. In *The Future Is Now: The Changing Face of Technical Services.* Dublin, Ohio: OCLC Online Computer Library Center, 39–42.

Catalogs have a simple purpose: connecting library users with material they want. Although the role of catalogers is changing, it is a change
that results in more jobs with paraprofessional status instead of professional. One contribution of catalogers is in the area of Universal Bibliographic Control (UBC). UBC is the concept that items should be cataloged
one time only and that the results should be shared worldwide. Another
important job that remains for catalogers is the bibliographic control of
electronic documents. Gorman sees the future of librarians as controlling
computer resources, as opposed to computers replacing librarians.

Harmon, Joseph C. 1996. The death of quality cataloging: Does it make a difference for library users? *The Journal of Academic Librarianship* 22, no. 4:
306–7.

The quality of cataloging directly affects access. As cataloging standards are lowered to save costs, the concomitant loss of access is not offset by the search capabilities of the library's local system. "No machine,
no matter how advanced, can extract data that are not there." Today's cost-
savings and cataloging shortcuts may have dramatic, negative consequences, and it will be difficult, at best, to recover the loss.

Holt, Glen. 1995. Catalog outsourcing: No clear-cut choice. *Library Journal*
120, no. 15: 34.

Many questions are raised in this half-page column about outsourcing of cataloging. Outsourcing may be a useful tool, but it is not a panacea. Outsourcing brings answers, as well as its own set of problems.

Holt, Glen. 1994. Public library cataloging and technical services: Changing work because of computers and networks. In *The Future Is Now: The Changing Face of Technical Services.* Dublin, Ohio: OCLC Online Computer Library Center, 21–27.

Two major changes are taking place in public library information access. One change is the transformation from automated catalogs to networked information search platforms. The other change is the need to find ways to increase productivity of technical services staff because of rising personnel costs. The combination of these two changes heralds an opportunity for technical services librarians to work along with public services librarians and computer programmers to develop new ways to provide access to information.

Hopkins, Judith. 1992. The ALCTS Commercial Technical Services Costs Committee. *Cataloging & Classification Quarterly* 15, no. 1: 106–9.

The committee focused on two aspects of library/vendor data exchange at the 1991 ALA annual convention program. Lynne Okonek, Cleveland Public Library, addressed cost savings realized by using the Data Research Associates' Library of Congress (LC) MARC (machine-readable cataloging) bibliographic database for a cataloging source, as an alternative to a bibliographic utility. Marsha Hamilton, Ohio State University, described tape loading of bibliographic and financial data from book vendors. Elaine Henjum, Florida Center for Library Automation, talked about authority control costs and questions to consider when selecting an authority vendor. Patricia Thomas, Stockton–San Joaquin Public Library, also addressed authority control issues.

Intner, Sheila S. 1994. Outsourcing: What does it mean for technical services? *Technicalities* 14, no. 3: 3–5.

The word "outsourcing" may be new, but the concept is not. Librarians have been outsourcing for nearly 100 years. However, the targets for outsourcing, and the degree to which outsourcing is being used, have changed. Current and future possibilities relating to technical services, serials, and acquisitions activities are explored by the author.

Kresge, Lynda S. 1997. ALCTS hosts forums on outsourcing at midwinter. *ALCTS Newsletter* 8 (2): 17, 20.

This is a brief report on two ALCTS outsourcing programs held at the ALA 1996 midwinter conference. One program entitled "Outsourcing Technical Services: The Selection Process" was a panel discussion by librarians from both libraries and vendors. The second panel's topic was "Changing Relationships among Publishers, Vendors, and Librarians in an Age of Outsourcing: Whose Job Is It Anyway?" and it included book vendors, subscription agents, publishers, and book reviewers.

Marcum, James W. 1997. "Outsourcing" at LITA/LAMA. *Library Administration & Management* 11 (2): 123–24.

> At the spring 1997 LITA/LAMA conference in Pittsburgh, outsourcing was the subject of two sessions and two roundtable discussions. A variety of speakers involved in outsourcing projects underscored issues, pitfalls, and rewards. The final discussion centered on the prospect of outsourcing the entire library function. The general consensus was that librarians have repeatedly faced major challenges in the past and the way to keep professional control is to look for ways to achieve major cost savings and to maintain core competencies.

Martin, Murray S. 1995. Outsourcing. *The Bottom Line: Managing Library Finances* 8, no. 3: 28–30.

> The rush to outsourcing or privatization may be the case of finding the answer before asking the question. Librarians, however, have taken advantage of privately operated services where these fit with their libraries' goals. Librarians are expected to continue outsourcing as long as they know that outsourcing brings them the most results for the money.

Miller, William. 1995. Outsourcing: Academic libraries pioneer contracting out services. *Library Issues: Briefings for Faculty and Administrators* 16, no. 2: 1–4.

> Miller offers an overview of outsourcing, as it has related to libraries in the past 100 years and as it is currently being viewed. Outsourcing is necessary to fulfill the obligations of academic librarians to operate efficiently with fewer resources, but it will probably stop short of contracting out the entire operation of the library.

Outsourcing cataloging expedites handling of special formats, benefits small libraries. 1995. *Action for Libraries* 21, no. 2: 1–2.

> Librarians who are under pressure to reduce costs and accomplish more with current or fewer staff are turning to outsourcing for all or a portion of cataloging. The OCLC network, Bibliographic Center for Research (BCR), provides contract cataloging for all material, including foreign languages. The benefits of outsourcing are fast turnaround, low error rates, and cost containment. When catalog records are uploaded to OCLC, they are a benefit to the library community, in terms of interlibrary loan and cooperative cataloging.

Renaud, Robert. 1997. Learning to compete: Competition, outsourcing, and academic libraries. *The Journal of Academic Librarianship* 23 (2): 85–90.

> The future of academic libraries will be shaped by competition from new sources such as other campus units and the private sector. Librarians have traditionally viewed themselves as noncompetitors. Renaud takes precepts from modern competition theory and applies them to academic libraries. Librarians need to understand the barriers to entering new markets and to exiting old markets. Outsourced activities need to be done at

a lower cost and they need to link seamlessly with existing library operations. Tasks that can remain in the library should be viewed as the source for competitive advantage.

Rider, Mary M. 1996. Developing new roles for paraprofessionals in cataloging. *The Journal of Academic Librarianship* 22 (1): 26–32.

Roles for paraprofessionals in the cataloging departments of academic libraries are expanding to include subject heading and call number assignment which have typically been done by professional librarians. Rider encourages paraprofessional staff training and development, expanded job responsibilities, and participation in professional organizations. Professional librarians will have more time to devote their expertise to achieving the goals of the library.

Ruschoff, Carlen. 1995. Cataloging's prospects: Responding to austerity with innovation. *The Journal of Academic Librarianship* 21, no. 1: 51–57.

This survey of the literature reveals how librarians have responded to the reality that technical services departments are caught in the vise of diminishing budgets. Simplification of standards, cooperative cataloging ventures, streamlining of operations, and artificial intelligence have been explored as possible solutions to alleviate the pressure on technical services operations.

Rush, James E. 1994. A case for eliminating cataloging in the individual library. In *The Future Is Now: The Changing Face of Technical Services.* Dublin, Ohio: OCLC Online Computer Library Center, 1–13.

Money spent on local cataloging is viewed as wasteful. This argument is supported by examples of repetitive cataloging by Palinet members. Catalog record examples are used to demonstrate that most local changes do not contribute to increased access for the library user. To the contrary, local modifications often result in the deletion of useful data from the record. Either way, local modifications are costly.

Smith, Patricia. 1994. Book vendor-supplied cataloging: Impacts for technical services. *Colorado Libraries* 20, no. 3: 14–16.

Smith provides an overview of the changing role of book vendors vis-à-vis outsourcing of technical services functions. Much progress has been made by vendors toward the realization of integrated acquisitions and cataloging processes. Even when this becomes a reality, technical services staff will be essential for the ongoing analysis and design processes, as well as for training other library staff members.

Varner, Carroll H. 1995. Outsourcing library production: The leader's role. In *Continuity & Transformation: The Promise of Confluence.* Proceedings of the Seventh National Conference of the Association of College and Research Libraries, Pittsburgh, Pennsylvania, March 29–April 1, 1995. Edited by Richard AmRhein. Chicago: Association of College and Research Libraries, American Library Association, 445–48.

When faced with outsourcing, the technical services subculture within the organized structure of academic libraries is presented with either an opportunity or a threat. The key for library leaders, when transforming the new technical services roles into a positive future, is in staff development, involvement, and training.

Wilson, Karen A. 1994. Vendor-supplied cataloging and contract cataloging services: A report of the ALCTS Creative Ideas in Technical Services Discussion Group. American Library Association. Midwinter Meeting. Los Angeles, February 1994. *Technical Services Quarterly* 12, no. 2: 60–63.

Five roundtable discussions were held on the subject of vendor-supplied services. The pros and cons of projects in process were reviewed. The consensus was that librarians need to work with vendors to improve outsourcing services. Librarians also need information on which to base cost analyses, in order to make informed decisions about the feasibility of outsourcing.

Woo, Christina. 1994. Is outsourcing on its way in? *CARL Newsletter* 17, no. 3: 4–5.

These brief notes report on a full-day program on outsourcing, featuring five speakers from a range of perspectives, including public and academic libraries and book and cataloging vendors. Outsourcing has its place, its pitfalls, and its advantages. The speakers related their experiences with all aspects.

Library Case Studies: Academic Libraries

California State University San Marcos

Herlihy, Catherine S. 1992. Bibliographic records: An experiment in buying DLC copy. *Technicalities* 12, no. 8: 11–15.

Creating access to an opening-day collection for a new library, with limited staff, was a challenge at California State University San Marcos. The library's book vendor, Academic Book Center, worked with MAR-CIVE, Inc. to obtain LC copy and book processing materials. The conclusion was that the advantages outweighed the disadvantages. The author encourages others to explore this alternative.

Colorado School of Mines

Stomberg, Lisa. 1996. The underutilization of government document collections: Can outsourcing provide access solutions? *Colorado Libraries* 22 (1) 42–43.

U.S. government depository libraries are faced with many issues in the management of the sheer volume of federal publications. The acquisition of documents is profile-driven and it requires only annual revisions. The cataloging of the materials is a much more labor-intensive task, but it is a necessary step in adding documents to the library's catalog. At Arthur Lakes Library, the solution was to outsource cataloging of GPO materials to MARCIVE. Bibliographic maintenance and authority control remain as concerns, but the outsourcing of cataloging will enable the library to provide improved access to the document collection.

Florida Gulf Coast University

Cook, Eleanor. 1997. ACQflash: Outsourcing in Florida. ACQNET [acqnet-l @listsserv.appstate.edu], January 16.

This is a listserv news release describing total outsourcing of all book purchasing and technical services for a new campus library of Florida Gulf Coast University. The University teamed with OCLC, Solinet, and Academic Book Center to acquire cataloging, bibliographic maintenance, retrospective conversion, authority control, and physical processing as well as an opening day collection, collection analysis, an ongoing approval plan, standing orders, and firm order services.

Front Range Community College, Larimer Campus

Dornseif, Karen. 1995. Outsourcing cataloging: An alternative for small libraries. *Colorado Libraries* 21, no. 1: 48–49.

The Larimer campus of the Front Range Community College was faced with limited space and staff. To handle a cataloging backlog of approximately 700 records, library staff contracted with their OCLC network, BCR. This arrangement proved to be successful and staff continued the contract for the outsourcing of ongoing cataloging. Bibliographic maintenance remains a problem, but all new material is added to the library's CARL online catalog and holdings are contributed to OCLC.

Loyola University Chicago

Two TECHPRO projects under way for Loyola University. 1994. *Information Today* 11, no. 10: 52.

Loyola University Chicago's staff established two special projects with OCLC's TECHPRO service. One was the cataloging of approximately 7,000 titles in a special religion and philosophy collection. The other project arose because library staff faced a rapidly increasing book budget, with no corresponding increase in staff. The library's book vendor, Academic Book Center, sent title slips to TECHPRO for the cataloging of approval books. This approach to outsourcing enabled the library's staff to meet their goal to have approval material on the shelf within 10 days of arrival.

Waite, Ellen J. 1995. Reinvent catalogers! *Library Journal* 120, no. 18: 36–37.

In this response to Gorman's "The Corruption of Cataloging" article (see p. 196), the author argues that outsourcing of cataloging at Loyola University Chicago serves the ultimate goal of ensuring that patrons receive the information they need. In terms of timeliness of cataloging, volume of cataloging, and the contribution to interlibrary loan resources, "perfect and precise" cataloging descriptions are not an issue that affects the library's mission. Both Gorman and Waite seem to agree that librarians are the ones capable of bringing the "electronic network" under control.

Michigan State University

See also Library Case Studies for Ohio State University
    Vendor Articles

Bazirjian, Rosann. 1995. ALCTS Automated Acquisitions/In-Process Control Systems Discussion Group. American Library Association Conference, Miami Beach, June 1994. *Technical Services Quarterly* 12, no. 4: 55–57.

Bazirjian offers a brief introduction to three speakers who address the topic of integrating vendor products and services into the automated acquisitions environment. Elizabeth Parang, University of Nevada Las Vegas, discusses how the library uses B. H. Blackwell's CONNECT and Yankee Book Peddler's FOLIO. Kay Granskog talks about Michigan State University's PromptCat pilot project, and Marda Johnson addresses PromptCat from OCLC's perspective.

Granskog, Kay. 1994. PromptCat testing at Michigan State University. *Library Acquisitions: Practice & Theory* 18, no. 4: 419–25.

This article outlines Michigan State University's positive experience with the prototype of OCLC's PromptCat service. A PromptCat test was conducted from October to December 1993, and included 2,764 titles for both approvals and firm orders supplied by Yankee Book Peddler. PromptCat was not priced, so the library could not evaluate its cost effectiveness. There was a high degree of accuracy in the match between the records delivered and the books received.

Hyslop, Colleen F. 1995. Using PromptCat to eliminate work: MSU's experience. *Library Acquisitions: Practice & Theory* 19, no. 3: 359–62.

Much of the information overlaps Granskog's article, but the emphasis in this article is on viewing PromptCat as a monograph check-in system. The problem that CIP records present to the workflow is raised. The benefits, in terms of volume of cataloging throughput by a reduced staff, bring the goal of monograph check-in one step closer to the library's serials check-in throughput statistics.

Hyslop, Colleen F. 1994. PromptCat prototype: Accelerating progress in technical services. In *The Future Is Now: The Changing Face of Technical Services.* Dublin, Ohio: OCLC Online Computer Library Center, 33–38.

Change in technical services is inevitable. It is best to acknowledge past accomplishments and then to participate in and shape changes. Original and copy cataloging procedures and sources will change, but the outsourcing trend will probably fall short of full privatization. Book vendors and bibliographic utilities, with services such as OCLC's PromptCat, will play an increasing role in cataloging.

Ohio State University

El-Sherbini, Magda. 1995. Contract cataloging: A pilot project for outsourcing Slavic books. *Cataloging & Classification Quarterly* 20, no. 3: 57–73.

This is an evaluation of a successful pilot project in which 100 Slavic titles were sent from Ohio State University to OCLC's TECHPRO service for contract cataloging. The first analysis was based on quality. Despite some errors, the records were considered acceptable because access points often were not affected. The second analysis was based on cost. The TECHPRO per-title cost was calculated to be $31.65, compared to $56.32 per title for in-house cataloging. The outsourcing cost does not include the library's staff time to research and correct errors made by TECHPRO's staff.

El-Sherbini, Magda. 1992. Cataloging alternatives: An investigation of contract cataloging, cooperative cataloging, and the use of temporary help. *Cataloging & Classification Quarterly* 15, no. 4: 67–88.

The author provides a report from Ohio State University Library on a 1991 project for cataloging of Korean and Greek material. An investigation of commercial vendors, cooperative arrangements with other libraries, and temporary assistance led OSU's staff to the conclusion that this project would best be served by a cooperative agreement with a library of similar size and background.

Rider, Mary M. 1995. PromptCat: A projected service for automatic cataloging—results of a study at The Ohio State University Libraries. *Cataloging & Classification Quarterly* 20, no. 4: 23–44.

Ohio State University, an OCLC PromptCat test site, uses Baker & Taylor, Inc. as their approval and firm order vendor. The emphasis of this evaluation is the accuracy of catalog record selection and editing. The library's staff recognize the trend to merge acquisitions and cataloging functions to save costs. The study divided two weeks of records into two groups. The results of the analysis are that the record selection was accurate and it was most often the record that would have been selected by library staff. One recommendation for making the service more viable was the upgrading of CIP records.

Rider, Mary M., and Marsha Hamilton. 1996. PromptCat issues for acquisitions: Quality review, cost analysis and workflow implications. *Library Acquisitions: Practice & Theory* 20, no. 1: 9–21.

Drawing on Ohio State University's (OSU) experience with Prompt-Cat, as well as Michigan State University's testing, considerations and guidelines for other users of the service are provided. OSU's rough estimates indicate that PromptCat may reduce copy cataloging costs by one third. For libraries to realize this cost savings and to maximize benefits of the service, it may be necessary to examine and perhaps redesign the internal workflow, as well as evaluate local editing practices. This internal review needs to be sensitive to staffing issues. Libraries also need to work with local systems and materials vendors to streamline the process. Although PromptCat is an OCLC product, the data originate with the materials vendor and they are destined for use in the library's local system. All must function well for a library's staff to successfully use PromptCat.

Stanford University

BGHDS956 Report: American Library Association Big Heads Meeting. 1995. AUTOCAT [autocat@ubvm.cc.buffalo.edu], July 26.

Two case studies on the why and how of reengineering are presented. Catherine M. Tierney, Stanford University Libraries, explained their redesign of technical services and the use of outsourcing as a method of reallocating organizational resources. William Gosling and Wendy Lougee, University of Michigan, discussed the emerging digital library.

Gozzi, Cynthia I. 1994. Technical processing, today and tomorrow: A scenario for one large research library. In *The Future Is Now: The Changing Face of Technical Services.* Dublin, Ohio: OCLC Online Computer Library Center, 28–32.

The way in which the technical processing environment has already changed at Stanford University, and possibilities for future changes, are examined. The influence of internal and external complexities is considered. Outsourcing is one element in the mix.

Propas, Sharon W. 1995. Ongoing changes in Stanford University Libraries technical services. *Library Acquisitions: Practice & Theory* 19, no. 4: 431–33.

This is an overview of a three-year project to reorganize technical services. The impetus for this reorganization is threefold: (1) save $750,000 in technical services for reallocation within the library; (2) divert funds to construct a new technical services building; and (3) create a model for the research library technical services operations of the twenty-first century. Reexamining workflow and outsourcing services, while involving staff in the process and avoiding layoffs, were primary goals of the planning process.

Stanford University Libraries. Redesign Team. 1995. *Redesigning the Acquisitions-to-Access Process: Final Report of the Stanford University Libraries Redesign Team.* Stanford: Stanford University Libraries. (http://www-sul.stanford.edu/depts/diroff/ts/redesign/redesign.html)

Stanford University's Redesign Team's goal was to save $750,000 by reengineering library procedures from the acquisitions-to-access processes. This document is a thorough and thoughtful analysis of the courses of action best suited to Stanford University Libraries. It can serve as a model for others faced with analyzing their operations in light of their own goals. The focus is on handling material as few times as possible and at the point in the workflow where it makes optimum sense. Vendor partnerships are one tool in accomplishing these objectives.

Wilson, Karen A. 1995. Outsourcing LC copy cataloging and physical processing: A review of Blackwell's outsourcing services for the J. Hugh Jackson Library at Stanford University. *Library Resources & Technical Services* 39, no. 4: 359–83.

This article offers an assessment of a one-year pilot project for outsourcing copy cataloging and physical processing supplied by Blackwell North America, Inc. and B. H. Blackwell, Ltd. A historical overview of outsourcing is provided as a background to the library's project. The quality of the vendors' cataloging and book processing were tracked and found to be equal to the library staff's output in terms of quality. The recycling of CIP records to match full records, and the effect of LC's error rate on the success of outsourcing, are also explored.

Texas A&M University

Kellough, Patrick H., and Christine E. Thompson. 1987. Network/library cooperative cataloging: The AMIGOS-Texas A&M experience. *Technicalities* 7, no. 5: 8–10.

In this 1986 project, the library sent two special collections to AMIGOS for cataloging and the provision of cards. Each collection, the Jeff Dykes Range Livestock and the Science Fiction Research, consisted of over 20,000 titles. Due to the valuable and fragile nature of the collections, AMIGOS's staff worked from photocopies of the title pages and versos. Contract cataloging, at the time this project was done, was a novel concept. The advantages of per-item cataloging costs, even with cleanup factored in, and the volume of cataloging completed per year, were clear advantages of outsourcing.

Tufts University

Block, Rick J. 1994. Cataloging outsourcing: Issues and options. *Serials Review* 20, no. 3: 73–77.

Before outsourcing, library staff must understand what outsourcing should accomplish. Electronic resources continue to grow, and cataloging expertise will continue to be needed to make these resources accessible. Project-based outsourcing definitely has a place, but librarians should analyze their situations thoroughly before implementing total outsourcing of technical services.

University of Alberta

Distad, Merrill, and Brian Hobbs. 1995. The client still ranks first in University of Alberta Library's restructuring. *Library Acquisitions: Practice & Theory* 19, no. 4: 435–38.

> A mandate to reduce the University of Alberta Library's operating budget by 20 percent by 1997 prompted a major restructuring of the organization. The plan did not rely on layoffs to achieve this goal. Instead, an emphasis was placed on outsourcing cataloging for shelf-ready books to Information Systems Management/Library Technical Services (ISM/LTS). Internal staff concentrate on cataloging gift and free material, as well as being reassigned to other library tasks, particularly in public services. Pros and cons of this restructuring are discussed.

Gibbs, Nancy J. 1994. ALCTS/Role of the Professional in Academic Research Technical Services Departments Discussion Group. *Library Acquisitions: Practice & Theory* 18, no. 3: 321–22.

> This report includes notes from the presentations by three speakers: Gary Shirk, Yankee Book Peddler; Keith Schmiedl, John Coutts Library Services; and Seno Laskowski, University of Alberta. The speakers presented views and shared outsourcing experiences. Outsourcing was a relatively new topic at the time, but the impact it would have was predicted by the participants in these discussions.

Martin, Murray S., and Ernie Ingles. 1995. Outsourcing in Alberta. *The Bottom Line: Managing Library Finances* 8, no. 4: 32–34.

> The University of Alberta entered into a public/private partnership with ISM/LTS and, together, a new MARC*ADVANTAGE* product was developed. ISM/LTS's staff provide cataloging for most material. Rare books along with Chinese-, Japanese-, Korean-, and other foreign-language materials were noted as exceptions at that time. The joint effort enabled the library's staff to respond to a sizable budget cut, without endangering the library's mission, service goals, or staff.

University of North Dakota

Harken, Shelby E. 1996. Outsourcing: Ready, set, go? A cataloger's perspective. *Cataloging & Classification Quarterly* 23 (2): 67–87.

> Lessons learned from relatively unsuccessful outsourcing projects at the University of North Dakota Library are expressed in sections labeled "Who," "What," "When," "Where," "Why," and "How." Points to consider before outsourcing and specifications to include in outsourcing contracts are mixed together in the sections. Harken emphasizes that quality must not be sacrificed because cataloging will be shared and redistributed. Librarians also can't afford not to do cataloging right the first time.

University of North Texas

Farkas, Doina. 1997. Outsourcing of AV cataloging at UNT libraries. *OLAC Newsletter* 17 (1): 24–26.

> Farkas begins by stating that outsourcing is not for every library and that it should be a local decision made by staff at individual libraries. Farkas describes a 1996 pilot project for outsourcing cataloging of audio-visual materials. Professional Media Services Corporation was selected to provide both the materials and the cataloging services. The 10 steps in the technical processing workflow during the pilot are outlined.

Wright State University

Doepker, Bonnie. 1996. Letter to the editor. *The Journal of Academic Librarianship* 22, no. 4: 308.

> A former Wright State Cataloging Department member uses Clare Dunkle's *JAL* January 1996 article as a springboard to launch her defense of Wright State staff during the early 1990s (before outsourcing). The focus is on external circumstances, such as system migration, merging of two university library cataloging departments, and loss of key personnel, as the cause of low productivity and low staff morale.

Hague, Dale. 1994. Outsourcing cataloging: A rational viewpoint. LIBADMIN [libadmin@umab.bitnet], January 21.

> Miami University Libraries (Ohio) participates in several cooperative endeavors with Wright State University Libraries, and the latter's decision to outsource all cataloging caused MUL's staff to evaluate this option. Outsourcing is not a panacea and, after careful consideration, it was decided that it is not the right choice for MUL.

Hirshon, Arnold. 1996. Letter to the editor. *The Journal of Academic Librarianship* 22, no. 5: 392.

> In this reply to Bonnie Doepker's letter to the editor of *JAL*, the focus is on three key points. Hirshon defends the decision not to publish Wright State's cost data because he believes that each institution's staff must conduct their own costs studies as a step in their decision-making process. The production rate of the cataloging staff is another important issue that Doepker and Hirshon do not see from the same perspective. Last, Hirshon maintains that organizational changes at Wright State were not unusual for an academic library in the 1990s. The organizational changes do not explain or excuse the cataloging staff's low rate of production. The staff members were certainly not incompetent, but the production situation did not improve and the solution is now history.

Hirshon, Arnold. 1994. The lobster quadrille: The future of technical services in a re-engineering world. In *The Future Is Now: The Changing Face of*

Technical Services. Dublin, Ohio: OCLC Online Computer Library Center, 14–20.

Reengineering is not about marginal productivity increases. It is a radical change of the entire process. "Why do we do what we do at all?" is the question that must be asked and answered. Outsourcing is a reengineering strategy. The short-term and long-term effects of reengineering technical services are discussed, including Wright State University staff's own outsourcing decision.

Hirshon, Arnold. 1994. Outsourcing cataloging: Reflections upon a rational viewpoint. LIBADMIN [libadmin@umab.bitnet], January 25.

This is a response to and elaboration on Hague's LIBADMIN message. The factors used in calculating cataloging costs and the necessity of setting a cost savings target, as well as working with one's administration to ensure that savings are reinvested in the library, are points emphasized in this response. Different solutions developed by librarians to achieve similar goals makes the profession richer. Hirshon does not advocate a procrustean approach.

Hirshon, Arnold. 1993. Cataloging outsourcing: Wright State Univ. response (Pt. 1 of 2). AUTOCAT [autocat@ubvm.cc.buffalo.edu], December 16.

The author provides part one of a two-part response issued by Hirshon and Karen Wilhoit, respectively, in reply to AUTOCAT listserv discussions regarding the decision to outsource all cataloging at Wright State University. It is incumbent on all librarians to maximize use of the fiscal resources with which they are entrusted and to continually improve library service. Outsourcing is only one solution, but it was the solution that fit Wright State University's situation.

Hirshon, Arnold. 1993. Wright State cataloging update. AUTOCAT [autocat@ ubvm.cc.buffalo.edu], December 8.

This brief update was written at the time when library staff in general were reviewing responses to Wright State's RFP for contract cataloging of all material. These comments were posted in response to an AUTOCAT message about how Wright State University's staff handled authority control and local cataloging decisions. As Hirshon states, authority control was not in the RFP and is handled separately in a batch mode. Local decisions are covered in the cataloging contract.

Hirshon, Arnold, Barbara Winters, and Karen Wilhoit. 1995. A response to "Outsourcing cataloging: The Wright State experience." *ALCTS Newsletter* 6, no. 2: 26–28.

In this joint response to David Miller's article (see below), and on behalf of several Wright State University staff members, the authors reiterate that outsourcing is not for every institution. It cannot also be said, however, that outsourcing is not for any institution. Reengineering raises issues that must be examined if individuals are to keep their libraries' future in their own hands.

Miller, David. 1995. Outsourcing cataloging: The Wright State experience. *ALCTS Newsletter* 6, no. 1: 7–8.

This is a report of a presentation by Barbara Winters, Wright State University, at the New England Library Association Conference in October 1994. The talk focused on the reasons leading to the decision to contract for all cataloging and authority work. The motivations were not purely based on the bottom line, since they encompassed unusually low cataloging productivity rates and low-quality output. An explanation of the reasons to outsource all work versus only a portion of it is included. As always, there is the caveat that this measure, although suited to Wright State University, may not fit the situation in other libraries.

Wilhoit, Karen. 1994. Outsourcing cataloging at Wright State University. *Serials Review* 20, no. 3: 70–73.

Wilhoit looks at the operational details and mechanics of outsourcing all cataloging, from the perspective of the head of bibliographic control at Wright State University. With cost cutting and service improvements as goals, outsourcing was clearly a success, but one not achieved easily.

Wilhoit, Karen. 1993. Cataloging outsourcing Wright State Univ. response (Pt. 2 of 2). AUTOCAT [autocat@ubvm.cc.buffalo.edu], December 16.

In this second part of a two-part response, the head of the Bibliographic Control Department at Wright State University addresses quality control and related matters. Twenty years ago, Wright State's staff made a decision to create brief records on OCLC. These records served a purpose, but they were also an Achilles' heel. With the recent decision to outsource all cataloging, the library's managers want to make it clear that all original cataloging now will follow national standards. Local modifications to records are specified in the cataloging contract. Authority control is outsourced under a separate agreement. The resultant records are designed to meet both local and national standards.

Winters, Barbara A. 1994. Cataloging outsourcing at Wright State University: Implications for acquisitions managers. *Library Acquisitions: Practice & Theory* 18, no. 4: 367–73.

Low productivity by Wright State University's cataloging staff, coupled with a 25 percent error rate and continued lack of improvement, served as the impetus for the decision to outsource all cataloging. The process to set this decision in motion is outlined by Winters. Pros, cons, and other thoughts on managing technical services operations, as inevitable changes reshape the library landscape, are examined.

Library Case Studies: Public Libraries

Atlanta–Fulton Public Library

Agnew, Grace. 1993. Contracting for technical services: Shelf-ready services for books. In *Against All Odds: Case Studies on Library Financial Manage-*

ment. Edited by Linda F. Crismond. Fort Atkinson, Wis.: Highsmith Press, 217–28.

> Expansion of the library facility, coupled with shrinking budgets and diminishing staff levels, formed the impetus for examining technical services operations. Goals were to increase efficiencies, release staff for other work, and implement technological innovations. Through the RFP process, Brodart was selected to provide cataloging and shelf-ready material. The project was a success, due to clearly communicated expectations, well-documented library procedures, and a responsive vendor.

Charleston County Library

Walker, Thomas M. 1996. Outsourcing: A customer's perspective on the process and the potential. *The Bottom Line: Managing Library Finances* 9, no. 2: 14–17.

> Charleston County Library in South Carolina began outsourcing in 1986. Brodart was selected to provide opening-day collections for a new main library and four branches. MARC catalog records with embedded item information and physical processing were part of the outsourcing agreement. When Hurricane Hugo destroyed two community libraries, another project was implemented with Book Wholesalers, Inc. (BWI) to supply replacement titles. Physical processing, and the addition of copy level data directly into the library's DRA database via a modem connection, was provided by BWI. The "can" and the "should" of outsourcing library operations in general are explored. Pilot projects are recommended as the best way to evaluate value-added services.

Hawaii State Public Library System

ACQNET. [serial online] Boone, N.C.: Eleanor Cooke, no. 1 , 1990– .

> ACQNET (Acquisitions Librarian's Electronic Network) and ACQ-FLASH (time-sensitive postings from ACQNET) have been forums for much of the discussion on Hawaii's outsourcing program. To subscribe, send the following electronic mail message to: listserv@lester.appstate.edu: sub acqnet-l [first name last name].

Donnelly, Christine. 1997. Library books deal a "disaster." *Honolulu Star-Bulletin* January 9: 1, 9. http://starbulletin.com/97/01/09/news/index.html

> This is a local press report on the Hawaii State Library contract with Baker & Taylor for book selection. The opposing viewpoints on the issue of outsourcing book selection are personified by Pat Wallace representing those against the decision and by Bart Kane, Hawaii State Librarian, defending his position.

Farmanfarmaian, Roxane. 1997. Hawaii libraries vs. Baker & Taylor: Better times ahead? *Publishers Weekly* 244 (9): 16.

A 50 percent budget cut engendered the state librarian's decision to outsource book selection with Baker & Taylor. The urgency of the situation precipitated implementation before any of the groundwork such as selection profiles and database access was laid. The performance complaints can be seen as stemming from the startup situation rather than from any inherent flaw in the concept of outsourcing public library book selection.

Farmanfarmaian, Roxane. 1996. B&T, local wholesaler choose books for Hawaii libraries. *Publishers Weekly* 243 (42): 15.

Hawaiiana constitutes 10 percent to 15 percent of the Hawaii State Public Library System's acquisitions. Baker & Taylor, a mainland firm, partnered with the largest wholesaler on the islands, Booklines Hawaii, to select and provide local materials. This arrangement includes a weekly conference call between Booklines staff and a rotating group of librarians from each of the 49 libraries to discuss and resolve selection issues.

Flagg, G. 1997. Angry Hawaiian librarians denounce B&T outsourcing. *American Libraries* 28 (1): 12–13.

Implementation issues have created controversy over the decision to outsource book selection in the Hawaii State Public Library System. Looking to an outside source is viewed by critics as a threat to professionalism while advocates see outsourcing as a necessary cost-cutting measure. This well-publicized arrangement has certainly demonstrated that there can never be too much communication before or after the decision to outsource has been made.

Flagg, G. 1997. Hawaii bill would prohibit library outsourcing. *American Libraries* 28 (3): 17–18.

This is a brief article describing a situation with potentially far-reaching consequences. Legislation has been introduced in the Hawaii State Senate to prohibit outsourcing of book selection and to limit materials selection decisions to state library system employees.

Honolulu is talking. . . . 1996. *Newsweek* 121 (18): 8.

The subject of public library book selection does not often warrant coverage by *Newsweek*. This short article makes the point that individuals are usually under fire for banning books, not for buying them. In Hawaii, State Librarian Bart Kane is under fire for the implementation "kinks" in his plan to outsource book selection for 49 branch libraries although he states that his plan saved 124 jobs.

Intner, Sheila S. 1997. Stream of consciousness discord in paradise: Outsourcing in Hawaii and other librarian-vendor quarrels—an ALA report. *Technicalities* 17 (3): 2–3, 9.

Intner observes that there is a lot of emotion and very few facts about the Hawaii outsourcing controversy and it's time to sort out the rhetoric from the reality. She calls for substantive information on which to base an ALA resolution and other professional judgments.

Intner, Sheila S. 1997. Stream of consciousness: Outsourcing selection in Hawaii—the next installment. *Technicalities* 17 (4): 2–3.

>The anti-outsourcing movement in Hawaii may be testimony to the power of the Internet rather than proof that outsourcing is not viable. If legislation passes to give Hawaii librarians a voice in materials selection, it should have some positive local impact. However, the national spotlight on this situation will cause other librarians to question the concept of outsourcing public library book selection.

Oder, Norman. 1997. Hawaii outsourcing controversy grows. *Library Journal* 122 (4): 15–16.

>Baker & Taylor, the outsourcing vendor selected by the Hawaii State Public Library System, has already addressed concerns about initial selection decisions. However, for some librarians within the system, the first impression is the lasting impression and they are moving to prohibit all such outsourcing contracts.

Oder, Norman. 1997. Outsourcing model—or mistake? The collection development controversy in Hawaii. *Library Journal* 122 (5): 28–31.

>Outsourcing is defined as giving responsibility for certain tasks to an outside firm. Successful outsourcing depends on how this process is managed. The exigencies of putting outsourcing in place without benefit of a pilot project, widespread staff buy-in, and adequate selection profiling are at the heart of the Hawaii controversy.

Oder, Norman, and Susan DiMattia. 1996. Hawaii/B&T outsourcing deal causing controversy. *Library Journal* 121 (19): 12.

>The success or failure of the outsourcing of book selection in the Hawaii State Public Library System remains to be seen. Start-up problems caused many to predict the doom of the entire project. In fact, many implementation issues have already been addressed. One significant step was the formation of a selection advisory committee to assist in resolving profiling issues and facilitating communication between the library staff and Baker & Taylor staff.

Olson, Renee. 1996. Hawaii's newest volcano: Dissent erupts over outsourcing. *School Library Journal* 42 (11): 10–11.

>Some critics say that entrusting book selection to a book vendor is like allowing the fox to guard the hen house. Proponents see vendor-assisted selection as the basic tenet of an approval plan. In the book selection process, typically the communication between vendor staff and library staff culminates in a selection profile that is continuously refined. In the Hawaii situation, there wasn't time to put the profiles in place before funds had to be expended. Olson also raises interesting issues about the nature of library collections: Are collections unique? To what degree do public library collections vary? Is maintaining uniqueness worth the cost? Can uniqueness be profiled?

The outsourcing dilemma: Polar opposites Bart Kane and Patricia Wallace debate the merits of the Hawaii model. 1997. *American Libraries* 28 (5): 54–56.

This article is a provocative dialog between Hawaii State Librarian Bart Kane and Patricia Wallace, chair of ALA's Hawaii Working Group, and is facilitated by an *American Libraries* reporter. Kane points to circulation statistics which belie the argument that effective selection can only be done by local selectors, and he raises issues regarding the uniqueness of collections. Wallace maintains that selection is a core competency of librarians and to remove this responsibility is a threat to professional librarians and will result in the degradation of the collection.

Outsourcing from Kane to Abel. 1997. *American Libraries* 28 (4) 68–69.

Outsourcing was a frequent topic of discussion at the 1996 ALA midwinter meeting. Several speakers emphasized the need for good contracts and the definition of mutual obligations of librarians and vendors in an outsourcing arrangement. Hawaii State Librarian Bart Kane talked about the three R's of outsourcing—risk, resistance, and resilience. He also emphasized that new ventures need to have a sound financial and philosophical basis.

Riverside City and County Public Library

Johnson, Thomas L. 1986. Cataloging service contracts: The Riverside experience. *Technicalities* 6, no. 6: 13–15.

Hemet Public Library and Palo Verde Valley Library District contracted with Riverside (Calif.) City and County Public Library for copy cataloging of new material, excluding nonbook items. Details, procedures, and benefits of the contract arrangement are discussed.

Library Case Studies: Special Libraries

Exploring outsourcing. 1997. *Information Outlook* 1 (3): 31, 46.

This is a discussion of the Special Libraries Association publication entitled *Exploring Outsourcing: Case Studies of Corporate Libraries.* It is clear from the study that it is time for corporate librarians to plan strategically for the future. The study also revealed that few corporations did strategic planning before outsourcing and no company in the study had effective measures in place for analyzing the anticipated benefits of outsourcing.

Portugal, Frank. 1997. *Exploring Outsourcing: Case Studies of Corporate Libraries.* Washington, D.C.: Special Libraries Association.

The Special Libraries Association commissioned this pilot study to examine outsourcing and corporate libraries. Thirty-two companies were considered and seven representative sites were targeted for in-depth study through a questionnaire that is included in the report. Five of the libraries had outsourced selected library functions while two companies had completely outsourced their libraries.

Baker & McKenzie

Kniffel, Leonard. 1995. Giant Chicago law firm dismisses library staff. *American Libraries* 26, no. 6: 491–96.

Following a decision to reduce overhead, all library staff at Baker & McKenzie's Chicago office were eliminated. Outsourcing of library operations was a surprise to staff. The devaluation of their skills, implicit in the dismissals, became the catalyst for the formation of the American Association of Law Libraries' task force on the value of library services supplied by professionally trained librarians.

Miles, Kevin. 1996. Outsourcing in private law libraries since the Baker & McKenzie action. *The Bottom Line: Managing Library Finances* 9, no. 2: 10–13.

The dismissal of all library staff at Baker & McKenzie was the impetus for this article. Attitudes toward outsourcing of library operations are divided. This polarization is briefly recapped, using quotations from the literature. The author conducted an outsourcing survey on the Private-LawLib listserv in October 1995. Many law librarians may not have had Internet access, but conclusions drawn from 42 responses indicate that outsourcing has a secure place in law librarianship, just as it has in other professions.

Saint-Onge, Michael. 1995. Outsourced law library serves as a wake-up call. *National Law Journal* 17, no. 46: 3.

Federal government mandates to outsource date back to 1955, and this concept has made its way into the private sector. One example of this trend was the termination of the entire library staff at Baker & McKenzie's Chicago office. This article examines the catalyst that brought about this change, as well as exploring why it should not have happened and what action law librarians can take.

Lexmark International, Inc.

Hatfield, Deborah. 1994. Partnerships in information services: The contract library. *Special Libraries* 85, no. 2: 77–80.

Hatfield offers a twist on outsourcing partnerships. The University of Kentucky Libraries, under contractual arrangement, serve as the professional corporate library for Lexmark International. This is a model of success, which was achieved by careful planning and communication.

Microsoft Corporation

Gershenfeld, Nancy. 1994. Outsourcing serials activity at the Microsoft Corporation. *Serials Review* 20, no. 3: 81–83.

> Redeployment and better utilization of staff drove Microsoft managers to outsource their serials management. They issued an RFP and, based on the responses, contracted with Readmore, Inc. to work on-site. The initial problems were not insurmountable, and this experiment in partnership has ultimately proven to be successful.

Outsourcing Acquisitions

See also Checklists, Manuals, and Surveys
    Library Case Studies for Ohio State University
    Library Case Studies for Wright State University
    Vendor Articles

Cargill, Jennifer. 1984. When purchasing commercially available technical services makes sense. *Technicalities* 4, no. 2: 7–9.

> This article pre-dates the outsourcing literature of the 1990s. The focus is on using commercial technical services in support of approval plans, continuations, periodicals, out-of-print services, and management reports. These services are commonplace in libraries during the 1990s, but the how-to advice, especially in regard to communication with vendors, holds true for any outsourcing endeavor.

Charles, John, and Shelley Mosley. 1997. Keeping selection in-house. *Library Journal* 122 (5): 30.

> This brief article enumerates traits of effective selectors in public libraries. The thesis is that local collections can only effectively be built by local selectors because they have access to the collection, the community, and the local media.

Montgomery, Jack G. 1995. Outsourced acquisitions?—let's meet the challenge. *Against the Grain* 7, no. 2: 66–68.

> The current literature makes it clear that outsourcing is not a fad. Continually eroding budgets and staffing levels ensure that outsourcing will be in our futures. It is up to library staff to be proactive and take a leadership role in outsourcing.

Ogburn, Joyce L. 1994. An introduction to outsourcing. *Library Acquisitions: Practice & Theory* 18, no. 4: 363–66.

> This brief discussion of outsourcing, as a business strategy and as it has been applied to library practices, reflects on a phenomenon forced by financial constraints. This paper also serves as an introduction to four views presented in a special outsourcing section of this journal.

Ray, Ron L. 1993. The dis-integrating library system: Effects of new technologies in acquisitions. *Library Acquisitions: Practice & Theory* 17, no. 2: 127–36.

> In the 1980s, the focus of library automation was on the integrated library system (ILS). Within the ILS, the acquisitions module plays a supporting role to public access and cataloging modules. In the 1990s, the emergence of electronic ordering, and other developments by materials vendors, offers distinct advantages. The linking or interfacing of vendor systems with the ILS is a costly proposition. Thought must be given to the optimal way to shape the technology of the acquisitions process.

Saunders, Laverna M. 1995. Transforming acquisitions to support virtual libraries. *Information Technology and Libraries* 14, no. 1: 41–46.

> Saunders examines reengineering of collection development and acquisitions in light of the virtual library. The virtual library concept, and the shift toward networked and local electronic resources, will transform libraries, jobs within the library, and local systems.

Outsourcing Public Services

Calabrese, Alice, and Jay Wozny. 1995. The CLS bottom line: It's more than money, it's service. *The Bottom Line: Managing Library Finances* 8, no. 2: 18–22.

> Staff at the Chicago Library System (CLS) serve a sizable and diverse group of libraries, including Chicago Public Library, Chicago Public Schools, 225 special libraries, and 52 academic libraries in the state. Achieving CLS's goals, with only a staff of four, is a challenge. Outsourcing of major services, including automation, interlibrary loan, reference, delivery, continuing education, and Internet access, either with vendors or through arrangements with member libraries, enables CLS's staff to fulfill the library system's mission.

Weaver, Barbara F. 1993. Outsourcing—a dirty word or a lifeline? *The Bottom Line* 7, no. 1: 26–29.

> Two outsourcing projects are discussed. Outsourcing of interlibrary loan delivery in New Jersey and Rhode Island reduced delivery costs and enabled the continuation of interlibrary loan services. In addition, the entire operation of the Regional Library for the Blind and Physically Handicapped in Rhode Island was successfully outsourced to cut costs.

Weaver, Sherrill L., and Harold A. Shaffer. 1995. Contracting to provide library service for a distance graduate education program. *The Bottom Line: Managing Library Finances* 8, no. 3: 20–27.

> Walden University's staff contracted with Indiana University Libraries for the provision of library services for a distance education summer session held at Indiana University. This "intersourcing" led to a multiyear

agreement and averted a crisis in protectionism, which could have sabotaged the endeavor. It is a model solution for other programs.

Woodsworth, Anne, and James F. Williams II. 1993. *Managing the Economics of Owning, Leasing, and Contracting Out Information Services.* Brookfield, Vt.: Ashgate.

A major shift has occurred from the 1980s, when information technology was viewed as giving organizations a competitive edge. In the 1990s, information technology, although an integral part of business, is costly and is not necessarily a function that must be supported within the company. Many organizations are outsourcing operations not linked directly to profit. This book provides a framework for decision makers to review the information services within their organizations.

Vendor Articles

Baker, John. 1994. Blackwell's in a new marketplace. *Serials Review* 20, no. 3: 78–81.

B. H. Blackwell's journal consolidation service, PLUS, provides for the outsourcing of serials check-in, claims, anti-theft tagging, labeling, ownership stamping, and online access to journal status information.

Crismond, Linda F. 1994. Outsourcing. *Against the Grain* 6, no. 3: 52–53.

Special considerations of outsourcing audiovisual materials, versus print, are discussed, including selection, acquisitions, and cataloging.

Crismond, Linda F. 1994. Outsourcing from the a/v vendor's viewpoint: The dynamics of a new relationship. *Library Acquisitions: Practice & Theory* 18, no. 4: 375–81.

Outsourcing of audiovisual material is, in many ways, different from print. The key to success on an emotional level is for library staff to view the contractor as an extension of their team, not as an adversary. The key to success on a practical level is to know the costs and practices of internal operations, in order to communicate expectations to the contractor and to accurately assess costs for each approach.

Diogenes: A new concept in cataloging. 1996. *The Research Libraries Group News* 39: 7–8.

Diogenes is an automated copy cataloging service co-developed by RLG and RetroLink using the RLIN database as a resource. Stanford University Libraries incorporated the Diogenes service in the redesign of their materials handling process to shift copy cataloging from a manual task to an automated one. Yale Law Library used Diogenes to facilitate reclassification.

Duchin, Douglas. 1989. Looks like the ball is in our court—library support services from vendors. *Journal of Library Administration* 10, no. 1: 71–80.

Much of what was predicted in this 1989 article has come to pass, and some services are still evolving. Library staff have requested more and more services from book suppliers as library budgets have been constrained. However, even if additional vendor services are provided at no charge, vendors do incur development costs and support costs that reduce ongoing profits. Options for the possibilities of more give and take between library staff and vendors are outlined, so that both can benefit and continue viable enterprises.

Fast, Barry. 1995. Outsourcing and PromptCat. *Against the Grain* 7, no. 2: 50.

Fast provides a brief examination of two questions: (1) Why can't libraries make their own technical services operations as productive as outsourcing? and (2) How can vendors make a profit? The answer to the first question lies in the different goals or "cultures" of libraries and for-profit businesses. The answer to the second question is that the profit motivation enables vendors, dedicated to the task, to operate quite efficiently. OCLC's PromptCat is cited as an example of the latter.

Griffin, David. 1989. The WLN cataloging service and the cataloging of serials. In *Advances in Serials Management* 3: 213–32.

WLN's cataloging service is an alternative for contract cataloging of all types of material, with particular strength in serials cataloging. Balancing production rates and quality is critical to WLN's success, because serials are difficult and time-consuming to catalog.

Johnson, Marda. 1995. Technical services productivity alternatives. *Library Acquisitions: Practice & Theory* 19, no. 2: 215–17.

Presented at the 1994 Charleston Conference, this paper describes three OCLC services that were either available or in development. The services are designed to accomplish functions typically performed within the library. TECHPRO, an established service, provides customized cataloging. PromptCat supplies copy cataloging for book purchases. PromptSelect, a service then under development, automates the book selection and ordering process.

Johnson, Marda. 1994. PromptCat development at OCLC. *Library Acquisitions: Practice & Theory* 18, no. 4: 427–30.

This article both supplements and reiterates information in Granskog's article on the PromptCat prototype. It outlines fine-tuning changes that OCLC's staff will make in the production version.

Secor, John R. 1995. Outsourcing: An opportunity to move beyond just another management technique to intended change. *Against the Grain* 7, no. 4: 26–29.

Outsourcing is one management tool for bringing big, complex organizations back to profitability. Leaders need to involve the organization's members in seeking change—change that will be a choice in which they will participate actively.

Shirk, Gary M. 1994. Outsourced library technical services: The bookseller's perspective. *Library Acquisitions: Practice & Theory* 18, no. 4: 383–95.

>   Businesses have been using outsourcing for some time and the for-profit sector's experiences are transferable to situations facing libraries, especially technical services functions. The author examines the roles that booksellers play and could play in the future of outsourcing. If partnerships are well crafted, risks can be minimized and substantial rewards can be gained by both parties.

Shirk, Gary M. 1993. Contract acquisitions: Change, technology, and the new library/vendor partnership. *Library Acquisitions: Practice & Theory* 17, no. 2: 145–53.

>   This paper explores how changes in technical services, economics, and politics are creating a new future for library-vendor relationships, especially as they relate to acquisitions functions. Some aspects of acquisitions have traditionally been provided by vendors. Issues that would arise if all acquisitions functions were provided by a book vendor are explored.

Shirk, Gary M. 1991. The wondrous web: Reflections on library acquisitions and vendor relationships. *The Acquisitions Librarian* 5: 1–8.

>   This is an argument for increased collaboration between book vendors and librarians. The author envisions replacing the often awkward current relationships with strategic alliances that will yield mutual benefits. Particular attention is paid to the bid process and how this should be reexamined.

Whitacre, Cynthia M. 1994. OCLC's TECHPRO service. *Serials Review* 20, no. 3: 77–78.

>   TECHPRO, OCLC's contract cataloging service, began in 1985. It is designed to accommodate ongoing or one-time projects. The primary markets are larger academic and public libraries with backlogs or special groups of material to be cataloged, as well as corporate and special libraries without sufficient cataloging staff.

Wittenberg, R. Charles. 1996. "Reengineering" and the approval plan: New process or new perspective? *The Acquisitions Librarian* 16: 61–67.

>   Technical services cost-saving measures, such as receiving "approval" books shelf-ready, are affecting traditional selector functions because processed books are non-returnable. Wittenberg suggests a solution which maintains the integrity of the selection process—a three-tiered approach to approval plans: (1) a core of high-confidence titles which are processed and non-returnable, (2) another level of standard, non-processed approval books, and (3) a standard slip plan for material on the periphery of the collection. Bibliographers are involved in balancing the mix as well as making decisions about individual titles at levels 2 and 3.

ABOUT THE AUTHORS

Susan B. Bailey is Assistant Head of the Catalog Department at the General Libraries of Emory University, where she does original cataloging of audiovisual material and oversees authority control work. Her interest in authority control developed while working on projects that involved both in-house and outsourced retrospective conversion of catalog records in the early 1980s at Georgia State University. She is active in ALCTS and is a member of the ALCTS Audiovisual Committee for 1996–98. Bailey has an M.P.A. from Georgia State University and an M.Ln. from Emory University.

Frances G. Bordonaro is Cataloging Unit Manager at the Fort Worth Public Library, a position she has held since 1990. Before that time, she was a cataloger at Fort Worth Public and at the Suffolk Cooperative Library System in New York. Balsam has a library degree from the Graduate School of Library Science at Simmons College.

Stephen Bosch is the Information Access Librarian at the University of Arizona Library, where he has worked for over 15 years. During that time, he has served in various positions as acquisitions librarian, coordinator for collection development in the humanities, and acting head acquisitions librarian and coordinator for collection development. He has been a member of several ALCTS committees and was co-author of the ALCTS publication *Guide to Selecting and Acquiring CD-ROMs Software and Other Electronic Publications*. Bosch has an M.A. in Chinese history and an M.L.S. from the University of Arizona.

Kathy Carter is Head of the Cataloguing Services Division of the University of Alberta Library. She has previously held the position as supervisor of the serials cataloguing and processing unit, as well as served as coordinator of the monograph retroconversion project. Carter has a B.A. from the University of Calgary and a B.L.S. from the University of Alberta.

Marylou Colver is a Senior Account Manager in the Technical Services Division of Blackwell North America, Inc. She has worked in libraries and has been in library automation since 1979. Colver was a member of the ALCTS Commercial Technical Services Committee from 1992 to 1996. She has an M.L.S. from the University of California at Berkeley.

Ellen Crosby is Head of Cataloging at the Indiana Historical Society. She has taught cataloging, technical services, and research methods courses in the College of Library and Information Science, University of South Carolina, and is currently an adjunct professor for Indiana University School of Library and Information Science. She acquired experience as a cataloger in public and academic libraries in Idaho and Oregon. Crosby has a Ph.D. from Indiana University and an M.Libr. from the University of Washington.

Selden Deemer is Library Systems Manager at the General Libraries of Emory University, a position he has held since 1985. He has been involved with library automation since 1980 and was the 1996 chair of the International Sirsi Users Group. Deemer has an M.L.S. from the University of California, Los Angeles.

Catherine A. Dixon is Assistant Director at the Fort Worth Public Library. She manages technical services, interlibrary loan, computer services, collection development, and volunteers, and serves as the Friends liaison. She was formerly the head of technical services at New Orleans Public Library, and began her career as a local history/genealogy and regional reference librarian. Dixon has an M.L.S. from Emory University.

Janice E. Donahue is Assistant Director for Technical Services at Florida Atlantic University in Boca Raton. She is the former head of the cataloging department at Florida Atlantic University, and was previously head cataloger at Georgia College in Milledgeville, Georgia. Donahue has an M.S. in library science from Florida State University.

Ann Fiegen is the Catalog Management Librarian at the University of Arizona, where she previously served as head of the authority work team. She has experience working with a variety of MARC database loads, and has planned several cataloging and authority work outsourcing projects. Her publications and interests include research in technical services costs and staffing. She currently serves on the ALCTS Committee on Cataloging: Description and Access. Fiegen has an M.L.S. from the University of Arizona.

Patricia Haber is the Book Selection Coordinator for Albuquerque Public Library. She has worked at Albuquerque Public Library for 22 years and has been in her current position for 15 years. She has also worked at the New York State College in Buffalo. Haber has an M.L.S. from the University of Buffalo.

Dawn Hale is Head of Cataloging at the Milton S. Eisenhower Library of the Johns Hopkins University, a position she has held since 1986. She has 10 years of outsourcing experience, including outsourcing of authority work to Blackwell North America, Inc.; contracting with free-lance catalogers to catalog Arabic-, Persian-, and Mongolian-language material; and employing TeleSec Library Services to assist with nonbook and major microform set cataloging, copy cataloging, and postcataloging authority work. She served as chair of the ALCTS Commercial Technical Services Committee in 1992–93, and was co-editor of the ALCTS publication, *Outsourcing Cataloging, Authority Work, and Physical Processing: A Checklist of Considerations.* Hale has an M.L.S. from Drexel University and an M.M. from Temple University.

Carol G. Henderson is Instructional Dean at Central Oregon Community College. Before her appointment as dean, she held the position of faculty librarian at the library, supervising reference, cataloging, and material processing. Before moving to Oregon in 1986, she served as head of technical services at Keene State College in New Hampshire. Henderson has an M.A. in librarianship and information science from the University of Denver and a Ph.D. in educational policy and management from the University of Oregon.

Sandra Herzinger is Chair of the Cataloging Department at the University of Nebraska–Lincoln, a position she has held since 1979. During that time, departmental staff have been involved in several outsourcing projects, an insourcing project, and a major, in-house retrospective conversion operation. She is active in ALCTS and served as chair of the ALCTS Commercial Technical Services Committee for 1995–96. Herzinger has an M.S. in library science from the University of Illinois.

Ernie Ingles is Executive Director of Learning Systems at the University of Alberta. He is responsible for the library system, the departments of computing and network services, museums and collections, and archives and records management, as well as telecommunications, the bookstore, printing and duplication services, the university press, and other university service units. His library experience includes service as a reference librarian at the University of British Columbia, head of the department of rare books and special collections at the University of Calgary, executive director of the Canadian Institute for Historical Microreproductions, university librarian at the University of Regina, and library director at the University of Alberta. He is active in the Canadian library community, has published extensively, and has received numerous awards. Ingles has an M.A. in history from the University of Calgary and an M.Libr. from the University of British Columbia.

Cecily Johns is Deputy University Librarian at the University of California, Santa Barbara, a position she has held since 1985. She is also responsible for technical services and the library's integrated online system. Before 1985, she was the associate university librarian for collections and information services at the University of Cincinnati. She is the general editor of *Selection of Library Materials for Area Studies,* Part I and II, published by the American Library Association. Johns has an M.A. in English from the University of Kansas and an M.L.S. from the University of California, Los Angeles.

Robert E. Mayer is the Head Public Services Librarian/Assistant Director in the J. Hugh Jackson Library at Stanford University's Graduate School of Business. He has held various positions in cataloging and technical services both at the Jackson Library and at Georgia State University in Atlanta. Mayer has an M.A. in Russian language and literature, a Russian area certificate, and an M.L.S. from the University of Wisconsin–Madison.

William Miller is Director of Libraries at Florida Atlantic University in Boca Raton, where he also teaches courses in English. He is serving as president of the Association of College and Research Libraries for 1996–97. He previously worked in libraries at Michigan State University, Bowling Green State University, and Albion College. Miller has an M.L.S. from the University of Toronto and a Ph.D. in English and American literature from the University of Rochester.

Lynne Partington is Head of the Cataloguing Section, University of Manitoba Libraries. She was formerly head of original cataloguing and supervised the libraries' two retrospective conversion projects. Since 1986, she has been a Cataloguing in Publication coordinator for the National Library of Canada. She is a member of ALA and a past convener of the Manitoba Library Association Technical Services Interest Group. Partington has an M.L.S. degree from the University of Toronto.

Paul Reist is a Research Librarian in the J. Hugh Jackson Library at Stanford University's Graduate School of Business. He has also held positions at the library of the *San Francisco Chronicle* and at the Bank of America. Reist has an M.A. in history from the University of California, Los Angeles, and an M.L.S. from the University of California, Berkeley.

Gene Rollins is Library Systems Manager for the San Antonio Public Library, where he has worked since March 1996. His previous positions include chief of technical services, coordinator of databases and automation, and reference librarian at Houston Public Library; and head of acquisitions at the University of Houston Libraries and Harris County (Texas) Public Library. Rollins has an M.L.S. from the University of Texas.

Aimee Ruzicka is Manager of the Chubb Law & Business Library in Warren, New Jersey, and has served as manager and law librarian for Chubb & Son Inc.'s library since 1979. She has also held the position of state law librarian for the Alaska Court System in Anchorage, Alaska. Ruzicka has an M.S.L.S. from the University of Tennessee/Knoxville.

Julie Swann is the Catalog Librarian for Slavic languages and English and American literature at the University of Nebraska–Lincoln. She has served as the resource person for both outsourcing and insourcing projects in her position as catalog librarian. She is active in ACRL's Slavic and East European Section committees. Swann has an M.A. in Russian language and literature from the University of Texas Arlington and an M.L.S. from Indiana University.

Suzanne Sweeney is Library Systems Manager and Manager of Staff Client Services for the J. Hugh Jackson Library at Stanford University's Graduate School of Business. Before this, she held the position of head cataloging librarian at Jackson Library. She has also served as head, technical processing, for the Beaumont (Texas) Public Library, as well as serials cataloger and head, conversion projects, at the University of Houston. Sweeney has an M.L.S. from the University of North Texas.

George Talbot is a Cataloguer in the Cataloguing Section of the Bibliographic Database Management Department at the University of Manitoba Libraries. He has also held the positions of head of original cataloguing and record maintenance sections, as well as acting head of the cataloguing department and acting coordinator of technical services at the University of Manitoba. He is the libraries' bibliographer for bibliographic tools and has served as the bibliographer for library science. Since 1986, he has been a co-coordinator of the National Library of Canada's Cataloguing in Publication Office serving Manitoba and Saskatchewan publishers. He is a member of ALA and is currently convener of the Manitoba Library Association Technical Services Interest Group. Talbot has an M.L.S. from the University of Oklahoma.

Isao Uesugi is the Technical Services Librarian at College of the Canyons. He is the former head, OPAC management/Innopac system coordinator at The Libraries of The Claremont Colleges, and was previously head of cataloging services at the libraries. He teaches political science at California State Polytechnic University, Pomona, in addition to his full-time duties at Claremont. Uesugi has an M.L.S. from San Jose State University and a Ph.D. in government from the Claremont Graduate School.

Karen A. Wilson is the Head Technical Services Librarian/Assistant Director in the J. Hugh Jackson Library at Stanford University's Graduate School of Business. She has also held the position of head of public services at Jackson Library. She began her career in public libraries in Southern California and has also worked as a catalog librarian and reference librarian in the Martin P. Catherwood Library at Cornell University's New York State School of Industrial and Labor Relations. She is active in ALCTS and was a member of the ALCTS Commercial Technical Services Committee from 1995 to 1997. Her publications cover topics in library technical services and outsourcing. Wilson has an M.A. in librarianship from San Jose State University.

INDEX

227